Study Guide

LIFESPAN DEVELOPMENT

Second Edition

LIFESPAN DEVELOPMENT

Second Edition

Kelvin L. Seifert
Robert J. Hoffnung
Michele Hoffnung

Manolya Bayar
Harford Community College

HOUGHTON MIFFLIN COMPANY   BOSTON   NEW YORK

Sponsoring Editor: Kerry Baruth
Assistant Editor: Sara Wise
Senior Manufacturing Coordinator: Sally Culler
Senior Marketing Manager: Pamela J. Laskey

Printed in the U.S.A.

ISBN: 0-395-96772-4

2 3 4 5 6 7 8 9-B+B-03 02 01 00

CONTENTS

TO THE STUDENT

This study guide was prepared to help you master the information provided in the text *Lifespan Development,* Second Edition and to facilitate your study and retention of the important theories, facts, and concepts related to developmental psychology.

In developing a study guide, we recognize that most students have devised their own ways of studying and learning new material. We encourage you to try those means you have found useful to make studying interesting and productive. At the same time, having access to a study guide developed especially for a text may help you study more efficiently and effectively, particularly as this may be introductory material for you.

The study guide contents parallel the textbook contents, and the study guide contains the following information for each chapter:

1. A list of *learning objectives*, drawn specifically from the textbook's coverage. They describe what you are expected to be able to do to show that you have learned the material in the chapter.

2. A detailed chapter *outline* that summarizes the main points of the chapter and contains helpful hints for learning.

3. A series of *fill-in-the-blank statements* related to the *key concepts* of the chapter. The answers to these questions appear at the end of each chapter of this study guide.

4. A Multiple-Choice Self-Test Factual Questions and Multiple-Choice Self-Test Conceptual Questions. These tests are designed to test your knowledge of chapter content and to give you practice in taking multiple-choice tests based on this content. The answers to the tests, along with a detailed explanation of why the correct choice is right and the other choices are not, appear at the end of each study guide chapter.

We hope that this study guide will help you to learn the material in your textbook more easily and thoroughly, and we wish you success in your study of developmental psychology.

CHAPTER 1
Studying Lifespan Development

Learning Objectives:

1. Define what is meant by development and describe the nature of developmental change.
2. Describe the three domains of developmental psychology and indicate how they interact.
3. Describe Bronfenbrenner's ecological framework for understanding development.
4. Discuss the benefits of studying developmental psychology.
5. Sketch the history of lifespan developmental psychology and describe how certain historical situations contributed to the emergence of this field.
6. Identify and discuss the basic challenges of developmental psychology.
7. Describe the four features of the scientific method and explain how it is used in psychology.
8. Discuss the strengths and limitations of the cross-sectional approach.
9. Discuss the strengths and limitations of the longitudinal approach.
10. Describe sequential studies.
11. Differentiate between naturalistic and experimental studies.
12. Describe the experimental approach and be able to differentiate between experimental and control groups, and between independent and dependent variables.
13. Define correlation and explain its meaning.
14. Define and evaluate other methods for investigating developmental issues, including surveys, interviews, and case studies.
15. Discuss the ethical constraints on conducting research.
16. Define what is meant by informed consent and describe the special concerns that exist when children are involved as research participants.

Chapter Outline

I. The nature of lifespan development

Development refers to changes in a person's long-term growth, feelings, and patterns of thinking.

A. Three domains of development

Domains refer to the type or form of change. There are three domains, and they interact in many ways with one another.

1. **Physical development** includes bodily changes, the use of the body (e.g., motor skills, sexuality), and the effects of aging (e.g., eyesight, muscular strength).

2. **Cognitive development** refers to changes in methods and style of thinking, language ability and use, and strategies for remembering and recalling information.

3. **Psychosocial development** relates to changes in feelings or emotions, relationships with others, and development of a sense of self.

B. An example of development: Jodi

Bronfenbrenner's theory on ecological systems provides a framework for understanding the many contexts of development.

1. The microsystem consists of situations in which the individual experiences face-to-face contact with important individuals.

2. The mesosystem is the connections and relationships that exist between two or more microsystems.

3. Settings in which the person does not participate but that still have an influence are called the exosystem.

4. The macrosystem is the overall society, with its overarching institutions, practices, and patterns of belief.

II. Why study development?

A. Knowledge about development can lead to realistic expectations for children, adolescents, and adults.

B. Knowledge about development can aid appropriate responses to a person's actual behavior.

C. Developmental knowledge can increase recognition when departures from the normal are significant.

D. Developmental knowledge can enhance understanding of one's own development.

E. Knowledge about development can facilitate advocacy for the needs and rights of people of all ages.

III. The history of developmental study

A. Childhood and adolescence as concepts

1. Children were not always considered full-fledged members of society or even genuine humans. Children graduated to adult beings status early in life and took on major adultlike tasks.

2. Therefore, the period of adolescence was unknown, and teenagers assumed adult roles. Assuming major adultlike tasks was a factor in the early mortality of children.

• Focusing On: Wanted: A child and family policy

B. Early precursors to developmental study

Economic changes and the effects of industrialization made it known that children were working in factories and being abandoned.

C. The emergence of modern developmental study

1. Baby biographies were one of the earliest attempts to study development.

2. Gesell developed **norms,** or standards of normal development, by observing children at precise ages doing specific tasks.

3. Piaget observed behavior that illustrated cognitive skills.

IV. Lifespan Perspectives on Human Development

A. Continuity within Change

One challenge of lifespan psychology is to identify the factors that underlie developmental changes that happen over the very long periods of the lifespan. The field looks for continuities hidden within long-term changes.

B. Lifelong Growth

This theme highlights the potential for growth at all ages.

C. Changing Meanings and Vantage Points

The key events and themes of life can be viewed from several perspectives.

• A Multicultural View: Street Children: comparing Paraguay and North America

D. Developmental Diversity

Lifespan psychology is interested in differences in patterns of development created both by individual experiences and by social and cultural circumstances.

V. Methods of studying developmental psychology

A. Scientific methods

The **scientific method** refers to systematic procedures for objective observations and interpretations of observations.

1. Research begins with the formulation of research questions.

2. Each question is stated as a **hypothesis**—a statement that precisely expresses the research question.

3. After formulating hypotheses, researchers test them by conducting an actual study.

4. Following the study, researchers analyze and report their results. Then they make reasonable interpretations and conclusions about these results.

B. Variations in time frame

Psychologists can study people of different ages at one point in time. In addition, the same people can be studied at several points in time.

1. A **cross-sectional study** compares people of different ages at a single point in time.

2. A **longitudinal study** observes the same subjects periodically over a relatively long period, often years.

3. Both types of studies have advantages and limitations. For instance, **cohorts** cannot be distinguished in cross-sectional studies. Subjects in longitudinal studies may drop out or move away.

4. **Sequential studies** combine elements of cross-sectional and longitudinal studies.

• Working with Marsha Bennington, speech-language pathologist: Communication difficulties across the lifespan

C. Variations in control: Naturalistic and experimental studies

Developmental studies vary in how much they attempt to control the circumstances in which individuals are observed.

1. **Naturalistic studies** observe behavior as it normally occurs in natural settings.

2. **Experimental studies** arrange circumstances so that only one or two factors or influences vary at a time.

a. In experimental research, groups are arranged so that factors can be manipulated or held constant. A deliberately varied factor is called the **independent variable**. A factor that varies as a result of the independent variable is called the **dependent variable**.

b. The population refers to the group being studied. When every member of the population has an equal chance of being chosen for the study, the individuals selected form a **random sample**. If any person does not have an equal chance of being selected, the sample is biased.

c. Experimental studies use a number of precautions to ensure that their findings have **validity**, meaning that they measure or observe what they are intended to measure or observe.

d. One way to improve validity is to observe two sample groups, one an **experimental group**, or treatment group, and the other a **control group**. The experimental group receives the treatment or intervention related to the purposes of the experiment. The control group experiences conditions that are as similar as possible to the conditions of the experimental group but does not experience the crucial experimental treatment.

3. Most research studies look for correlations among variables.

      a.   A **correlation** is a systematic relationship.

      b.   When the behaviors or characteristics change in the same direction, the relationship is a positive correlation; when they change in opposite directions, it is a negative correlation.

      c.   The correlation coefficient, which falls between +1.00 and −1.00, summarizes the degree of relationship between two characteristics.

D. Variations in sample size

Developmental studies vary as to how many people are observed or interviewed.

    1.   **Surveys** are large-scale, specific, focused interviews of large numbers of people. Surveys have advantages and limitations.

    2.   **Interviews** are face-to-face directed conversations. Because interview studies take time, they usually focus on a smaller number of individuals than surveys do.

    3.   A **case study** examines one or a few individuals. In general, case studies try to pull together a wide variety of information about an individual case and then present the information as a unified whole. Case studies emphasize the relationships among specific behaviors, thoughts, and attitudes in the life of the subject.

VI. Ethical constraints on studying development

Sometimes ethical concerns limit the methods that can be used to study particular questions about development. Generally, researchers face four major ethical issues:

A. Confidentiality

If researchers collect information that might damage individuals' reputations or self-esteem, they should take care to protect the identities of the participants.

B. Full disclosure of purposes

Research subjects are entitled to know the true purpose of any research study in which they participate. Sometimes, however, telling subjects the truth about the study will make them distort their behavior. When this is the case, researchers need to balance dishonesty with making research more scientific. Purposeful deception may be permissible—but only when no other method is possible and when participants are fully informed of the deception and its reasons following the study.

C. Respect for individuals' freedom to participate

As much as possible, research studies should avoid pressuring individuals to participate.

D. Informed consent

With **informed consent**, each person shows that he or she understands the nature of the research, believes that his or her rights are protected, and feels free to either volunteer or refuse to participate.

VII.   Strengths and limitations of developmental knowledge

Key Concepts

Directions: Identify each of the key concepts discussed in this chapter.

1.   Long-term changes in a person's growth, feelings, patterns of thinking, social relationships, and motor skills are called _____.
2.   The broad changes and continuities that constitute a person's identity and growth from birth to death are called _____.
3.   A _____ is a realm of psychological functioning.
4.   Growth and changes in motor skills are examples of _____. Changes in thinking and reasoning skills are called _____. Changes in personality and social and emotional skills are called _____.
5.   Bronfenbrenner describes the contexts of development as _____. He outlines the _____, _____, _____ , and _____ as various sets of people, settings, and recurring events that are related to one another, have stability, and influence the person over time.
6.   During medieval times, children took on adult roles at about age _____ or _____. Consequently, the period we recognize as _____ today was unknown.
7.   _____ are behaviors typical at certain ages and of certain groups.
8.   The textbook identifies four lifespan perspectives on human development; these are _____, _____, _____, _____, and _____.
9.   Scientific research methods have common qualities. These are: _____, _____, _____, and _____.
10. A _____ is a precise prediction based on scientific theory; usually it can be tested by scientific research.
11. In a _____ study individuals of different ages are tested at one point in time. In a _____ study the same individuals are followed over a period of weeks, months, or years and tested multiple times.
12. A _____ is a group of people born in the same historical time. In _____ studies at least two cohorts are compared to each other and at different times.
13. When behavior is observed in its natural setting without interference from the experimenter, a _____ study is being conducted.
14. In experimental research, the _____ variable is manipulated by the experimenter and the effect of this manipulation on the _____ variable is measured.
15. If each member of a particular population has an equal chance of being selected into a sample, then the sample was chosen _____.
16. To the extent that research findings measure or observe what is intended, they are said to be _____.
17. In experimental research, the group that receives the experimental treatment is called the _____ group. The group that does not receive the experimental treatment is called the _____.
18. In _____ research the values of two variables move and change together.
19. In a _____, large numbers of people are asked to report their specific knowledge or opinions.
20. An _____ is intended to gather in-depth information through a face-to-face conversation.
21. A research study that uses one or a few individuals is called a _____ study.
22. An _____ is an agreement signed by research participants prior to making a decision about their participation.

Multiple-Choice Self-Test

Factual Questions

1. Which domain of development is primarily concerned with changes in feelings and relationships with others?
   a. Physical
   b. Cognitive
   c. Psychosocial
   d. Emotional

2. The interaction between the family and the workplace is an example of a(n)
   a. microsystem.
   b. mesosystem.
   c. exosytsem.
   d. macrosystem.

3. Contemporary society views children as innocent and in need of protection. This view leads to
   a. child abuse.
   b. respect from the community.
   c. insensitivity to the diversity of childhood experiences.
   d. nonuniform views about the nature of childhood.

4. In research, a precise testable prediction is called a
   a. norm.
   b. theory.
   c. study.
   d. hypothesis.

5. Which of the following is true of the longitudinal study?
   a. It tests the same participants repeatedly.
   b. Its participants are people who belong to several different cohorts.
   c. It takes a relatively short time to complete.
   d. It always involves the manipulation of multiple independent variables.

6. A questionnaire that includes specific questions about political attitudes, opinions and behaviors will most likely be used in
   a. experimental research.
   b. a naturalistic study.
   c. a survey.
   d. a correlational study.

7. An in-depth face-to-face conversation with a participant constitutes a(n)
   a. survey.
   b. naturalistic study.
   c. case study.
   d. interview.

8. In a negative correlation, as the values of one variable increase, the values of the other variable
   a. increase.
   b. decrease.
   c. remain the same.
   d. change randomly.

9. In an experimental study, the variable that is measured is called the _____ variable.
   a. independent
   b. dependent
   c. control
   d. experimental

10. An informed consent must include information about all of the following *except*
    a. confidentiality.
    b. full disclosure of the purpose of the study.
    c. respect for individuals' freedom to participate in the study.
    d. compensation for participation.

Conceptual Questions

1. Which of the following is the best illustration of cognitive development?
   a. Betsy is now able to tie her own shoelaces.
   b. Jamie is considering whether or not his friend intended to break his, Jamie's, Nintendo before he blames the friend.
   c. Trisha has learned to swim.
   d. Bobby has recently joined the school basketball team.

2. Dan's father has been transferred to another state. Dan must move with his family and leave behind his friends. Which level of Bronfenbrenner's ecological systems is influencing Dan?
   a. Microsystem
   b. Mesosystem
   c. Exosystem
   d. Macrosystem

3. Dr. Errol, a psychologist, is recording detailed descriptions of his son's behaviors, opinions, accomplishments, and so forth. Whose method of studying children is Dr. Errol using?
   a. Uri Bronfenbrenner's
   b. Jacqueline Goodnow's
   c. Arnold Gessell's
   d. Bernice Neugarten's

4. A lifespan developmental psychologist argues that traditions and customs of different cultures influence the experience of childhood differently. Which perspective of lifespan development is he referring to?
   a. Continuity within change
   b. Lifelong growth
   c. Changing vantage points
   d. Developmental diversity

5. A researcher hypothesizes that increased alcohol consumption reduces recall ability. What is the dependent variable in this hypothesis?
   a. Amount of alcohol consumed
   b. Ability to recall
   c. This is a correlational study; it does not have a dependent variable
   d. This is a correlational study; both amount of alcohol consumed and ability to recall are dependent variables.

6. Assume that ability to recall and alcohol consumption are correlated variables. Which of the following statements is true?
   a. Alcohol consumption causes a decline in recall ability.
   b. Alcohol consumption causes an increase in recall ability.
   c. As alcohol consumption increases, there is a corresponding decline in recall ability.
   d. As alcohol consumption increases, there is a random change in recall ability.

7. A researcher has been collecting data from the same one hundred subjects for the past five   years. Twice a year he contacts them and they complete various questionnaires and are interviewed on their political attitudes and behaviors. This researcher is conducting which type of study?
   a. Longitudinal
   b. Cross-sectional
   c. Naturalistic
   d. Case

8. A neuropsychologist is studying the effects of a new drug on depressive symptoms. He divides his thirty participants into three groups of ten each. The first group receives 10 milligrams of the new drug. The second group receives 15 milligrams of the new drug. The third group receives a sugar pill. Which is (are) the experimental groups of this study?
   a. The first
   b. The second
   c. The third
   d. The first and the second

9. Which of the following represents the strongest correlation?
   a. +1.90
   b. +0.75
   c. -0.95
   d. -0.50

10. If a scientist were conducting a study on aggressive behaviors with ten-year-old participants, she would have to get informed consent from
    a. the child participants.
    b. the parents of the child participants.
    c. the child participants and their parents.
    d. neither the parents nor the child participants.

Answer Key

Key Concepts

1. development
2. lifespan development
3. domain
4. physical development; cognitive development; psychosocial development
5. ecological systems; microsystem; mesosystem; exosystem; macrosystem
6. seven; eight; adolescence
7. Norms
8. continuity within change; lifelong growth; changing vantage points; developmental diversity
9. formulating the research question; stating questions as a hypothesis; testing the hypothesis; interpreting and publicizing the results
10. hypothesis
11. cross-sectional; longitudinal
12. cohort; sequential
13. naturalistic
14. independent; dependent
15. randomly
16. valid
17. experimental; control
18. correlational
19. survey
20. interview
21. case
22. informed consent

Multiple-Choice Self-Test / Factual Questions

1. Choice (c) is correct; the psychosocial domain covers emotions, personality, and social knowledge and skills. Choice (a), physical development, examines physical and biological changes. Choice (b), cognitive development, is concerned with thinking and reasoning skills, collectively called cognition. Choice (d), emotional development, is not one of the domains.

2. Choice (b) is correct; the mesosystem examines relationships between microsystems. Choice (a), the microsystem, refers to one-on-one and small-group interactions. Choice (c), the exosystem, refers to settings in the larger society that influence the individual, such as institutions. Choice (d), the macrosystem, examines social, cultural, and institutional patterns and assumptions that influence the individual.

3. Choice (c) is correct; viewing children in a uniform manner leads to an ignorance of the diversity of children with respect to race and ethnicity, economic resources, and so forth. Therefore, choice (d) is incorrect. This view does not lead to child abuse, choice (a), or respect for children, choice (b).

4. Choice (d) is correct; a hypothesis is a specific prediction based on theory. Choice (a), norms, are behaviors typical of particular ages and groups. Choice (b), a theory, is a broad and general explanation of a phenomenon. Choice (c), a study, is synonymous with the concept of conducting research.

5. Choice (a) is correct; longitudinal studies follow participants over weeks, months, and years and involve repeated testing. Choices (b) and (c) are characteristics of cross-sectional designs. One or more variables, choice (d), may be involved in longitudinal research.

6. Choice (c) is correct; in survey research, participants are questioned directly about their opinions, attitudes, and behaviors. Choice (a), experimental research, involves manipulating an independent variable and measuring the impact of the manipulation on the dependent/variable. In naturalistic studies, choice (b), participants are tested in their natural environments, without any interference from experimenters. Choice (d), correlational research, examines the relationship between two variables.

7. Choice (d) is correct; interviews are in-depth face-to-face conversations intended to gather specific information. In survey research, choice (a), participants are questioned directly about their opinions, behaviors, and attitudes. In naturalistic studies, choice (b), participants are tested in their natural environments, without any interference from the experimenters. Choice (c), a case study, is a research method that uses only one or just a few subjects.

8. Choice (b) is correct; in a negative correlation, as the values of one variable increase, the values of the other variable decrease. Choice (a), is incorrect in that the values of both variables increase if they are positively correlated. If variables are not correlated, as the values of one increase, the values of the other may remain the same, choice (c), or change randomly, choice (d).

9. Choice (b) is correct; the dependent variable is the outcome variable. Choice (a), the independent variable, is manipulated. Choices (c) and (d) are not recognized as variables in research.

10. Choice (d) is correct; although some research participants are compensated, compensation of participants is not required. Choices (a), (b), and (c) are all major parts of an informed consent.

Multiple-Choice Self-Test / Conceptual Questions

1. Choice (b) is correct; cognitive development includes the growth of thinking and reasoning skills, and these encompass decision-making ability. Choices (a), (c), and (d) are examples of physical development.

2. Choice (c) is correct; the exosystem includes the impact of institutions in which the person affected does not participate; in this case, the father's workplace. Choice (a), the microsystem, refers to one-on-one or small group interaction. Choice (b), the mesosystem, is the interaction of multiple microsystems. Choice (d), the macrosystem, is the influence of the larger society.

3. Choice (c) is correct; Gessell made extensive use of baby biographies. Choice (a), Bronfenbrenner, described the concept of ecological systems. Choice (b), Goodnow, examined the changing meaning of key life events and roles as one ages using household chores as an example. Choice (d), Neugarten, studied middle-aged and elderly adults.

4. Choice (d) is correct; a consideration of developmental diversity involves examining the factors that create differences in individuals' developmental patterns. Choice (a), refers to how we account for continuity as well as change in developmental patterns over time. Examining lifelong growth, choice (b), involves potential for growth throughout the lifespan. Choice (c)refers to the change and stability of meanings of key life events and roles across the lifespan.

5.   Choice (b) is correct; the dependent variable is measured - it is the outcome variable. In this case, the researcher would vary (manipulate) alcohol consumption, choice (a) (independent variable), and assess the effects of this variation on recall ability. Choices (c) and (d) are incorrect because the described study is not correlational.

6.   Choice (c) is correct; it refers to a negative association between the variables. Choices (a) and (b) are incorrect because correlation does not imply causation. Choice (d) is incorrect because it represents the absence of a correlation.

7.   Choice (a) is correct; the researcher is conducting a longitudinal study. In a cross-sectional study, choice (b), participants are tested only once. In naturalistic study, choice (c), data is collected without any interference from the experimenter, as the participants behave in their natural environments. Choice (d), a case study employs only one or a few participants.

8.   Choice (d) is correct; groups that receive the independent variable (the drug) are the experimental groups. Therefore, choices (a) and (b) are only part of the answer. Choice (c), the third group, receives the sugar pill instead of the independent variable and is the control group.

9.   Choice (c) is correct; correlation coefficients above +0.70 and below -0.70 are considered strong, and -0.95 is the strongest listed. Choices (b) and (d) are smaller and therefore weaker. Choice (a) is incorrect because correlation coefficients range between +1.00 and -1.00.

10.   Choice (c) is correct; both parents and children between ages five and nineteen need to be fully informed about the purposes, risks, procedures, and so forth of a research study. Choice (a) is incorrect in that children must be over nineteen years old to participate without the consent of their parents. If the child is under five years of age, the parent can consent; however, the child must be informed of the procedures of the study and must verbally assent to participate. Therefore, choice (b) is incorrect. Choice (d) is incorrect in that all human research participants must consent prior to participation.

CHAPTER 2
Theories of Development

Learning Objectives:

1. Define and describe the concept of developmental theory.
2. Discuss how developmental theories differ on the issues of maturation versus experience, active versus passive development, stages of development, and breadth of the theory.
3. Discuss the basic ideas in Freud's psychosexual theory of development, including the id, ego, and superego.
4. List and describe Erikson's eight psychosocial stages and compare them with Freud's five psychosexual stages.
5. Describe the object relation theories of Mahler and Stern.
6. Describe classical conditioning and be able to identify and define the key concepts, including conditioned stimulus, conditioned response, unconditioned stimulus, and unconditioned response.
7. Describe operant conditioning and be able to identify and define the key concepts, including reinforcement, punishment, and shaping.
8. Describe Bandura's social cognitive theory and identify the roles of observational learning, modeling, and vicarious reinforcement in his theory.
9. Discuss the basic ideas in Piaget's theory of development, including the notion of schemes, the processes of assimilation and accommodation, equilibrium, and social transmission.
10. List and describe Piaget's four stages of cognitive development.
11. Discuss the neo-Piagetian approaches and describe how they have influenced Piagetian thought.
12. Describe the basic features of the information-processing approach.
13. Differentiate among the sensory register, the short-term memory, and the long-term memory.
14. Describe developmental changes according to information-processing theory, including changes in control processes, metacognition, and the knowledge base.
15. Compare the contextual theories of Bronfenbrenner's ecological theory, Vygotsky's ZPD, Lerner's reciprocal changes, Elder's social trajectories, and ethology theory.
16. Discuss life-span applications of cognitive theories and contextual theories.
17. Describe the normative-crisis and timing of events models of development.
18. Compare and contrast the major theoretical schools in terms of their basic assumptions and key concepts.

Chapter Outline

I. The nature of developmental theories

    A. What is a developmental theory?

        Theories help organize and make sense of information about development. A good theory has several characteristics.

2. It provides meaningful explanations of developmental change.

3. The theory is open to scientific evaluation so that it can be revised or discarded.

4. The theory stimulates new thinking and research.

5. It provides guidance to parents and professionals in working with children, adolescents, and adults.

B. How developmental theories differ: Four developmental themes

1. Developmental theories differ in how much influence they attribute to maturation and how much to experience.

2. They differ in their view of developmental change as being continuous or stagelike in nature.

3. They differ in their view of individuals as active or passive participants in their own development.

4. They differ in how broadly they define various factors and contexts in developmental change.

II. Psychodynamic developmental theories

Psychodynamic theories propose that development is an active process influenced by inborn, biological drives and conscious and unconscious experiences.

A. Freudian theory

Freud, the creator of psychoanalysis, influenced psychodynamic theories of personality development and the causes and treatment of psychological problems.

1. Freud described a three-part structure of personality.

a. The **id**, which is present at birth, is unconscious. It tries to satisfy a person's biological needs and desires by motivating behavior that instinctively seeks to maximize pleasure and avoid discomfort without regard for the realities involved.

b. The **ego** is the largely rational, conscious, reality-oriented, problem-solving part of the personality. It functions according to the reality principle.

c. The **superego** is the moral and ethical part of the personality. It includes the child's emerging sense of conscience.

2. Freud believed development occurs through id/ego/superego conflicts within a series of psychosexual stages.

a. Each stage focuses on a different area of the body.

b. Conflicts may result in these stages.

b. Conflicts may result in these stages.

3. Defense mechanisms such as repression and projection protect the ego from conflicts.

4. Unresolved conflicts can lead to fixations. A fixation is a blockage in development

B. Erikson's psychosocial theory

Erikson, who studied with Freud's daughter, Anna, believed personality development involves a lifelong process through which an individual attempts to achieve a sense of identity by mastering a series of conflicts created by three interrelated developmental forces: the person's biological and physical strengths and limitations; his or her unique life circumstances and developmental history; and the particular social, cultural, and historical forces at work during the individual's lifetime.

1. Each of Erikson's eight stages of development involves a particular psychosocial crisis that individuals must successfully master to achieve an adult identity.

   a. **Trust versus mistrust** is the first stage (birth to one year). At this time, the child develops trusting relationships with others.

   b. b.For successful resolution of the crisis of **autonomy versus shame and doubt** (one to three years), the child must learn control over bodily functions and activities.

   c. During the **initiative versus guilt** stage (three to six years), the child tests the limits of self-assertion and purposefulness.

   d. **Industry versus inferiority** (six to twelve years) is the stage where the child experiences the challenge of mastering many new social and intellectual tasks.

   e. During the **identity versus role confusion** stage (twelve to nineteen years), individuals attempt to form an identity and coherent self-concept.

   f. During the **intimacy versus isolation** stage (nineteen to twenty-five years), the young adult must develop close and committed relationships with others.

   g. The crisis of **generativity versus stagnation** (twenty-five to fifty years) occurs in adulthood and midlife. Here the individual attempts to help future generations.

   h. The older adult (fifty and older) confronts the crisis of **ego integrity versus despair**.

2. According to Erikson, people never fully resolve any of their psychosocial conflicts. Rather, they achieve more or less favorable ratios of positive to negative outcomes.

•   Focusing On: Erik Erikson's identity crisis: An autobiographical perspective

C. Other psychodynamic approaches

Other theories reflect Freud's belief in the significance of early childhood relationships and both conscious and unconscious inner experiences. An example is **object relations** theory.

1. Mahler proposed a four-phase model by which children learn to develop a psychological sense of self.

2. Kohut argued that a newborn's sense of self is initially fragmented and incomplete.

3. Stern described the infant's process of developing a sense of self in four overlapping, interdependent stages, each of which defines a different area of self-experience and social relatedness.

D. Applications of psychodynamic developmental theories throughout the lifespan

III. Behavioral learning and social cognitive learning developmental theories

Learning is generally defined as relatively permanent changes in observable behavior as a result of experience. Learning experiences that occur during the course of a person's life are the source of developmental change. The behavioral learning theories of Pavlov and Skinner have provided key concepts for understanding how learning experiences influence development and for helping individuals learn new, desirable behaviors and alter or eliminate behaviors that are problematic.

A. Pavlov developed the notion of **classical conditioning** while studying digestion in dogs.

B. Skinner pioneered the notion of **operant conditioning**.

1. Operant conditioning is based on the simple concept of **reinforcement**.

2. **Punishment** weakens a response by either adding an unpleasant stimulus or removing a pleasurable one.

3. Shaping occurs when small changes in behavior are reinforced to bring the behaviors closer to a desired behavior.

C. Bandura's social cognitive theory views developmental change as a process resulting from
the **observational learning** and interactions between the child and the physical and social environment.

D. Applications of learning theories throughout the lifespan

IV. Cognitive developmental theories

Cognitive theories examine the development of children's thinking and problem solving.

A. Piaget's cognitive theory describes cognition and intelligence.

Key principles of Piaget's theory

1. Piaget believed thinking develops in a series of increasingly complex stages, each incorporating and revising those that precede it.

2. People move from stage to stage through the processes of direct learning, social transmission, and physical maturation.

3. Direct learning occurs when the child experiences changes related to a **scheme**, which is a pattern of thought and action.

4. **Assimilation** is the process by which the child interprets experiences on the basis of concepts he or she already knows.

5. **Accommodation** occurs when the already existing schemes are modified to better fit new ideas or experiences.

6. **Adaptation** is the result of the interplay of assimilation and accommodation and refers to a deepening and modification of a scheme.

B. Neo-Piagetian approaches

These approaches to cognitive development are new or revised models of Piaget's basic approach.

1. Case proposed that cognitive development results from increases in the available capacity of the child's mental space.

2. Fischer's theory accepts Piaget's basic idea of stages, but instead of schemes uses the term *skills* to describe cognitive structures that apply to particular problem-solving tasks. These skills are more task specific than Piaget's schemes.

C. Information-processing theory

Precise, detailed steps involved in mental activities are the focus of **information-processing theory**.

1. Key principles in information-processing theory

   a. The sensory register takes in information from the environment.

   b. Information that is attended to is transferred to short-term memory.

   c. Information is saved permanently in long-term memory.

2. Developmental changes in information processing

   a. As children grow older, they experience several cognitive changes that allow them to process information more efficiently and comprehensively.

   b. Changes take place in control processes, which direct attention toward particular input from the sensory register and guide the response to new information.

    c. As children grow older, they develop **metacognition**--or the awareness and understanding of how thinking and learning work. This understanding helps children assess task difficulty and plan strategies for approaching a task.

    d. As children grow older, they also increase their knowledge base.

  D. Applications of cognitive developmental theories throughout the lifespan

V. Contextual developmental theories

Contextual approaches view development as a process involving the pattern of reciprocal transactions between the child and the system of physical, social, and cultural developmental contexts in which those interactions occur.

  A. Bronfenbrenner's ecological systems theory

  B. In Bronfenbrenner's ecological approach, the context in which the developing individual exists; the person's cognitive, socioemotional, and motivational capacities; and his or her active participation are central ingredients for developmental change. Bronfenbrenner describes four ecological settings in which development occurs.

  C. Vygotsky's sociohistorical theory

  D. Vygotsky proposed that the development of cognitive ability is a function of individuals' social interactions with others more capable than themselves, and he asserts that **learning occurs within the zone of proximal development**, the range between what a person is capable of attaining alone and what she or he can achieve with the assistance of a more capable individual.

  E. Richard Lerner's contextual approach emphasizes the dynamic, interactive relationships between individual development and the development of the contexts in which his or her development occurs.

  F. Glen Elder suggests that education, work and family create the social trajectories that guide individual development.

  G. Ethological theory, in the context of human development, focuses on an individual's innate behavioral and psychological characteristics that constrain physical and behavioral development.

  H. Applications of contextual developmental theories throughout the lifespan

• A Multicultural View: Cultural context and cognitive development

VI. Adulthood and lifespan developmental theories

  A. **Normative-crisis model** of development

This model assumes that developmental changes occur in distinct stages and that all individuals follow the same sequence.

    1. Each stage is qualitatively unique, each becoming more complex and developed.

2. Vaillant's styles of adult coping are based on longitudinal research; according to his model, development is a lifelong process influenced by relationships with others and coping styles.

3. Levinson, using biographical data from men, identified three eras in male adult life: early adulthood, middle adulthood, and late adulthood. Each era is characterized by transitions.

B. **Timing of events** model

   1. Life events are seen as markers of developmental change.

   2. Life events may be normative.

      a. Normative life events are transitions that follow an age-appropriate social timetable.

      b. An internalized social clock tells the person if he or she is "on time."

   3. Life events may be nonnormative.

      Nonnormative life events occur at any point in time.

   4. According to the timing of events model, changes during adulthood are less closely tied to the predictable physical and cognitive maturational changes that occur during childhood and adolescence. Adults play much more active and self-conscious roles in directing their own development through decisions and choices.

VII.   Developmental theories compared: Implications for the student

• Working with Jeffrey Friedman, clinical social worker: The value of developmental theory for helping children, adolescents, and their families

Key Concepts

Directions: Identify each of the key concepts discussed in this chapter.

1. A good theory should behave the following characteristics; it should _____, _____, _____, _____, and _____.
2. Developmental theories differ with respect to four major themes; these include _____, _____, _____and _____.
3. According to _____ theories, development is a dynamic and active process, influenced by biological drives and conscious and unconscious experiences.
4. Psychoanalysis was developed by _____.
5. The _____ is a part of the personality that is motivated to increase pleasure and avoid pain.
6. The _____ is a part of the personality that functions according to the reality principle.
7. The _____ is a part of the personality that is morally aware.
8. The psychosexual theory includes five stages; these are _____, _____, _____, _____, and _____.
9. The ego uses _____ in order to protect itself from conflicts.
10. According to Freud, unresolved id-ego and ego-superego conflicts can lead to a _____.

11. According to Erik Erikson, development is a _____ process that lasts from _____ to _____.

12. Erikson claims that development occurs in a series of _____ stages; at each stage the individual faces a particular _____.

13. During the first psychosocial crisis, the infant must develop _____ over _____. The successful resolution of this crisis leads to _____, the belief that one's wishes are attainable.

14. During the second psychosocial stage, the child who gains the ability to be independent and self-directed develops _____ , whereas _____ develop if the child loses self-respect because he or she cannot meet his or her own standards. The successful outcome of this stage is the virtue of _____, capacity to make choices freely and knowledgeably.

15. The successful resolution of the third psychosocial stage leads to the development of _____, autonomous and purposeful exploration of new activities and ideas. In contrast, if _____ develops, the child becomes self-critical because he or she fails to fulfill parental expectations. The virtue of this stage is _____.

16. When school-age children become confident of their ability to learn and master new skills they develop _____, and the virtue of _____ is the result. If children repeatedly experience failure they will develop _____.

17. During adolescence the individual's task is to develop an integrated sense of self, an _____. Those who fail to accomplish this will experience _____. The successful resolution of this crisis leads to the virtue of _____.

18. The task of young adulthood is to establish _____ with another individual, and those who are able to do this experience the virtue of _____. If this crisis is not successfully resolved, the outcome is _____.

19. Middle-aged adults seek to be _____, or to feel that they are able to contribute to future generations through their activities. The virtue that develops from this is _____, or concern for others. Middle-aged individuals who fail at this task develop _____.

20. Older adults and the elderly who are satisfied with the life they have lived develop _____ and gain the virtue of _____. In contrast, an unsuccessful resolution of this stage leads to _____.

21. _____ refers to the child's relationships with the important people in his or her environment and the process by which their qualities become part of the child's personality and mental life.

22. Margaret Mahler proposes that during the first three years of life a psychological sense of self develops through four phases; these are the _____, _____, _____, and _____ phases.

23. Daniel Stern outlines four stages of development of the self; these are called _____, _____, _____, and _____.

24. The intimate and enduring relationship between an infant and his or her caregiver is called _____.

25. _____, a Russian scientist, developed classical conditioning.

26. In classical conditioning a _____ stimulus brings about the same response as a stimulus that _____ elicits the response after being paired with it repeatedly.

27. In the original classical conditioning experiments, the dog's salivation to the bell is called the _____.

28. If the frequency of behavior increases in response to repeated rewarding of the behavior, then _____ has occurred.

29. Stimuli that increase the probability of behavior occurrence are called _____.

30. _____ decreases the probability of behavior occurrence either by adding an unpleasant stimulus to or by removing a pleasant stimulus from the environment.

31. According to Bandura, developmental change occurs through _____, and learning is _____, meaning that it results from the interactions between the developing person and his or her social and physical environment.

32. When children _____ the behaviors of others, they are directly reinforced. When children _____ the behaviors of others, the reinforcement is indirect or vicarious.

33. The set of therapy techniques based on operant conditioning and social cognitive learning is called _____.

34. According to Piaget, a _____ is a child's existing patterns of behaviors and thoughts that allow him or her to understand the world.
35. Piaget identified three complementary mechanisms that lead to changes in a child schemes; these are _____, _____, and _____.
36. Cognitive developmental theories that are new or revised models of Piaget's basic approach are called _____.
37. Case's theory explains that cognitive development is the result of increases in the child's _____.
38. Fischer's theory discusses specific _____ rather than _____ to describe the cognitive structures children use for solving problems.
39. _____ explains cognition through precise and detailed features or steps involved in mental activities.
40. The first memory store, which holds information obtained through the senses very briefly, is called the _____. From here, the information is transferred to _____, which corresponds to momentary awareness. If this information is processed further, it moves into _____.
41. The concept of _____ refers to knowledge and thinking about cognition.
42. _____ theories view development as a process of reciprocal, patterned interactions between the individual and his or her social and physical environment.
43. Bronfenbrenner's _____ theory proposes four interactive and overlapping contextual levels that influence development; these are called _____, _____, _____, _____.
44. According to Vygotsky, the _____ refers to the range and level of tasks that a child is yet unable to accomplish without assistance from those with more knowledge.
45. The _____ refers to the path development takes over an individual's lifespan.
46. _____ theory attempts to apply the principles of evolutionary biology to behavioral and psychological characteristics.
47. The _____ model views developmental change in terms of distinct periods or stages that are influenced by physical and cognitive performance. Two examples of this model are Vaillant's _____ and Levinson's _____.
48. The _____ views developmental change in terms of important life events that are expected to be completed according to culturally determined timetables.

Multiple-Choice Self-Test

Factual Questions

1. Theories that claim that developmental change is caused by events in the environment that elicit responses from the individual adopt the view that the individual is a(n) _____ contributor to his or her own development
   a. maturational
   b. experiential
   c. active
   d. passive

2. The socially aware and reality-oriented part of the personality is called the
   a. id.
   b. ego.
   c. superego.
   d. conscious.

3. According to Freudian theory, during the latency stage sexual activity
   a. centers around the mouth, and feeding is important.
   b. centers around the anus, and toilet training is important.
   c. centers around the genitals, and mature sexual activity is important.
   d. is suspended, and physical and intellectual activities are important.

4. A child who has developed initiative
   a. can independently explore new activities and ideas.
   b. can independently start and complete tasks successfully.
   c. has developed an integrated sense of self.
   d. has gained the capacity for fidelity.

5. Removing a pleasant stimulus from the environment is an example of
   a. reinforcement.
   b. punishment.
   c. modeling.
   d. shaping.

6. During the preoperational stage of cognitive development the child
   a. achieves object permanence.
   b. can solve problems using logic.
   c. has an egocentric view of the world.
   d. can think abstractly.

7. Short-term memory
   a. lasts only about a second.
   b. can hold about seven items.
   c. holds information exactly as it receives it.
   d. is the first memory store.

8. Who advanced the concept of the zone of proximal development?
   a. Alfred Bandura
   b. Robbie Case
   c. Jean Piaget
   d. Lev Vygotsky

9. Which theoretical approach is based on the principles of evolutionary biology?
   a. Ethological
   b. Information-processing
   c. Social-cognitive
   d. Psychodynamic

10. Normative-crisis theories focus primarily on which kind of development?
    a. Cognitive
    b. Physical
    c. Child
    d. Personality

Conceptual Questions

1. Nine-year-old Nigel feels very guilty for having lied to his dad. The guilt is a product of the
    a. ego.
    b. id.
    c. conscience.
    d. ego-ideal.

2. For the past two years, Tommy has been working in various jobs during his summer vacations and on days when he does not have classes. He is trying to determine the best career for himself so that he can major in this area. Tommy is attempting to develop
    a. initiative.
    b. an identity.
    c. industry.
    d. autonomy.

3. After witnessing her friend's drowning in a pool, Karen becomes intensely afraid of pools. In this case, the pool is the
    a. unconditioned stimulus.
    b. unconditioned response.
    c. conditioned stimulus.
    d. conditioned response.

4. Whenever the family goes to a restaurant, Jon's dad holds out the chair for his mother as she seats herself. Similarly, Jon has been helping his sister whenever they go to a restaurant and enjoys behaving in a gentlemanly fashion. Jon's behavior indicates
    a. imitation.
    b. modeling.
    c. shaping.
    d. behavior modification.

5. Steve's mother notices that he seems to study longer and with better concentration whenever she turns off the radio. In this case, the mother's behavior of turning off the radio is
    a. positively reinforced.
    b. negatively reinforced.
    c. punished by the removal of a pleasant stimulus.
    d. punished by the addition of an unpleasant stimulus.

6. Four-year-old Jody encounters a helicopter for the very first time and, pointing to it, calls it an airplane. This behavior demonstrates the Piagetian concept of
    a. assimilation.
    b. accommodation.
    c. adaptation.
    d. egocentrism.

7. Twelve-year-old Lisa knows that she learns better and quicker if she repeatedly listens to information. Usually, she records her lessons and listens to the tapes she has made. Lisa has acquired
   a. a knowledge base.
   b. cognitive mechanics.
   c. a schema.
   d. metacognition.

8. The relationship between a married couple is an example of the
   a. microsystem.
   b. mesosystem.
   c. exosystem.
   d. macrosystem.

9. Adam is learning to read, and he's having trouble with letters that are silent within a word. His teacher and parents are doing their best to help him. Their help demonstrates the concept of
   a. the zone of proximal development.
   b. scaffolding.
   c. social trajectories.
   d. adaptation.

10. Eighteen-year-old Tina wants to get married because the women in her family have always married by their twentieth birthday. Tina's view is most consistent with
    a. the normative-crisis model of development.
    b. Vaillant's "adaptive mechanisms" approach.
    c. the timing of events model of development.
    d. Levinson's "seasons of adult lives" approach.

Answer Key

Key Concepts

1. be internally consistent; provide meaningful explanations; be open to scientific evaluation; stimulate new thinking and research; provide guidance
2. maturation versus experience; process versus stage; active versus passive; broad versus narrow
3. psychodynamic
4. Sigmund Freud
5. id
6. ego
7. superego
8. oral; anal; phallic; latency; genital
9. defense mechanisms
10. fixation
11. psychosocial; birth; death
12. eight; psychosocial crisis
13. trust; mistrust; hope
14. autonomy; shame and doubt; will
15. initiative; guilt; purpose

16. industry; competence; inferiority
17. identity; role confusion; fidelity
18. intimacy; love; isolation
19. generative; care; stagnation
20. ego integrity; wisdom; despair
21. Object relations
22. autistic; symbiotic; separation-individuation; object constancy
23. emergent self; core self; subjective self; sense of verbal self
24. attachment
25. Ivan Pavlov
26. neutral; naturally
27. conditioned response
28. operant conditioning
29. reinforcements
30. Punishment
31. observational learning; reciprocally determined
32. imitate; model
33. behavior modification
34. scheme
35. assimilation; accommodation; adaptation
36. neo-Piagetian
37. mental space
38. skills; schemes
39. Information-processing theory
40. sensory register; short-term memory; long-term memory
41. metacognition
42. Contextual developmental
43. ecological systems; microsystem; mesosystem; exosystem; macrosystem
44. zone of proximal development
45. social trajectory
46. Ethological
47. normative-crisis; adaptive mechanisms; seasons of adult lives
48. Timing of events

Multiple-Choice Self-Test / Factual Questions

1. Choice (c) is correct; conditioning theories, as the stem of the question describes, assume that the individual has a highly active role in his or her own development. Therefore, choice (d) is incorrect. Choices (a) and (b) are inappropriate responses within the context of this particular question.

2. Choice (b) is correct; the ego operates according to the reality principle. Choice (a), the id, operates according to the pleasure principle. Choice (c), the superego, operates according to the morality principle. Choice (d), the conscious, is the aware part of the ego.

3. Choice (d) is correct; between six and twelve years of age, which corresponds to the elementary school years, children are in the latency stage and focus their energies on intellectual and physical activities. Choice (a) corresponds to the oral stage, choice (b) corresponds to the anal stage, and choice (c) corresponds to the genital stage.

4. Choice (a) is correct; the Eriksonian stage of initiative versus guilt corresponds to tree to six years of age, and during this time children can purposefully pursue and achieve tasks if they develop initiative. Choice (b) corresponds to the development of industry, choice (c) corresponds to the development of identity, and choice (d) corresponds to the virtue that is the result of a sense of identity.

5. Choice (b) is correct; punishment can occur in one of two ways; removal of a pleasant stimulus or the addition of an unpleasant stimulus. The intent of punishment is to reduce the frequency of behavior. Choice (a), reinforcement, is any stimulus that can increase the probability of behavior. Choice (c), modeling, refers to learning the behaviors and personality traits of models, such as parents. Choice (d), shaping, occurs when a child learns new responses that he or she is not yet capable of.

6. Choice (c) is correct; preoperational children lack the cognitive capacity for viewing the world from alternative perspectives. Piaget called this limitation egocentrism. Choice (a), object permanence, is achieved in the sensorimotor period. Choice (b), logical problem-solving ability, is achieved in the concrete operational period. Choice (d), abstract reasoning ability, emerges in the formal-operational period.

7. Choice (b) is correct; the capacity of short-term memory is about seven items. Choices (a), (c), and (d) are all characteristics of the sensory register.

8. Choice (d) is correct; the zone of proximal development refers to the level of tasks that a child cannot yet accomplish without assistance. According to Vygotsky, a contextual developmental theorist, this is where most developmental tasks occur. Choice (a), Alfred Bandura, is a social cognitive learning theorist and described the concept of observational learning. Choices (b) and (c), Piaget and Case, are cognitive developmental theorists; Case's theory is neo-Piagetian and based on the information-processing approach.

9. Choice (a) is correct; the ethological theory combines the principles of evolutionary biology and ethology to explain behavioral and psychological characteristics. Choice (b), the information-processing approach to cognitive development, is a neo-Piagetian perspective. Choice (c), the social cognitive approach, focuses on observational learning through imitation and modeling. Choice (d), the psychodynamic approach, contends that development is an active process that is influenced by both inborn, biological drives and conscious and unconscious processes.

10. Choice (d) is correct; normative-crisis theories primarily focus on the development of personality during the adult years. They are less focused on cognitive, choice (a), physical, choice (b), and child development, choice (c).

Multiple-Choice Self-Test / Conceptual Questions

1. Choice (c) is correct; the conscience is the part of the superego that prevents wrong and bad behaviors and punishes such behaviors with guilt. Choice (a), the ego, is the reality-oriented part of the personality. Choice (b), the id, is the pleasure-oriented part of the personality. Choice (d), the ego-ideal, is the part of the superego that promotes morally correct and good behavior.

2. Choice (b) is correct; the task of adolescence is to establish a mature sense of self, an identity. This is achieved in various areas, including career identity, religious identity, political identity, and sexual identity. Choice (a), establishing initiative, is the task of preschool years. Choice (c), establishing industry, is the task of elementary school years. Choice (d), establishing autonomy, is the task of toddlers and preschoolers.

3. Choice (c) is correct; the pool, which is originally a neutral stimulus (i.e., it does not produce fear), becomes a fearful object after being paired with drowning, a stimulus that naturally elicits fear (the unconditioned stimulus), choice (a). The other choices are incorrect because they refer to responses rather than to stimuli. In this case, the unconditioned response, choice (b), is fear of drowning, and the conditioned response, choice (d), is fear of pools.

4. Choice (b) is correct; modeling involves learning the personality traits and behaviors of a parent and brings indirect reinforcement. Therefore, it goes beyond simple imitation, choice (a), which brings direct reinforcement for copying behaviors. Choice (c), shaping, is the learning of new responses that one is currently unable to perform. Choice (d), behavior modification, is the umbrella term for the set of therapy techniques that are based on operant conditioning principles.

5. Choice (b) is correct; negative reinforcement increases the frequency of behavior by removing an unpleasant stimulus from the environment after the occurrence of the desired response. Choice (a), positive reinforcement, is the addition of a pleasant stimulus to the environment in order to increase the frequency of a desired behavior. Choices (c) and (d) are incorrect because the intent of punishment is to reduce the frequency of undesirable behavior.

6. Choice (a) is correct; the Piagetian concept of assimilation is understanding new information by relating to existing knowledge. Choice (b), accommodation, involves the modification of existing information (knowledge base) so that the new information can fit in and make sense. Choice (c), adaptation, is the product of the combined processes of assimilation and accommodation. When adaptation occurs, developmental change has occurred. Choice (d), egocentrism, is Piaget's term for describing the preoperational child's limitation of viewing the world only from his or her own perspective.

7. Choice (d) is correct; metacognition is knowledge and thinking about cognitive processes, such as knowing how one's memory works. Choice (a), knowledge base, refers to a child's existing knowledge and skills. Choice (b), cognitive mechanics, refers to intellectual problems in which culture-based knowledge is important, such as reading. Choice (c), a schema, is an organized way of mentally representing the world.

8. Choice (a) is correct; the microsystem refers to one-on-one or small-group interactions. Choice (b), the mesosystem, is the interactions between various microsystems. Choice (c), the exosystem is the settings and events that influence the person indirectly, even though he or she does not participate in them. Choice (d), the macrosystem, refers to the cultural and social values, beliefs, policies, and so forth, that influence the person.

9. Choice (b) is correct; Vygotsky's concept of zone of proximal development, choice (a), refers to the level of difficulty at which the child needs assistance in order to solve a problem. The assistance he or she receives from those with greater knowledge is called scaffolding. Choice (c), a social trajectory, is the path that a person's development takes over the course of his life. Choice (d), adaptation, is a Piagetian concept that results from the combined processes of assimilation and accommodation.

10. Choice (c) is correct; timing of events theories explain development in terms of culturally determined timetables that dictate the timing of important life events. Choice (a), the normative-crisis model of development, focuses on developmental change in terms of distinct stages that are influenced by physical and cognitive performance. Vaillant's, choice (b), and Levinson's, choice (d), theories are examples of the normative-crisis model of development.

CHAPTER 3
Genetics, Prenatal Development, and Birth

Learning Objectives:

1. Identify and describe the mechanisms and means through which genetic information is transferred and define DNA, genes, and chromosomes.
2. Differentiate between meiosis and mitosis.
3. Distinguish between genotype and phenotype.
4. Compare dominant and recessive genes and how these mechanisms influence the expression of various traits including by polygenic transmission of traits.
5. Describe how and when sex is determined and discuss sex-linked recessive disorders.
6. Define genetic imprinting.
7. Describe the characteristics of the major genetic disorders, including chromosomal abnormalities and gene-based abnormalities.
8. Describe the methods used for detecting genetic disorders during the prenatal period and identify the circumstances in which genetic counseling is recommended.
9. Discuss the key concepts of behavioral genetics.
10. Describe methods for studying the heredity-environment issue, including adoption and twin studies.
11. Define conception.
12. Identify and describe the three stages of prenatal development.
13. Discuss concerns about infertility and common treatments.
14. Identify and discuss the physical and psychological factors that affect the mother during pregnancy.
15. Address issues of family planning and discuss current attitudes toward contraception and bortion.
16. Discuss biological risks in the prenatal period in terms of canalization and critical periods.
17. List common teratogens and their possible effects on prenatal development.
18. Discuss the problem of domestic violence during pregnancy.
19. Discuss the importance of prenatal care, good nutrition, and maternal health during pregnancy.
20. Describe each of the stages of birth.
21. Describe and evaluate different childbirth settings and practices.
22. Discuss childbirthing problems and adjustments.

Chapter Outline

I. Genetics

   Inheritance affects a large number of human qualities.

II. Mechanisms of genetic transmission

Genetic information is combined and transmitted through gametes (i.e., **ovum** and **sperm**), which contain genetic information in molecular structures called **genes**, which form threads called **chromosomes**.

A. The role of DNA

   1. The genes are made of deoxyribonucleic acid (DNA) molecules, which have a double helix (spiral) chemical structure that allows their division and duplication.

   2. DNA transmits genetic information at conception, when the sperm and ovum unite creating a **zygote**.

B. Meiosis and mitosis

   1. Gametes divide through meiosis, resulting in twenty-three chromosomes.

   2. All other cells divide by mitosis, resulting in forty-six chromosomes.

III. Individual genetic expression

A. Genotype and phenotype

   1. The **genotype** of an individual is the set of genes he or she inherits that may influence a particular trait.

   2. The **phenotype** is the physical and behavioral characteristics a person actually exhibits at a particular point in development. The phenotype results from all of the interactions of the genotype with environmental influences.

B. Dominant and recessive genes

   1. A **dominant gene** will influence a phenotype even when paired with a recessive gene.

   2. A **recessive gene** must be paired with another recessive gene to be able to influence the phenotype.

   3. Traits that exhibit the phenotype of recessive genes, such as blue eye color, result from the pairing of two recessive genes.

C. Transmission of multiple variations

   1. The genes responsible for eye color, or any other specific trait, often take on a variety of forms called **alleles**.

   2. When a person inherits identical alleles from each parent for a specific trait, he or she is said to be homozygous for that trait.

   3. When a person inherits different alleles for a trait, he or she is said to be heterozygous for that trait.

          4.   Codominance is a situation where the characteristics of both alleles are independently expressed in a new phenotype.

    D. Polygenic transmission

          1.   Because polygenic pheotypes vary by small degrees, environment can influence them in relatively important ways.

          2.   Since the influence of these genes is small, the environment can influence phenotypes.

    E. The determination of sex

          1.   One chromosomal pair determines development as a male or a female.

          2.   Females have a matched pair of longer chromosomes, called XX; males have one longer and one shorter chromosome, an XY pair.

          3.   A large number of genetic abnormalities are linked to genes on the X chromosome and are called **sex-linked recessive traits**. One of these traits is hemophilia, for which males are at greater risk because there is no location on the shorter Y chromosome for a dominant gene to block the influence of the abnormal hemophilia gene.

          4.   In genetic imprinting genes are chemically marked or imprinted in a way that identical sections of the same chromosome will result in different phenotypic outcomes, depending upon whether the chromosome was inherited from the mother or the father. This imprint may disappear in the next generation.

IV. Genetic abnormalities

    A. Disorders due to abnormal chromosomes include Down syndrome, Klinefelter syndrome, and Turner syndrome.

    B. Abnormal genes, even though transmitted through a normal pattern of forty-six chromosomes, may create serious medical problems for the child after birth.

          1.   Dominant gene disorders

              These disorders require only one abnormal gene to affect a child (e.g., Huntington disease).

          2.   Recessive gene disorders

               These disorders require a pair of recessive genes (e.g.,**sickle-cell disease**).

          3.   Multifactorial disorders

               Disorders that result from a combination of genetic and environmental.

V. Genetic counseling and prenatal diagnosis

Some genetic problems can be reduced or avoided through counseling for couples who may carry genetic disorders. The parents' medical and genetic histories and tests are used to estimate the chances of having a healthy baby.

• A Multicultural View: Cultural differences and genetic counseling

VI. Relative influence of heredity and environment

Research supports the important role of heredity, as well as environmental factors, plays in individual developmental differences. Behavior genetics is the study of how genotype and environmental experience jointly influence phenotype.

A. Key concepts of behavior genetics

1. **Behavior genetics** is the study of how genotype and environmental experience jointly influence phenotype.

2. **Range of reaction** refers to the range of possible phenotypes a particular genotype might exhibit in response to environmental influences.

B. Adoption and twin studies

1. **Adoption studies** measure the effects of genetics and environment on development.

2. **Twin studies** compare pairs of identical twins raised in the same family with pairs of fraternal twins raised in the same family.

3. **Twin adoption studies** compare pairs of identical twins who are raised apart since birth in different environments.

4. Linkage and association studies allow research to identify polymorphisms, which are certain segments of DNA that are inherited together, and those polymorphisms that are coinherited with a particular trait in families unusually prone to that trait.

VII. Stages of prenatal development

Prenatal development takes place in the **germinal, embryonic**, and **fetal** stages.

A. Conception

Conception occurs when a sperm cell penetrates and fertilizes an egg cell.

B. The germinal stage (first two weeks)

1. The blastocyst is differentiated into three layers: the ectoderm, the endoderm, and the mesoderm.

2. The blastocyst moves down the fallopian tube into the uterus for implantation.

       3.   The embryonic stage begins with implantation, and the fully implanted blastocyst is referred to as the embryo.

  C. The embryonic stage (third through eighth weeks)

       1.   Growth in the embryonic and fetal stages follows a cephalocaudal (head-to-tail) and a proximodistal (near-to-far) pattern.

       2.   The head, blood vessels, heart, and most vital organs begin to develop before the arms, legs, hands, and feet.

       3.   The **placenta** forms, through which oxygen and nutrients reach the fetus.

       4.   The **umbilical cord** connects the embryo to the placenta; it provides nutrients and carries away waste products.

       5.   The **amniotic sac** surrounds the embryo and protects it.

  D. The fetal stage (ninth week to birth)

       1.   The fetal stage is marked by the development of the first bone cells. The embryo is now called the fetus.

       2.   By the third month, the fetus is able to move its head, legs, and feet. By the fourth month, the mother may feel quickening, or fetal movement.

       3.   The beginning of the seventh month is considered the age of viability.

       4.   At the end of nine months, the fetus is on average 7.5 pounds and almost 20 inches long.

  E. The experience of pregnancy

       1. Physical complaints such as nausea are common.

       2. Normal weight gain is about 30 pounds and is dispersed in organs, baby, and bodily fluid.

       3. Pregnancy is a powerful experience for both mother and father. It raises the question "Am I ready to be emotionally and economically responsible for this baby?"

• Working with Katie Glover, ob-gyn nurse practitioner: Preparing for childbirth

VIII. Infertility, Contraception, Abortion

  A. About 15 percent of couples are unable to conceive or carry a pregnancy to term after one year of unprotected intercourse.

  B. In about 80 to 90 percent of couples receiving medical treatment, it is possible to discover a clear medical reason for infertility.

  C. New technologies are now available to help couples deal with infertility.

• Focusing On: Technological alternatives to normal conception

    D. Contraception refers to voluntary methods of preventing unintended pregnancy.

    E. Abortion

IX. Prenatal influences on the child.

Canalization refers to the tendency of genes to influence development and to resist environmental factors that would change that pattern. Risk factors can interfere with canalized processes that lead to the development of specific organs.

  A. Harmful substances.

The **critical period** refers to a limited period of time during which certain developmental changes are particularly sensitive to disruption. Any substance or other environmental influence that can interfere with or permanently damage an embryo's growth is called a **teratogen**. A teratogen's effect is dependent on several factors, such as timing of exposure, intensity and duration of exposure, the number of other harmful influences, and biogenetic vulnerability.

    1. Medicinal drugs. Drugs that may cure illness and relieve pain may negatively affect fetal development.

        a. Thalidomide was widely prescribed for reducing morning sickness in the late 1950s and early 1960s. Babies of mothers who took thalidomide had deformed arms, legs, and faces and suffered deafness and brain damage.

        b. Diethylstilbestrol (DES) was taken by pregnant women to prevent miscarriages. Babies of mothers who took DES seemed normal but developed serious problems later in life such as structural abnormalities in the vagina and uterus in girls and an increased risk for testicular cancer in boys.

    2. Nonmedicinal drugs

        a. Babies born to mothers who consume too much alcohol may have fetal alcohol syndrome (FAS) and fetal alcohol effects (FAEs).

        b. Symptoms of FAS include central nervous system damage, physical abnormalities of the heart, head, face, and joints, and mental retardation.

        c. Even moderate drinking during pregnancy can be dangerous to the fetus.

    3. Maternal diseases. Syphilis may cause fetal death, and gonorrhea may cause blindness.

    4. Pediatric AIDS.

About three-fourths of AIDS cases in children involve perinatal transmission from an infected mother to her baby.

     a. IV drug use by the mother causes most cases of perinatal AIDS.

     b. Most children infected perinatally show symptoms before age one, but some remain free of symptoms for several years.

     c. The drug AZT administered to an AIDS-infected woman during late pregnancy and labor and given to her child immediately after birth may help reduce the chance of having an HIV-infected baby.

   5. Environmental hazards.

There are physical and biological hazards to the developing fetus present in the workplace.

B. Domestic violence.

Seven to eight percent of pregnant women are beaten by their partners. One percent of all pregnant women with no history of being battered will be abused during pregnancy.

C. Maternal age and physical characteristics.

The mother's age and health can lead to complications at birth.

   1. Women over age 35 may be at risk for complications related to infertility and Down syndrome.

   2. Teenage mothers often have nutritional deficiencies and may not get adequate prenatal care. Babies born to teenage mothers are more likely to be premature and have low birth weight.

D. Prenatal health care.

   1. Adequate early prenatal health care is critical to infant and maternal health. Race and socioeconomic status play a major role in determining whether adequate early prenatal health care is obtained. Programs can help high-risk mothers. These programs involve regular home visits and education.

   2. Diet and nutrition. Poor nutrition leads to increased risk of prematurity and infant mortality. Babies of mothers with poor diets have lower birth weights and have an increased risk for congenital malformations.

   3. Stress and health. Prolonged anxiety just before or during pregnancy is likely to increase medical complications. Emotional stress is related to spontaneous abortion as well as to labor and birth problems.

X.   Birth

After about thirty-eight weeks in the womb, the baby is considered "full term," or ready for birth. **Fetal presentation** refers to the body part closest to the mother's cervix. There are three types of presentation: cephalic, breech, and transverse.

A. Stages of labor

1.   During the last weeks of pregnancy, it is common for the mother to experience false labor, or Braxton-Hicks contractions.

2.   The first stage of labor usually begins with relatively mild contractions, leading to stronger contractions and the dilation of the cervix to accommodate the baby's head.

3.   Toward the end of the first stage, which may take from eight to twenty-four hours, a period of transition begins, and the baby's head begins to move through the birth canal.

4.   The second stage of labor is from complete dilation of the cervix to birth, lasting from one to two hours.

5.   During the third stage of labor, which lasts between five and twenty minutes, the afterbirth (consisting of the placenta and umbilical cord) is expelled.

B. Childbirth settings and methods

Traditionally, childbirth was attended by a midwife and was seen as a natural process. With the advent of modern technology, more births took place in medical settings. This resulted in decreased mortality rates, but birth was now seen as a medical event controlled by physicians.

1.   Hospital births

Birthing rooms are becoming more popular in hospitals.

2.   Nonhospital settings

a.   Freestanding birth centers are nonhospital facilities that provide family-centered maternity care.

b.   Home births are another birthing alternative, with a nurse-midwife or physician monitoring labor if the pregnancy has been predetermined to be low risk.

3.   Prepared childbirth

Methods of **prepared childbirth** help parents rehearse the sensations of labor.

a.   Programs emphasize educational, physical, and emotional preparation for the birth process and use of a coach.

b.   Women who participate in the Lamaze method report more favorable effects.

c.   Fathers' involvement in preparing for and participating in delivery has positive effects.

d.   Midwives and doulahs are also used increasingly for delivery and early care of the mother and infant.

4. Medicinal methods

Despite good psychological preparation, the mother may experience considerable pain, which can be made bearable through pain-reducing drugs such as narcotics or other sedatives.

   a. The most common anesthetics are epidural and spinal, which allow the mother to remain awake and alert during birth.

   b. A general or local anesthetic delays the recovery of the mother as well as the bonding between mother and child.

C. Problems during labor and delivery

   1. Faulty power is the failure of the uterus to contract strongly enough to make labor progress to actual delivery. Induced labor can be stimulated by the hormone oxytocin.

   2. A faulty passageway condition occurs when the placenta develops so close to the cervix that it blocks the baby's passage down the birth canal during labor. This condition is called placenta previa.

   3. A faulty passageway can also occur when the placenta partly separates from the wall of the womb.

   4. A faulty passenger condition is when problems exist with the baby's position or size. Usually babies enter the birth canal headfirst, but occasionally one turns in the wrong direction during contractions. Forceps are sometimes used to remedy the situation.

   5. In a cesarean section, the mother receives a general anesthetic and the baby is removed surgically. Techniques for this surgery have improved; however, a common criticism is that too many cesareans are performed.

   6. In most hospitals, electronic fetal monitoring is used to record uterine contractions and the fetal heart rate.

   7. Mothers who have physical disabilities face special challenges.

D. Birth and the family

   1. The majority of births occur without significant problems.

   2. A newborn can create stress in the family.

XI. Looking back/looking forward

   A. Continuity within change

   B. Lifelong growth

   C. Changing meaning and vantage points

   D. Developmental diversity

Key Concepts

Directions: Identify each of the key concepts discussed in this chapter.

1. Reproductive cells are called ____. The male reproductive cell is the _____ and the female reproductive cell is the _____.
2. A _____ is the basic unit of heredity. It is carried on _____, which are threadlike, rod-shaped structures containing genetic information that is transmitted from parents to children.
3. Human reproductive cells contain _____ chromosomes.
4. _____ are made up of _____, the complex protein code of genetic information that directs the functioning of each cell.
5. When male and female gametes meet, the resulting cell is called a _____.
6. Reproductive cells divide by the process of _____; this process yields two new cells, each of which contains _____ chromosomes.
7. Normal body cells divide by the process of _____; this process yields two daughter cells each of which contains _____ chromosomes.
8. The observable physical and behavioral traits of a person are called the _____. The set of genetic traits inherited by an individual is the individual's _____.
9. When genes are paired with one another, the one with the greater influence in determining characteristics that are physically observable is called the _____ gene. The gene whose information does not physically manifest is called the _____ gene.
10. An alternative form of a gene is called an _____.
11. Traits such as hair and skin color, alcoholism, and depression that are the result of the combination of many genes are called _____.
12. The sex of the child is determined by the chromosome carried on the _____. If this gamete is carrying the _____ chromosome, then the child will be female; if the gamete is carrying the _____ chromosome, then the child will be male. All ova carry the _____ chromosome.
13. Recessive traits that result from genes carried on the X chromosome are called _____.
14. A new mode of inheritance in which genes are chemically marked in such a way as to activate the chromosome pair contributed by either parent is called _____.
15. Down syndrome is also called _____ because it is generally caused by an extra twenty-first chromosome. This disorder typically results in some degree of _____ in the affected individual.
16. Huntington disease is an example of a _____ disorder, disorders that require only one gene from either parent to affect a child. Sickle-cell disease is an example of a _____ disorder, disorders that occur when the fetus inherits a pair of recessive genes, one from each parent.
17. The concept of the _____ refers to the possible phenotypes an individual with a particular genotype may exhibit in response to the environmental influences he or she experiences.
18. _____ compare the degree of physical and behavioral similarity between adoptive children and members of their adoptive families with the degree of similarity between these same children and the members of their biological families.
19. _____ compare pairs of identical twins raised in the same family with pairs of fraternal twins raised in the same family.
20. _____ compare pairs of identical twins who have been raised apart since birth in different environments.
21. The three stages of prenatal development are called _____, _____, and _____ stages.
22. The pattern of development that proceeds from head to tail is called _____. A _____ pattern of development proceeds from the center of the body outward.
23. The organ that delivers nutrients and oxygen from the mother to the fetus and waste products from the fetus to the mother is called the _____.

24. Blood vessels that connect the embryo to the placenta are collectively called the _____.
25. The protective fluid-filled sack that surrounds the embryo is the _____.
26. An inability to conceive or carry a pregnancy to full term after one year of unprotected intercourse is termed _____.
27. The termination of a pregnancy before the embryo or fetus is capable of independent life is called _____.
28. _____ refers to the tendency of many developmental processes to unfold according to genetically determined patterns despite a wide range of environmental conditions.
29. A _____ is any period during which development is highly susceptible to positive or negative events or influences.
30. _____ are substances that can harm the developing embryo or fetus if ingested by a pregnant woman.
31. If a pregnant woman consumes too much alcohol during pregnancy, her child may be born with _____.
32. The _____ virus is associated with the development of AIDS.
33. _____ refers to the body part of the fetus that is closest to the mother's cervix.
34. Labor is divided into _____ stages.
35. _____ are people, usually women, who give care to a woman during pregnancy and delivery and for about one month following the birth of the baby.
36. A _____ allows parents to rehearse or simulate labor and delivery before the actual delivery of the baby.
37. Currently, more than ----- percent of births in the United States occur in hospitals.
38. When vaginal birth is not possible, the baby may be removed through a surgical procedure called a _____.
39. _____ is used to record uterine contractions and the fetal heart rate during labor.

Multiple-Choice Self-Test

Factual Questions

1. When a cell divides by the process of mitosis, each of the resulting cells has
   a. twenty-three chromosomes.
   b. twenty-three genes.
   c. forty-six chromosomes.
   d. forty-six genes.

2. The actually observable physical and behavioral traits of an individual are known as a(n)
   a. phenotype.
   b. genotype.
   c. karotype.
   d. allele.

3. Hemophilia is an example of
   a. genetic imprinting.
   b. a sex-linked recessive trait.
   c. trisomy 21.
   d. a disorder caused by an abnormal chromosome.

4. The restriction placed by genetics on the effects of environmental influences on phenotypes is called
   a. canalization.
   b. heritability.
   c. genotype.
   d. range of reaction.

5. Studies that compare identical twins who have been raised apart in different environments since birth are called
   a. adoption studies.
   b. twin studies.
   c. twin adoption studies.
   d. linkage studies.

6. The moment that marks the meeting of the sperm and the egg is known as
   a. conception.
   b. the germinal stage of pregnancy.
   c. the embryonic stage of pregnancy.
   d. the fetal stage of pregnancy.

7. Which of the following structures allows the exchange of nutrients and wastes between the mother and the embryo?
   a. The amniotic sac
   b. The placenta
   c. The umbilical cord
   d. The zygote

8. Under which of the following conditions is abortion prohibited or *not* permitted by nations that belong to the United Nations?
   a. Abortion is necessary to preserve the woman's health.
   b. Pregnancy resulted from a rape.
   c. The woman wants an abortion.
   d. The nation is already overpopulated, and abortion is mandated by federal law.

9. Teratogens are
   a. periods during which development is particularly vulnerable.
   b. the predictable unfolding of developmental processes.
   c. substances ingested by pregnant women that can harm the developing embryo or fetus.
   d. sedatives prescribed to pregnant women in the 1950s and 1960s that led to birth of babies with defects, including shortened limbs.

10. Babies born to teenagers are
    a. healthier because the mother is younger and therefore healthier.
    b. not different in health status from babies born to women in their mid- to late twenties.
    c. more likely to be premature and to have lower birth weights.
    d. more likely to be male.

Multiple-Choice Self-Test

Conceptual Questions

1. Sheralee has blue eyes. She probably inherited a _____ gene for eye color from her mom and a _____ one from her father.
   a. recessive; dominant
   b. dominant; recessive
   c. dominant; dominant
   d. recessive; recessive

2. Grace has brown hair. Her genotype is likely to be
   a. homozygous dominant.
   b. heterozygous.
   c. homozygous recessive.
   d. heterozygous or homozygous dominant.

3. Who is more likely to give birth to a baby with Down syndrome?
   a. A teenager
   b. An alcoholic
   c. A woman over the age of thirty-five
   d. A woman who has a blood relative with Down syndrome

4. Which of these couples is *least* likely to seek prenatal genetic counseling?
   a. Couples who are blood relatives to each other
   b. Couples with a family history of mental retardation
   c. Couples who have at least one child with congenital heart disease
   d. Couples who have a family history of cancer

5. Gerry was born to parents who were mildly mentally retarded. She was then adopted by a couple with above-average intelligence levels. Gerry's intellectual ability is likely to be
   a. very similar to the intellectual capacities of her biological parents.
   b. very similar to the intellectual capacities of her adoptive parents.
   c. higher than the intellectual capacities of her biological parents.
   d. higher than the intellectual capacities of her adoptive parents.

6. At one of her visits to the doctor for a prenatal checkup, Judy tells her doctor that that very morning she felt the movement of the baby for the first time. In which month of pregnancy is Judy most likely to be?
   a. Third
   b. Fourth
   c. Fifth
   d. Sixth

7. Sammy was born deaf, with very short arms and brain damage. What is the most likely cause of for his condition?
   a. His mother abused alcohol during pregnancy.
   b. His mother took thalidomide during pregnancy.
   c. His mother had syphilis during pregnancy.
   d. The fetus contracted gonorrhea in the birth canal.

8. The drug AZT is administered to Sharon during labor because Sharon
   a. is infected with AIDS.
   b. has syphilis.
   c. has gonorrhea.
   d. abused alcohol during pregnancy.

9. Dora is in labor. Midway through the process the doctor tells her that her contractions have considerably declined in strength. Under the circumstances, which of the following is likely to be true?
   a. Dora has untreated placenta previa.
   b. The baby is in a breech position.
   c. The doctor will now have to induce labor.
   d. The condition of cephalopelvic disproportion has occurred.

10. Nancy and her doctor have agreed that she will deliver her baby by caesarrean because this will be the safest delivery for both her and the baby. Which of the following is probably true?
    a. Nancy has inactive herpes.
    b. There is suspected cephalopelvic disproportion.
    c. Nancy gave birth to her first child through a C-section.
    d. Nancy suffers from placenta previa.

Answer Key

Key Concepts

1. gametes; sperm; ovum
2. gene; chromosomes
3. forty-six
4. Chromosomes; DNA
5. zygote
6. meiosis; twenty-three
7. mitosis; forty-six
8. phenotype; genotype
9. dominant; recessive
10. allele
11. polygenic
12. sperm; X; Y; X
13. sex-linked recessive traits
14. genetic imprinting
15. trisomy 21; mental retardation
16. dominant gene; recessive gene
17. range of reaction
18. Adoption studies
19. Twin studies
20. Twin adoption studies
21. germinal; embryonic; fetal
22. cephalocaudal; proximodistal
23. placenta

24. umbilical cord
25. amniotic sac
26. infertility
27. abortion
28. Canalization
29. critical period
30. Teratogens
31. fetal alcohol syndrome
32. HIV
33. Fetal presentation
34. three
35. Midwives
36. prepared childbirth
37. 90
38. caesarean-section
39. Electronic fetal monitoring

Multiple-Choice Self-Test / Factual Questions

1.   Choice (c) is correct; mitosis yields two daughter cells, each containing the same number of chromosomes as the parent cell. Twenty-three chromosomes, choice (a), are present in the new cells that result from the process of meiosis. Choices (b) and (d) are incorrect because each chromosome contains thousands of genes.

2.   Choice (a) is correct; the phenotype is the traits of an individual as they are physically or behaviorally expressed. Choice (b), genotype, refers to the genetic makeup of the individual. Choice (c), a karotype is a picture of the twenty-three pairs of chromosomes of an individual. Choice (d), an allele, is an alternate form of a gene.

3.   Choice (b) is correct; genetic abnormalities caused by genes carried on the X chromosome are called sex-linked recessive traits. Choice (a), genetic imprinting, refers to chemically marking genes for the purpose of activating a particular gene contributed by one or the other parent. Choice (c), trisomy 21, is also known as Down syndrome. Choice (d), hemophilia, is not caused by an abnormality in a particular chromosome, as are some other conditions such as Down syndrome.

4.   Choice (d) is correct; range of reaction refers to the concept that heredity places a restriction on the extent of influence the environment can have on a particular trait. Choice (a), canalization, is the tendency for developmental processes to unfold in predictable patterns set by heredity despite environmental variations. Choice (b), heritability, is an index of the influence of heredity on various traits. Choice (c), genotype, refers to the person's genetic makeup.

5.   Choice (c) is correct. Choice (a), adoption studies, compare the similarity between adopted children and adoptive parents to the similarity between adopted children and their biological parents. Twin studies, choice (b), compare identical twins raised in the same family to fraternal twins raised in the same family. Choice (d), linkage studies, attempt to identify polymorphisms that are coinherited.

6.   Choice (a) is correct; conception occurs when the sperm penetrates the egg, usually in the fallopian tubes. Choices (b), (c), and (d) are the first, second, and third stages of pregnancy, respectively, that follow conception.

7.   Choice (b) is correct; the placenta is the organ of exchange between the mother and the embryo. Choice (a), the amniotic sac, is filled with fluid and surrounds and protects the embryo. Choice (c), the umbilical cord, connects the embryo to the placenta. Choice (d), the zygote, is the single cell that results from conception.

8.   Choice (d) is correct; none of the nations that are members of the United Nations use abortion as a method of population control. Choices (a), (b), and (c) are each used by some or all of the nations.

9.   Choice (c) is correct; teratogens are harmful substances if ingested by pregnant women. Choice (a) is the definition of a critical period. Choice (b) is the definition of canalization. Choice (d) is the definition of thalidomide.

10.   Choice (c) is correct; teenage mothers are less likely to receive adequate nutrition and prenatal care and often give birth to low-birth-weight and premature babies. These babies also have higher mortality rates during the first year of life. Therefore, choices (a) and (b) are incorrect. Choice (d) is incorrect in that the age of the mother (or the father) does not influence the sex of the baby; the child's sex is determined by the father's Y chromosome.

Multiple-Choice Self-Test / Conceptual Questions

1.   Choice (d) is correct; blue eye color is a recessive trait. In order for this eye color to appear in the phenotype of the person, an allele for it must be received from both parents. Choices (a), (b), and (c) will all lead to a phenotype of brown eye color because it is dominant.

2.   Choice (d) is correct; when two dominant alleles are paired to produce a particular trait (homozygous dominant) or when a dominant allele is paired with a recessive allele (heterozygous), the phenotype of the individual exhibits the dominant form of the trait. Therefore, choices (a) and (b) are partial answers. Homozygous recessive, choice (c), genotypes are the result of the pairing of two recessive alleles for a trait.

3.   Choice (c) is correct; maternal age is correlated with the incidence of Down syndrome. The risk for having such a baby increases significantly after age 35 probably because these mothers have been exposed to environmental hazards for a longer period of time and their ovaries and ova have been undergoing progressive deterioration. Therefore, choice (a) is incorrect; younger women are less likely to have babies with Down syndrome. Alcohol use and abuse, choice (b), has not been linked to Down syndrome. Choice (d) is incorrect in that Down syndrome is not inherited unless either the mother or the father is afflicted.

4.   Choice (d) is correct; although cancer does have some genetic links, specific forms of cancer are not strongly inherited traits. Choices (a), (b), and (c) are all good reasons for seeking prenatal genetic counseling. Each of the conditions described may produce an embryo with a genetic disorder.

5.   Choice (c) is correct; the relative influences of heredity and environment on development are explained by the concept of the range of reaction. Although the environment does affect development, the extent of the impact is bounded by genetics. Consequently, although intellectual capacity will be influenced positively in an intellectually enriched environment, the increase will not be drastic. Therefore, choices (a) and (b) are incorrect because (a) ignores environmental influences and (b) ignores genetic influences. Choice (d) is incorrect because it too ignores genetic limits placed on development.

6.   Choice (b) is correct; the movement of the fetus inside the womb, called quickening, usually occurs around the sixteenth week (fourth month) of pregnancy. Choice (a) is too early and choices (c) and (d) are too late.

7.   Choice (b) is correct; in the 1950s and early 1960s, thalidomide was prescribed to pregnant women to calm nerves, induce sleep, and reduce morning sickness. Although it was advertised as a safe drug, thousands of babies born between 1958 and 1962 had birth defects related to this drug, including deafness, short or missing limbs, brain damage, facial deformities, and seizure disorders. Choice (a), excessive alcohol use during pregnancy, leads to babies born with fetal alcohol syndrome. These infants are difficult to arouse, sluggish, and have distinctive facial features. Choice (c), if the mother has untreated syphilis, the disease may be transmitted to the fetus. In most cases, the fetus dies in the third trimester of pregnancy or soon after birth. Fetuses that contract gonorrhea in the birth canal, choice (d), develop eye infections and may become blind if not treated with silver nitrate or penicillin eye drops soon after birth.

8.   Choice (a) is correct; AZT is a drug used in the treatment of AIDS and may be administered to AIDS-infected women during late pregnancy or during labor to reduce the risk of transmitting the HIV infection to the fetus. AZT does not treat the symptoms of syphilis, choice (b), gonorrhea, choice (c), or alcohol abuse, choice (d).

9.   Choice (c) is correct; when the contractions of the uterus are not strong enough to progress to delivery, labor may be induced with drugs. Choice (a), placenta previa, occurs when the placenta covers the cervix and blocks the baby from moving down the birth canal. Choice (b), a breech presentation, refers to the baby entering the birth canal bottom first. Choice (d), cephalopelvic disproportion, refers to the baby being too big to pass through the mother's pelvis and the vaginal canal.

10.   Choice (d) is correct; if placenta previa occurs and the placenta is covering the birth canal, preventing the baby from descending, then a C-section is the safest form of delivery. Choice (a), inactive herpes, is not accepted as a valid reason for performing a C-section. Choice (b), cephalopelvic disproportion, must be confirmed by strong and frequent contractions in order for a C-section to be allowed; suspected cephalopelvic disproportion is an inadequate reason for a C-section. Choice (c) is incorrect in that if conditions do not mandate it, a previous delivery by a C-section is not an acceptable reason for a second such delivery.

CHAPTER 4

Physical and Cognitive Development in the First Two Years

Learning Objectives:

1. Discuss physical growth in infancy and compare discontinuity in infancy with discontinuity in adulthood.
2. Describe the physical characteristics of the neonate.
3. Describe the Apgar Scale for neonate assessment.
4. Describe infant sleep patterns in terms of type and duration.
5. Summarize current knowledge about Sudden Infant Death Syndrome (SIDS).
6. Discuss the infant's sensory and reflex abilities at birth and throughout the first two years.
7. Define and explain the cephalocaudal principle and the proximodistal principle.
8. Describe the development of motor skills during the first years considering gender differences.
9. Discuss the nutritional requirements during infancy and outline the pros and cons of breast versus bottle feeding.
10. Discuss concerns about poor nutrition and overnutrition during infancy.
11. Define low-birth-weight infants and discuss related consequences.
12. Describe current trends in infant mortality in the United States and elsewhere.
13. Describe habituation and indicate how it is used to study recognition and memory.
14. Discuss visual thinking and object perception including the development of constancy and depth perception.
15. Describe the infant's ability to localize sounds, the development of anticipation of visual events, and categorical thought.
16. List the major characteristics and achievements of each of Piaget's six stages of sensorimotor development.
17. Describe infant learning, including operant conditioning and imitation.
18. Trace phonological development in the infancy period.
19. Trace semantic development in the infancy period.
20. Describe the individual differences in language development and explain how parents influence early language.

Chapter Outline

I. Physical development. Physical and cognitive development during infancy shows more obvious growth, more discontinuity, but less diversity than at any other stage in the lifespan.

II. Appearance of the young infant

    A. The first few hours

        1. The **neonate** may be covered with vernix and lanugo.

        2. The head may be elongated from the compression of the skull bones at the fontanelles.

    B. Is the baby all right?

        The **Apgar scale** helps determine the health status of the newborn by measuring heart rate, efforts to breathe, muscle tone, skin color, and reflex irritability at one and five minutes.

    C. Size and bodily proportions

        1. At birth, a typical baby weighs about 7.5 pounds and is about 20 inches long.

        2. Babies' physical appearance may have consequences for attachment.

III. Sleep, arousal, and development of the nervous system

    The **central nervous system** consists of the brain and spinal cord. The brain grows rapidly from before birth through the second year. Weight gain in the brain results from the development of fibers to form connections among **neurons** and the formation of myelin—a fatty sheath encasing neurons and nerve fibers—by certain brain cells called glia.

    A. Sleep

        1. Infants sleep an average of sixteen hours per day.

        2. Newborns divide their sleeping time about equally between active sleep, or **REM sleep**, and quieter sleep, or **non-REM sleep**, and they waken frequently but unpredictably.

        3. Parents' response to infant sleep and arousal can be one of frustration. An attempt should be made for a regular routine.

    B. Infants show various states of arousal; however, the largest share of time goes to deep sleep. As they get older, their patterns of arousal begin to resemble those of older children.

• Focusing On: Sudden infant death syndrome

IV. Visual and auditory acuity

    A. Infants can see at birth, but without the clarity of focus or acuity characteristic of adults with good vision. Infant vision is nearsighted but improves rapidly.

    B. Auditory acuity refers to sensitivity to sounds.

       1.   Infants can hear at birth, but not as well as adults can.

       2.   Sudden noises produce a dramatic startle reaction called the Moro reflex.

   C.   By taking an interest in the environment, the child creates conditions where he or she can begin organizing (or perceiving) sights and sounds and attaching meanings to them.

V.   Motor development

   A.   Early reflexes

   Motor development begins with more than two dozen inborn **reflexes**, most of which disappear in the first few months.

   B.   The first motor skills

       1.   **Motor skills** are voluntary bodily movements and can be divided into gross motor skills and fine motor skills.

       2.   Skills generally develop according to the **cephalocaudal principle** (head to tail) and **proximodistal principle** (near to far).

       3.   Gross motor development in the first year is increasingly marked by purposefulness.

       4.   Early, crude reaching disappears fairly soon after birth, only to reappear at about four or five months as two separate skills, reaching and grasping.

       5.   By the age of twelve or thirteen months, babies typically take their first independent steps.

       6.   Differences exist in motor development among cultures.

       7.   During the first two years, the genders do not differ in competence.

           a.   Boys and girls pass major developmental milestones at about the same time.

           b.   Boys show more activity than girls and girls spend more time using their emerging fine motor skills, perhaps due to differences in parental encouragement and genetics.

VI.   Nutrition during the first two years

   Compared with older children, infants eat less in absolute amounts, but in proportion to body weight they need to consume much more than children or adults do.

   A.   Breast milk versus formula

       1.   Health experts generally recommend human milk as the sole source of nutrition for the first six months of life, because it seems to give infants greater protection from diseases and other ailments.

       2.   Infants can be gradually introduced to solid foods after about six months.

B. Poor nutrition

Malnutrition in North America is related to dietary deficiencies in vitamin A, vitamin C, and iron. Vitamin A and C deficiencies seem to create deficits in motor ability. Iron deficiency appears to create deficits in cognitive performance.

C. Overnutrition means too many calories, too much of the wrong nutrients, and not enough of other nutrients.

1. In calorie-loving societies, overeating can lead to becoming **obese**.

2. Contrary to what some parents fear, weight in infancy correlates very little with weight in childhood and even less with weight in adulthood.

VII. Impairments in infant growth

A. Newborns are considered **low-birth-weight** infants if they weigh less than twenty-five hundred grams, or 5.5 pounds.

1. Causes of low birth weight include maternal factors such as malnourishment during pregnancy, smoking, drinking alcohol, or consuming drugs. Teenage mothers or poor mothers who lack prenatal care also tend to have low-birth-weight babies. Multiple births also tend to result in small-for-date babies.

2. Consequences for the infant of low birth weight include neurological development that contributes to weak organization of reflexes such as grasping and startling, immaturity of muscle development, and difficulty regulating sleep. Neurological limitations may persist for the first two or three years of life.

3. Parents of low-birth-weight infants may feel distant from their newborn which can cause problems in the developing relationship if the parents are not patient and mature.

B. **Failure to thrive** occurs when an infant or preschooler fails to grow at normal rates for no apparent reason. Causes of failure to thrive are complex.

C. Infant mortality

1. In the past several decades, health-care systems have improved their ability to keep infants alive.

2. The **infant mortality rate** in the United States and Canada is two or three times lower than in many Third World countries. However, mortality in the United States is higher than in nineteen other developed nations.

3. The strongest correlate with mortality is not race, but level of family income.

VIII. Cognitive development

Perception is a psychological process that involves the brain's immediate organization and interpretation of sensation. **Cognition** refers to all the processes involved in thinking and other mental activities.

IX.   Studying cognition and memory in infants

    A.   Arousal and infants' heart rates

        1.   One way to understand an infant's cognition is to measure heart rate (HR) with a small electronic stethoscope.

        2.   The changes in HR are taken to signify variations in arousal, alertness, and general contentment.

        3.   When HR slows down, it suggests heightened attention or interest.

    B.   Recognition, memory, and infant habituation

        1.   Babies' responses to the familiar and the unfamiliar provide infant psychologists with a second means of understanding infant perception and cognition.

        2.   Psychologists study infants' tendency to get used to and therefore ignore stimuli as they experience them repeatedly; this tendency is called **habituation**.

        3.   Typically the researcher presents the baby with a study stimulus to which the infant habituates. Then the study stimulus is presented along with other stimuli. If the baby recognizes the original stimulus, she or he will look at the new stimuli longer   and HR will slow down.

        4.   Habituation is important not only because it provides a way to study infants' learning and development, but also because it suggests that infants have memories well before they acquire language.

X.   Infant perception and cognition

Infant cognition consists not only of growing complexity of perception, the organization of sensations, but also non-verbal cognitions including rudimentary reasoning and problem solving.

    A.   Visual thinking in infancy

        1.   Object perception

            Early studies suggested that two-day-old infants recognize human faces; more recent studies have shown that infants are drawn more to the interesting contours, complexity, and curvature of the face than to its humanness.

            a.   Object constancy refers to the perception that an object remains the same in some way despite constant changes in the sensations it sends to the eye.

            b.   Size constancy is the perception that an object stays the same size even when viewed at different distances.

        2.   Depth perception refers to a sense of how far away objects are or appear to be.

        a.   The **visual cliff** experiment demonstrates that infants acquire this skill at about two or three months.

        b.   Babies old enough to crawl show significant fear of the visual cliff.

   3. Anticipation of visual events

      Infants as young as two months develop expectations about the environment that show a variety of rule-governed qualities.

B. Auditory thinking in infancy

   1. Infants just two months old have a limited ability to locate sounds, as shown by the way they orient their heads toward the noise of a rattle. But several seconds are needed before orienting toward the sound.

   2. Infants are better able to locate relatively high-pitched sounds than low-pitched sounds. Infants prefer sounds in the middle range of pitches.

   3. Babies appear to be able to coordinate what they see with what they hear.

   2. Categorical thought: The reversal shift.

      One series of studies, using the concepts of reversal shift and nonreversal shift, demonstrated that infants are capable of "thinking" in terms of underlying, abstract categories. Cognition, in the sense of deliberate reasoning, seems to be continuous from infancy.

XI. Cognitive change during infancy: Piaget's stage theory

    At first, infant cognition, or thought, has little to do with the symbolic forms that develop in most children and adults. Instead, it emphasizes active experimentation with and manipulation of materials. Truly symbolic thought does not emerge until the end of infancy.

A. Stages of sensorimotor intelligence

   1. Piaget's theory of cognitive development outlines infant intelligence, describing infant thought in terms of sensory perceptions and motor actions, or **sensorimotor intelligence**.

   2. Two major trends are demonstrated across Piaget's six stages of infancy.

        a.   Infants show a trend toward symbolic thinking.

        b.   Infants form cognitive structures called **schemes**, organized patterns of actions or concepts that help them make sense out of and adapt to their environment. These initial schemes lead to later cognitive structures that Piaget called operations.

   3. Piaget argued that sensorimotor intelligence develops by means of two complementary processes: **assimilation**, which consists of interpreting new experiences in terms of existing schemes, and **accommodation**, which involves modifying existing schemes to fit new experiences.

a. Stage 1: early reflexes (birth to one month). Inborn reflexes are quickly modified in response to the newborn's experiences.

b. Stage 2: primary circular reactions (one to four months). The baby begins building
and differentiating action schemes quite rapidly. Within a month or so, these schemes become very repetitive—hence, the term **circular reactions**. Also at this time, babies begin to vary in their preferences for schemes.

c. Stage 3: secondary circular reactions (four to eight months). The infant expands attention beyond his or her own body to include objects and events in the surrounding environment. New, repetitive actions motivated by external objects and events, called secondary circular reactions, show that the infant is beginning to acquire **object permanence**—the belief that objects have an existence separate from the baby's own actions and continue to exist even when she or he cannot see them.

d. Stage 4: combined secondary circular reactions (eight to twelve months). Here the infant intentionally chooses a scheme as a means toward an end and uses this means-end connection purposefully. The relatively fixed quality of schemes at this stage may derive from a heavy reliance on motor actions.

e. Stage 5: tertiary circular reactions (twelve to eighteen months). At this stage, the infant deliberately varies schemes to produce interesting results. The baby can now use trial and error in learning about properties of new objects by running through his or her repertoire of schemes. These variations involving systematic scheme applications are termed tertiary circular reactions.

f. Stage 6: the first symbols (eighteen to twenty-four months). At this time, the motor schemes previously explored and practiced begin to occur symbolically; that is, the child can begin to imagine actions and their results without actually trying them beforehand.

B. Assessment of Piaget's theory of infant cognition

Piaget's theory has stimulated research on infant cognition, much of which confirms the main features of his theory. Some research, however, has pointed out additional aspects of infancy that complicate Piaget's original presentation.

1. One question concerns Piaget's emphasis on motor limitations versus cognitive limitations. Some infant psychologists question Piaget's six stages because they believe that the stages confuse the child's motor abilities with his or her cognitive abilities. Object permanence, for example, implicitly depends on a child's capacity to conduct a search. Perhaps younger infants lack classic object permanence because they lack motor skills or use them clumsily.

2. Piaget may have failed to account properly for the effects of memory. He explained most infant thinking in terms of motor schemes: repeated, familiar actions that allow infants to know their environment.

XII.   Behavioral learning in infancy

One framework for studying the specific performance of infants is based on **behaviorism**, or learning theory, which focuses on changes in specific behaviors.

A.   Operant conditioning

1.   Studies have found that infants are capable of learning through operant conditioning. For instance, newborns will learn to suck on a pacifier more rapidly if doing so yields a tiny amount of sugar water.

2.   Infants are predisposed to learn these particular behaviors. All examples of operant conditioning in infants rely on those few behaviors that young babies can already do, which are mainly reflexive. Since reflexes occur easily, one may question whether infant responses constitute learning or general excitement.

B.   Imitation

1.   Research generally shows that babies engage in different kinds of imitation at different points during infancy.

2.   Infants imitate actions they can see themselves perform sooner than they imitate actions they can observe only in a model.

3.   Infants sometimes imitate actions that are relatively invisible to themselves.

XIII.   Language acquisition

Infants must acquire all three major aspects of language to become verbally competent and to listen with comprehension: language sounds (phonology), meaning (semantics), and organization (syntax).

A.   Phonology

1.   Sounds that speakers of a language consider distinctive and use to make the words of that language are called **phonemes**. English has about forty-one phonemes.

2.   Perceiving phonemes is important because it helps infants ignore meaningless variations. Language specialists suspect that humans are genetically and physiologically predisposed to notice phonemic differences.

3.   Sometime between four and eight months, infants begin babbling with increasing complexity and with the purpose of hearing themselves vocalize.

4.   Babbling seems to be intrinsically motivated. Studies involving babbling in deaf infants revealed that babies babble with their hands in ways analogous to the oral babbling of hearing infants.

5.   Parents and others appear to have an influence on babbling. Deaf babies babble months later than hearing babies and only when they hear sound that is amplified.

    B. **Semantics** and first words

       1. First words learned by children are nominals, particularly those that are used frequently or that stand out.

       2. Children's language differs in style, which is encouraged by differing family environments.

- A Multicultural View: Cognitive effects of talking to infants: A cross-cultural perspective

    C. Influencing language acquisition

       1. Asking questions and pausing, even when a child is too young to answer, can facilitate the child's learning turn-taking in language.

       2. By simplifying their language with the infant and keeping just ahead of the infant's own linguistic skill (**infant-directed speech**), parents can stimulate further development of language.

       3. The Harvard Preschool Project has shown that the most intellectually and socially competent infants have parents who direct large amounts of language at them.

       4. Professional caregivers can also influence language acquisition even though differences of intensity and frequency exist. The forms of influence resemble those of parents.

- Working with Gillian Luppiwiski, infant care provider: Fostering infants' thinking

XIV. The end of infancy

Key Concepts

Directions: Identify each of the key concepts discussed in this chapter.

1. The newborn infant is called the _____.
2. The Apgar scale is administered to newborns at _____ and _____ after birth.
3. The central nervous system consists of the _____ and the _____.
4. A nerve cell is known as a _____.
5. The relatively active period of sleep during which the eyes move is called -----. Deep sleep is referred to as _____.
6. In most non-Western cultures babies sleep with their _____.
7. The acronym SIDS stands for _____.
8. The infant's various levels of alertness and activity are known as _____.
9. Visual clarity of focus is called _____; sensitivity to sounds is called _____.
10. An involuntary, automatic response is called a _____. Motor skills that involve large muscles of the body are called _____. Those that involve small muscles, such as the hands, are called _____.
11. An infant's ability to use and control organs, reflexes, and skills related to the top of the body earlier than those farther down the body is referred to as the _____.

12. Growth that proceeds from the center of the body outward is called _____.
13. From the time they can move, boys show more _____ than girls.
14. A diet that contains too many calories and not enough balanced nutrition is called _____.
15. Babies who are born weighing less than 5 2 pounds (2,500 grams) are labeled _____.
16. When an infant's physical growth is significantly delayed and his behavior is apathetic, he is suffering from a condition called _____.
17. The frequency with which infants die compared to the frequency with which they live is called _____.
18. The brain's organization and interpretation of sensations into meaningful patterns is known as _____.
19. Thinking and reasoning processes, including all methods for obtaining knowledge, are called _____.
20. The infant's tendency to attend to new stimuli and to ignore familiar stimuli is called _____.
21. The classic laboratory experiment which is used to test the ability to perceive depth in infants is called the _____.
22. Infants can locate sounds starting at about _____ months of age. They require an average of seconds _____ before orienting toward a sound.
23. A _____ is an experimental procedure in which reinforcement is offered for discriminating a particular dimension, such as color, that periodically takes on new values; for example, red rather than blue.
24. A _____ is an experimental procedure in which the dimension that is being reinforced changes.
25. Piaget's first stage of cognitive development, corresponding to the first two years of life, is called the _____ stage. This stage is divided into _____ substages.
26. A _____ is an organization of behaviors or thoughts that allows infants to represent the world.
27. The method of using existing information to understand and make sense of new ideas and concepts is known as _____. When existing knowledge is modified so that new information fits, _____ has occurred.
28. Often-repeated actions, such as thumb sucking, were labeled _____ by Piaget.
29. Piaget claimed that when an infant gains the understanding that people and objects continue to exist even when they are not immediately visible to her, she has achieved _____.
30. The branch of psychology that examines the relationships between behaviors and their causes and consequences is _____.
31. Behaviorism has outlined two methods by which infants learn: _____ involves learning through rewards or reinforcements of desired behaviors, whereas _____ involves copying the behaviors of others.
32. _____ are sounds that combine with other sounds to form words.
33. The words of a language are called its -----; the meaning of words is called.
34. The ways in which and purposes for words and sentences are typically used in conversation refers to the _____ of language, and the organization of words into sentences refers to the _____ of language.
35. Infant vocalizations such as "ba ba ba" are known as _____.
36. When adults and older children talk with one-to two-year-old infants, they typically use _____.

Multiple-Choice Self-Test

Factual Questions

1. At one minute and five minutes after birth the neonate is administered the
   a. neonatal assessment scale.
   b. Apgar scale.
   c. reflex irritability scale.
   d. muscle tone scale.

2. An infant who is engaging in very limited movement, whose eyes open and close with a glazed look, and who is breathing regularly is in the _____ state of arousal.
   a. alert inactivity
   b. distress
   c. REM sleep
   d. drowsy

3. Which of the following skills is likely to emerge first in the sequence?
   a. Wiggling fingers
   b. Wiggling wrist
   c. Waving arm
   d. Waving hand

4. Low birth weight is defined as less than
   a. 5 _ pounds.
   b. 6 _ pounds.
   c. 5 pounds.
   d. 6 pounds.

5. Habituation studies allow psychologists to understand infants'
   a. expressive language skills.
   b. receptive language skills.
   c. memory skills.
   d. motor skills.

6. If an infant is searching for a toy that he cannot visually see, the infant has achieved
   a. depth perception.
   b. object constancy.
   c. nonreversal shift.
   d. object permanence.

7. Repeated actions that involve the infant's own body are known as
   a. primary circular reactions.
   b. secondary circular reactions.
   c. tertiary circular reactions.
   d. reflexes.

8. In which sensorimotor substage do children begin to use symbols?
    a. Fourth
    b. Fifth
    c. Sixth
    d. Seventh

9. The study of the meaningfulness of a language is known as
    a. phonology.
    b. semantics.
    c. pragmatics.
    d. syntax.

10. Children who have a referential style
    a. use words to express feelings and relationships.
    b. use familiar language routines or rituals.
    c. encounter adults who attempt to extend their language initiatives.
    d. use their first words to refer to objects and events.

Conceptual Questions

1. Four-day-old Sarah has been sleeping about twelve hours per day. Her parents should
    a. immediately call the pediatrician; she is sleeping too little.
    b. immediately call the pediatrician; she is sleeping too much.
    c. not worry; her sleep time is within the normal range.
    d. try to increase her sleep time by scheduling her feedings further apart.

2. When his cheek is touched, three-week-old Alec turns his head in the direction of the touch. This is an example of the
    a. Moro reflex.
    b. Babinski reflex.
    c. tonic neck reflex.
    d. rooting reflex.

3. At birth, Kelly's reflexes were somewhat sluggish and weak. Also, it was very difficult for her to regulate her own sleep, she lacked responsiveness, and she needed intensive care. Kelly
    a. was suffering from failure to thrive.
    b. will probably die in the first few weeks of life.
    c. was a low-birth-weight baby.
    d. needs to be breast fed in order to recover from these symptoms.

4. Three-month-old Ben is sitting in front of a large computer screen on which colorful and fun drawings are displayed. As Ben watches the drawings appear in various locations, a video camera films his eye movements. In which type of study is Ben participating?
    a. Visual cliff study
    b. Nonreversal shift study
    c. Reversal shift study
    d. Visual expectation paradigm

5. Jordan loves to suck on the beak of his rubber duck. He does this over and over again whenever he plays with the duck. Which sensorimotor substage is Jordan in?
   a. Second
   b. Third
   c. Fourth
   d. Fifth

6. After accidentally stepping on her rubber duck and hearing it squeak, Lara now bangs it against the wall to see if this too will make the duck squeak. Lara's behavior is an example of
   a. primary circular reactions.
   b. secondary circular reactions.
   c. tertiary circular reactions.
   d. symbolic representations.

7. Each time an infant cries, her mom or dad rush to pick her up. Operant conditioning theory would predict that the parents' behavior will
   a. reinforce crying in the long term.
   b. not affect the infant's crying behavior.
   c. lead to less crying in the long term.
   d. lead to less crying in the short term only.

8. Which of the following is evidence for the notion that babbling is *not* intrinsically motivated?
   a. Deaf infants babble with their hands.
   b. All physically normal infants begin to babble at about six months of age.
   c. The language to which the child is exposed does not influence the onset of babbling.
   d. Deaf infants babble orally only after they hear amplified sounds.

9. Which of the following words is a child most likely to learn first?
   a. Good
   b. Hot
   c. Dog
   d. Up

10. When eighteen-month-old Jimmy points to a picture of a car and says "car!!", his mother says "Yes, that is a big car. Just like daddy's car." The mother is engaging in
    a. infant-directed speech.
    b. caregiver speech.
    c. contextual dialogue.
    d. contingent dialogue.

Answer Key

Key Concepts

1. neonate
2. one minute; five minutes
3. brain; spinal cord
4. neuron
5. rapid-eye-movement sleep (REM-sleep); non-REM sleep

6.   mothers
7.   sudden infant death syndrome
8.   states of arousal
9.   visual acuity; auditory acuity
10. reflex; gross motor skills; fine motor skills
11. cephalocaudal principle
12. proximodistal
13. activity
14. overnutrition
15. low birth weight
16. failure to thrive
17. infant mortality
18. perception
19. cognition
20. habituation
21. visual cliff
22. two; two to three
23. reversal shift
24. nonreversal shift
25. sensorimotor; six
26. scheme
27. assimilation; accommodation
28. circular reactions
29. object permanence
30. behaviorism
31. operant conditioning; imitation
32. Phonemes
33. lexicon; semantics
34. pragmatics; syntax
35. babbling
36. infant-directed speech

Multiple-Choice Self-Test / Factual Questions

1. Choice (b) is correct; the Apgar is a quickly administered scale that reliably assesses infant functioning immediately after birth. Choice (a) is a general definition of the Apgar. Choices (c) and (d) are two of the five ratings of the Apgar; the others are skin color, efforts to breathe, and heart rate.

2. Choice (d) is correct. Choice (a), alert inactivity, corresponds to a relatively still body, eyes scanning, irregular breathing. Choice (b), distress, corresponds to agitated movements, crying, and flushed skin. Choice (c), REM sleep, corresponds to irregular eye movements, occasional twitches, jerks, and facial grimaces, rapid and irregular breathing.

3. Choice (c) is correct; gross motor skills, those that involve the larger muscles of the body, emerge earlier than fine motor skills, those that involve smaller muscles. Waving the arm involves the large muscles of the shoulder. In comparison, muscles of the fingers, choice (a), wrist, choice (b), and hand, choice (d), are smaller muscles.

4. Choice (a) is correct; the medically accepted definition of a low-birth-weight baby is one who weighs less than 5 ½ pounds or 2,500 grams. Therefore, the other choices are inaccurate.

5. Choice (c) is correct; although habituation studies may be used in the assessment of a variety of developmental skills, one skill that they always demonstrate is memory functioning. Choices (a) and (b), language skills, are not examined with habituation studies because if a child has language ability, then verbal assessment methods may be used. Choice (d) is incorrect in that these studies are commonly used to examine perceptual and conceptual skills, not motor skills.

6. Choice (d) is correct; object permanence is the Piagetian concept that explains the child's ability to understand that objects that are out of his sight continue to exist somewhere in the world. Choice (a), depth perception, is the ability to perceive the world in three dimensions. Choice (b), object constancy, is the recognition that an object remains the same despite the constant changes in its appearance based on its distance, orientation, and angle of viewing. Choice (c), nonreversal shift, is an experimental procedure in which reward is offered for recognizing a new dimension of difference between objects.

7. Choice (a) is correct; primary circular reactions involve repeated interactions with the infant's own body. Choice (b), secondary circular reactions, are repeated interactions with objects in the environment. Choice (c), tertiary circular reactions, are applications of existing schemes to novel objects and situations. Choice (d), reflexes, are involuntary movements or behaviors controlled by the spinal cord.

8. Choice (c) is correct; in the last substage of the sensorimotor period, eighteen to twenty-four months of age, the child gains the capacity to mentally represent the world through the use of symbols. In the fourth substage, choice (a), the child can intentionally select a particular scheme to achieve a certain end. In the fifth substage, choice (b), the child is using tertiary circular reactions. Choice (d) is incorrect in that the sensorimotor stage has only six substages.

9. Choice (b) is correct; semantics refers to meanings of words. Choice (a), phonology, examines the sounds of language. Choice (c), pragmatics, refers to the purposes for and ways in which words and sentences are typically used. Choice (d), syntax, refers to the organization of words into sentences.

10. Choice (d) is correct; referential-style children first use words that label objects and events, such as *truck*. Expressive-style children, choice (a), initially use words to express feelings, such as *happy*. Choice (b) refers to the concept of contextual dialogue. Choice (c) refers to the concept of contingent dialogue.

Multiple-Choice Self-Test / Conceptual Questions

1. Choice (c) is correct; newborns sleep an average of sixteen hours per day, and yet some may sleep as few as eleven hours and others as much as twenty-one hours. Therefore, the baby is sleeping neither too little, choice (a), nor too much, choice (b). Also, there is no need to attempt to increase her sleep time, choice (d).

2. Choice (d) is correct. Choice (a), the Moro reflex, appears in response to a loud noise. Choice (b), the Babinski reflex, appears when the bottom of the foot is stroked. Choice (c), the tonic neck reflex, appears when the baby is laid on his or her back.

3. Choice (c) is correct; low-birth-weight babies, who are often born prematurely, have not developed completely and show some distress after birth. However, unless the weight is extremely low or the prematurity significant, these infants survive and catch up. Therefore, choice (b) is incorrect. Choice (a), failure to thrive, refers to a failure to grow at normal rates. This condition is not necessarily present at birth. Choice (d) is incorrect in that low-birth-weight infants do recover and benefit from feedings with formula; breast feeding, although healthier for the infant, is not absolutely necessary to reverse the condition.

4. Choice (d) is correct; visual expectation paradigms, modified versions of the habituation procedure, are used in the assessment of an infant's ability to anticipate visual events. Choice (a), the visual cliff study, is used to assess depth perception in infants. Choice (b), the nonreversal shift, refers to an experimental procedure in which a dimension that is to be reinforced is changed. Choice (c), the reversal shift refers to an experimental procedure in which the value of a particular dimension being reinforced is changed.

5. Choice (b) is correct; repeated actions that involve outside objects are called secondary circular reactions, Piaget's third sensorimotor substage. Sucking on an object is an example of this. Substage two, choice (a), corresponds to primary circular reactions. Substage four, choice (c), corresponds to combined secondary circular reactions. Substage five, choice (d), corresponds to tertiary circular reactions.

6. Choice (c) is correct; tertiary circular reactions involve the baby's systematic search for different ways to produce the same outcomes. Choice (a), primary circular reactions, are repeated actions that involve the baby's own body. Choice (b), secondary circular reactions, are repeated actions involving environmental objects. Choice (d), symbolic representations, are possible in the last sensorimotor substage, when the baby can use symbols and no longer relies on concrete objects and events.

7. Choice (a) is correct; according to conditioning theory, picking up a crying infant serves as a positive reinforcement for crying behavior because it leads to the positive outcome of attention from the environment. However, research indicates that immediate response to an infant's cries actually leads to less crying. That is, research results do not support the predictions of the conditioning theory. Consequently, the other choices are inaccurate.

8. Choice (d) is correct; deaf infants' ability to babble orally only after being exposed to amplified sounds is evidence that unless there is an outside (extrinsic) influence, babbling will not occur. The other choices are all support for the notion that babbling is intrinsically motivated.

9. Choice (c) is correct; children's first words tend to be object labels (nouns, such as *dog*). Choices (a) and (b) are adjectives, and choice (d) is an adverb.

10. Choice (d) is correct; contingent dialogue refers to expanding on a child's verbalizations. Choices (a) and (b) are synonymous and refer to a form of speech that adults and older children use in speaking to a one- to two-year-old child; it consists of short sentences, simple vocabulary, clear enunciation, and a singsong pitch. Choice (c), contextual dialogue, refers to familiar language routines and rituals.

CHAPTER 5

Psychosocial Development in the First Two Years

Learning Objectives:

1. Discuss the process adults go through in making the transition to parenthood.
2. Describe the special relationship parents and infants develop especially caregiver-infant synchrony and coregulation.
3. Describe the father-infant relationship and compare it to the mother-infant relationship.
4. Discuss the roles that siblings, grandparents, other caregivers, and peers play in social interactions and contrast these roles with parent-infant relationships.
5. Describe the early emotions of the infant, including the range of expression and developmental patterns.
6. Describe the development of behavioral self-regulation during infancy.
7. Define what is meant by temperament and distinguish among the types: easy, difficult, and slow-to-warm-up.
8. Discuss the short- and long-term effects of temperament.
9. Identify and describe the four phases of attachment.
10. Describe the Strange Situation and indicate how it is used to assess attachment level.
11. Compare the four outcomes of attachment, including long-term consequences.
12. Discuss the similarities and differences in mothers' and fathers' roles in attachment and describe cultural variations.
13. Describe the effects of maternal employment and day care on attachment.
14. Compare family-leave policies in the United States and Europe.
15. Distinguish among the four attachment patterns of adulthood: autonomous, dismissing, preoccupied, and resolved-disorganized.
16. Define autonomy and indicate how parents might influence its development.
17. Differentiate among the four major theoretical positions (identification, operant conditioning, observational learning, and social referencing) concerning the development of autonomy.
18. Discuss the development of a sense of self.
19. List the characteristics of a socially competent toddler.

Chapter Outline

I.   Early social relationships

Infants seem to have a natural tendency to be social participants and are capable of many social responses shortly after birth.

A. The transition to parenthood represents a major life transition.

    1. There are changes in relationships with other adults, family roles, and interactions between father and mother.

    2. Participation by the husband in child care and housework can increase his empathy and appreciation of his wife's experience.

B. Caregiver-infant synchrony

    1. Social interactions between parent (or other caregiver) and infant involve an intricate pattern of close coordination and teamwork called **caregiver-infant synchrony**.

    2. Mothers and babies have "conversations" that resemble adult dialogues.

    3. Coordinating these "conversations" is the caregiver's responsibility until the baby is a few months old and capable of initiating social exchange.

    4. Joint attention and reciprocal turn taking help children develop self regulation.

    5. Problems with synchrony may reflect childrearing difficulties and can place the infant at risk for developmental problems.

C. Social interactions with other family members

Children live in a network of social relationships where other people make contributions to their social lives.

    1. Fathers spend about two or three hours per day in the care of infants and young children and play actively with their children.

    2. Most children grow up with siblings. They spend more time with siblings than with mothers or fathers. Conflict among siblings is most likely when parents are seen as giving preferential treatment.

    3. Grandparents are often secondary sources of advice and child care. Sometimes grandparents become primary caretakers for their child's infant.

D. Interactions with nonparental caregivers

    1. Infants also interact with nonparental caregivers, including day-care teachers, other relatives, and family friends.

    2. High-quality care for infants is best ensured by employing caregivers who are well-trained and supervised and responsive to the physical, cognitive, social, and emotional needs of infants and their families.

E.   Interaction with peers

    1.   Even young babies show considerable interest in other babies and in much the same way they show interest in their parents.

    2.   Infants become more social with experience.

    3.   Peer relationships during toddlerhood may promote the development of positive friendships later in childhood.

    4.   Repeated contact with a peer in a familiar setting with a familiar caregiver and minimal adult interference appears to facilitate the development of peer friendship.

II.   Emotions and temperament in infancy

Infants are capable of expressing emotions and needs through four different kinds of cries. Caregivers respond with basic routines to an infant's different cries.

A.   Emotions in infancy

    1.   Babies' expectations and understandings influence the degree of specificity of emotional expression.

    2.   There is general agreement that emotions can reliably be expressed at different ages from a few weeks old through toddlerhood.

    3.   Expressions of emotion are thought to play an important role in development by providing vital information to infants and their caregivers about ongoing experiences and interactions.

    4.   Infants become increasingly able to regulate their emotional states to a comfortable level to maintain interaction with their surroundings.

B.   Temperament

Temperament refers to an individual's pattern or style of reacting to a broad range of environmental events and situations. These patterns are present at birth; whether temperament is due solely to genetics is unclear.

    1.   In the now classic study of temperament, infants were rated on nine dimensions. Three patterns of temperament were found: easy babies, difficult babies, and slow-to-warm-up babies. A fourth group, mixed-pattern babies, did not fall neatly into the first three groups.

    2.   Temperament can be useful for predicting problems, but only for a minority of children with difficult or slow-to-warm-up temperaments.

    3.   Predictions of later temperament based on differences observed toward the end of the first year are somewhat more accurate than those made earlier.

4.   It is not clear to what extent environmental influences (e.g., infant-family fit, culture, historical period) play in supporting or modifying temperament throughout development.

III. Attachment formation

Attachment refers to the strong and enduring emotional bond that develops between infant and caregiver during the infant's first year of life and is characterized by reciprocal affection and a shared desire to maintain physical closeness. Most developmental psychologists believe that attachment relationships develop over time as a result of repeated infant-caregiver interactions.

A.   Phases of attachment formation

Attachments are thought to develop in a series of phases, which are partly determined by cognitive changes and partly by interactions that appear to develop quite naturally between infants and their caregivers.

1.   Phase 1: Indiscriminate sociability (birth through two months). In this phase, an infant uses her limited attachment behaviors less selectively than she will as she grows older.

2.   Phase 2: Attachments in the making (two through seven months). In this phase, most babies still generally accept certain forms of attention and care from comparative strangers and will tolerate temporary separation from parents.

3.   Phase 3: Specific, clear-cut attachments (seven through twenty-four months). In this phase, the baby's preference for specific people becomes stronger; therefore, separation anxiety and stranger anxiety appear near the beginning of this phase.

4.   Phase 4: Goal-corrected partnerships (twenty-four months and onward). By age two, the baby is capable of mental representation and is better able to understand the feelings and points of view of parents and to adjust his own accordingly.

B.   Assessing attachment: The "Strange Situation"

1.   The most widely used method for assessing attachment is the **Strange Situation**, in which infants are confronted with a cumulative series of stressful experiences such as being in an unfamiliar place, meeting a stranger, or being separated from a parent.

2.   Based on infant patterns of behavior in this situation, about 70 percent of infants showed **secure attachment** to the parent, about 10 percent displayed an **anxious-resistant attachment** pattern, and about 20 percent showed an **anxious-avoidant attachment** pattern.

C.   Consequences of different attachment patterns

1.   Secure attachment early in infancy leads to babies who tend to cooperate best with parents, comply with rules, and seek help from parents.

2.   Anxious-resistant infants may not learn as well from their parents, responding with anger and resistance to parental efforts to teach or help them.

3. Anxious-avoidant infants often avoid interaction with their parents and miss out on parent efforts to teach or help them.

4. Such differences persist into the preschool years.

- A Multicultural View: Cross-cultural variations in attachment

D. Influences on attachment formation

1. The quality of the infant-mother relationship is a strong determinant in the attachment process. A mother's capacity to respond sensitively and appropriately to her baby is more important than the amount of contact.

2. Differences in infant temperament are likely to affect the mother-infant relationships and the quality of attachment.

3. Being securely attached herself makes the mother more likely to have a child who is securely attached.

4. Children can form equally strong attachments with their fathers. Studies have found no differences in most babies' preferred attachment during their first two years.

5. The quality of fathers' interaction with their infants, their attitudes, and time spent are important variables.

6. The effects of maternal employment on the child are almost always influenced by a number of factors such as economic and cultural differences, the mother's "morale," the father's satisfaction with his wife's employment, husband-wife relationships, and other factors. Working mothers who experience high levels of separation anxiety are more likely to have infants who develop anxious-avoidant attachments.

7. There are many variables that determine the effects of day care and other forms of nonmaternal care on attachment. The majority of infants receiving full-time center care appear to be quite securely attached to one or both parents. The two sets of attachment, one for parent and the other for caregiver, tend to be independent of each other. Multiple attachments in other contexts are not only possible but may contribute to the child's well-being.

- Focusing On: Family-leave policies in the United States

- Working with Rachelle Turner, infant day care coordinator: Understanding infant social development

E. Longterm and intergenerational effects of attachment

Attachment patterns in infancy are predictive of attachment relationships throughout life.

IV. Toddlerhood and the emergence of autonomy

By the second year of life, the relatively secure base of attachment that most infants have achieved with their parents allows them to shift attention outward to the physical and social world. **Autonomy** is the ability to be independent and self-directed and to balance one's own demands for self-control with demands for control from others. Parents must support their child's efforts to be autonomous without overestimating or underestimating the child's capabilities, external dangers, and internal fears.

A. Sources of autonomy

1. Identification is the process by which children wish to become like their parents and other important attachment figures in their lives.

2. Operant conditioning stresses the importance of reinforcement for desirable behaviors, including behaviors that reflect self-control.

3. Observational learning espouses the view that the key to autonomy lies in the child's inherent tendency to observe and imitate parents and other nurturant individuals.

4. **Social referencing**, a common denominator in all three explanations of autonomy, refers to children's sensitivity to how their parents are feeling and their ability to use those cues as a basis for guiding emotional response.

B. Development of self

The sense of self that develops late in infancy shows up in everyday situations as well as in situations involving self-control. Researchers have used mirrors and television images of infants to assess infants' self-recognition capability.

1. Self-recognition never occurs in infants younger than fifteen months and increases to 100 percent at twenty-four months.

2. Infants initially use contingent cues and then noncontingent cues.

3. By the end of their second year, most children show an increasing appreciation of the standards and expectations of others about how they should behave toward people and things. For children, satisfaction is gained by initiating challenging activities or behaviors, and they often smile at the results. A two-year-old may also direct adults' behavior by inviting them to play, requesting help, or other such behaviors. Children frequently use language to express needs and wants, implying awareness of themselves as individuals.

C. Development of competence and self-esteem

Competence (skill and capability) develops out of a child's natural curiosity and desire to explore the world and the pleasure experienced in successful mastery and control of that world.

1. A number of capabilities are observed in a socially competent toddler.

2. Social competence is influenced by the parent-toddler relationship. Mothers support and encourage their toddler's curiosity and desire to explore.

3.   A natural outcome of such parenting is a strong sense of **self-esteem**—the child's feeling that he or she is an important, competent, powerful, and worthwhile person whose efforts toward autonomy and initiative are respected and valued by those around him or her.

V.   Looking back/looking forward

A.   Continuity within change

B.   Lifelong growth

C.   Changing meaning and vantage points

D.   Developmental diversity

Key Concepts

Directions: Identify each of the key concepts discussed in this chapter.

1.   Research indicates that _____ with the baby is the most important factor influencing the marital satisfaction of the couple after the birth of the first baby.
2.   Patterns of closely coordinated social and emotional interaction between caregiver and infant are known as _____.
3.   Although both parents play with infants, fathers tend to engage the infant in more _____ play.
4.   Conflict between siblings is most likely to occur when parents are seen as giving _____ to one child.
5.   When grandparents are relatively young, in good health, and live nearby, they can be sources of _____ and _____.
6.   More _____ than _____ go to child care facilities. The majority of children are cared for in _____ or in _____.
7.   Young children's behavior with peers is influenced by and related to the quality of _____.
8.   The infant's characteristic ways of feeling and responding that are present at birth and relatively stable over time and across situations are called _____.
9.   Thomas and Chess identified three general patterns of infant temperament. These are _____, _____, and _____ babies. Infants who do not fit into any of these groups are called _____ babies.
10. The intimate and emotional bond between infant and caregiver that is characterized by reciprocal affection and physical closeness is known as _____.
11. The concept of _____ refers to an infant's internalized perceptions, feelings, and expectations regarding social and emotional relationships with significant caregivers.
12. When an infant is experiencing _____ , she displays fear, clinging, crying, and related distress upon the departure of her caregiver. This behavior generally appears between _____ and _____ months.
13. A wariness and avoidance of unfamiliar people is called _____.
14. The _____ was originally developed by Mary Ainsworth. It is a procedure for studying _____.
15. Ainsworth identified three attachment classifications; these are _____, _____, and _____ attachment. A more recently added category is _____ attachment.

16. The mother's _____ is important in determining the quality of attachment that forms between the infant and the mother.

17. An infant who is securely attached to the mother is likely to have a _____ attachment with the father.

18. Working mothers who are highly anxious tend to have infants who develop _____ attachments.

19. Infants cared for in day care facilities show more _____ than do infants reared at home.

20. The _____ is an instrument used to evaluate the childhood attachment relationships adults had with their own parents and other caregivers.

21. According to Erikson, _____ refers to a person's ability to govern his own thoughts, feelings, and actions freely and responsibly while also overcoming feelings of shame and doubt.

22. The psychoanalytic concept of _____ refers to a child's wish to become like her parents and other significant attachment figures in her life.

23. The child's ability to detect parents' and other adults' feelings and to use this information to direct his own feelings is known as _____ , and it is important in the development of _____.

24. Robert White's definition of _____ is an individual's skill in successfully mastering, controlling, and exploring the world around him or her.

25. Skillful parenting leads to the development of _____; the child believes that he or she is an important, competent, worthwhile, and valued person.

Multiple-Choice Self-Test

Factual Questions

1. Fathers who are primary caregivers are more likely than secondary caregiver fathers to
   a. imitate baby's facial expressions and vocalizations.
   b. be less active when playing with the baby.
   c. play more ritual games, such as peek-a-boo.
   d. experience more daily hassles in the caregiver role.

2. Approximately what percent of infants, toddlers, and preschoolers are cared for in licensed care centers?
   a. 40
   b. 45
   c. 15
   d. 5

3. Development of peer relationships in toddlerhood is *not* facilitated by
   a. contact with a peer in familiar settings.
   b. contact with a peer in the presence of familiar adults.
   c. repeated contact with a peer.
   d. substantial adult intervention during contact with a peer.

4. According to Thomas and Chess, approximately _____ percent of babies have an easy temperament.
   a. 40
   b. 15
   c. 10
   d. 35

5. An infant whose attachment classification is anxious-resistant will
   a. accept comfort from a stranger.
   b. be an active explorer.
   c. stay very close to the mother.
   d. show very little involvement with the mother.

6. Shorter maternity leaves lead to
   a. anxious-avoidant mother-infant attachment.
   b. a lower quality of mother-infant interaction.
   c. a higher quality of mother-infant interaction.
   d. disorganized-disoriented mother-infant attachment.

7. Mothers whose adult attachment patterns are autonomous are likely to have _____ attachments with their own infants.
   a. secure
   b. anxious-resistant
   c. anxious-avoidant
   d. disorganized-disoriented

8. A child who feels shame and doubt has failed to develop
   a. identification.
   b. autonomy.
   c. a secure attachment.
   d. a goodness of fit with the parents.

9. When children wish to become like their parents, they are experiencing the process of
   a. identification.
   b. autonomy.
   c. a secure attachment.
   d. a goodness of fit with the parents.

10. The child's sensitivity to the feelings of his parents and other adults is called
    a. observational learning.
    b. self-recognition.
    c. competence.
    d. social referencing.

Multiple-Choice Self-Test / Conceptual Questions

1. Which of the following is a *poor* infant day care program?
   a. One that offers structured as well as free activities
   b. One in which the staff turnover is high
   c. One in which the staff-child ratio is high
   d. One in which class sizes are small

2. Stephanie is eight months old. Which emotion is she likely to begin expressing?
   a. Wariness
   b. Shame
   c. Surprise
   d. Fear

3. Ali loved taking a bath from the very first moment. Now, at seventeen months of age, he is only upset when leaving the bathtub. Ali's temperament may be described as
    a. easy.
    b. difficult.
    c. slow-to-warm-up.
    d. impulsive.

4. Jason is clearly differentiating between people and prefers his parents and maternal grandmother over everyone else. According to Bowlby, he is in the _____ phase of attachment formation.
    a. first
    b. second
    c. third
    d. fourth

5. Occasionally, Martha leaves her one-year-old baby with a baby sitter when she goes shopping. The baby doesn't cry when Martha leaves and tends to continue playing when she returns, without acknowledging her mother's arrival. The attachment between Martha and her baby is best described as
    a. secure.
    b. anxious-resistant.
    c. anxious-avoidant.
    d. disorganized-disoriented.

6. One-year-old Debbie has a disorganized-disoriented attachment style. She probably
    a. learns easily from her mother.
    b. responds with anger to her mother's attempts to teach her new skills.
    c. easily seeks and accepts help from her mother.
    d. receives either overly intrusive or rejecting responses from her mother.

7. Two-year-old David is raised in a group with same-age peers by community child care providers. David is probably
    a. in a day care center in the United States.
    b. in an Israeli kibbutz.
    c. a member of the Efe people of Zaire.
    d. in an orphanage.

8. Keith's score on the Adult Attachment Interview classifies him as *preoccupied*. Keith is likely to
    a. insist he cannot remember his childhood.
    b. describe his parents as loving.
    c. have difficulty in clearly explaining his relationships with his parents.
    d. value relationships with attachment figures, such as parents.

9. Five-year-old Jennie loves to put lipstick on her lips and asks her mother to polish her nails whenever her mother is polishing her own nails. Jennie also enjoys wearing her mother's high-heeled shoes around the house. Jennie's behavior is an example of
    a. autonomy.
    b. identification.
    c. competence.
    d. social referencing.

10. Fourteen-month-old Tyler is always ready to accept small gifts from strangers if they are smiling but turns away from them if they appear angry and fearful. Tyler's behavior is an example of
    a. autonomy.
    b. identification.
    c. competence.
    d. social referencing.

Answer Key

Key Concepts

1. paternal involvement
2. caregiver-infant synchrony
3. rough-house
4. preferential treatment
5. practical advice; child care
6. toddlers; infants; their own home; the caregiver's home
7. infant-parent attachment
8. temperament
9. easy; difficult; slow-to-warm-up; mixed pattern
10. attachment
11. working models
12. separation anxiety; nine; twelve
13. stranger anxiety
14. Strange Situation; attachment
15. secure; anxious-resistant; anxious-avoidant; disorganized-disoriented
16. responsiveness or sensitivity
17. secure
18. anxious-avoidant
19. social confidence
20. Adult Attachment Interview (AAI)
21. autonomy
22. identification
23. social referencing; autonomy
24. competence
25. self-esteem

Multiple-Choice Self-Test / Factual Questions

1. Choice (a) is correct; full-time primary caregiver fathers are more likely to act like mothers in their caregiver role. Choices (b) and (c) are incorrect in that all fathers are more active than mothers when playing with infants and are less likely to play ritual games. Choice (d) is incorrect because primary fathers experience fewer daily hassles than other fathers when caring for the baby.

2. Choice (c) is correct. About 40 percent, choice (a), are cared for by paid workers. About 45 percent, choice (b) are cared for by relatives. Choice (d) does not represent any care arrangement.

3. Choice (d) is correct; minimal adult interference facilitates the development of friendships. Choices (a), (b), and (c) are conditions conducive to the development of friendships in toddlerhood.

4. Choice (a) is correct. Choice (b), 15 percent, have slow-to-warm-up temperaments. Choice (c), 10 percent, have difficult temperaments. Choice (d), 35 percent, are mixed pattern babies.

5. Choice (c) is correct; anxious-resistant babies are likely to stay very close to their mothers. Consequently, they will not accept comfort from strangers, choice (a), and will not explore, choice (b). Choice (d), anxious-avoidant babies, show very little involvement with the mother.

6. Choice (b) is correct; when mothers return to work relatively soon after the birth of the baby, the interaction between the mother and the baby tends to suffer, especially for mothers who report depressive symptoms. Therefore, choice (c) is incorrect. Nevertheless, most infants of working mothers are securely attached regardless of the length of the mother's maternity leave. Consequently, choices (a) and (d) are incorrect.

7. Choice (a) is correct. Anxious-resistant infant-parent attachment, choice (b), was not reported to be related to a specific adult attachment pattern. Adults with dismissing attachment patterns are more likely to have anxious-avoidant attachments with their children, choice (c). Adults with unresolved attachment patterns are likely to have disorganized-disoriented attachment patterns with their children, choice (d).

8. Choice (b) is correct; autonomy is the positive outcome of Erikson's second psychosocial crisis and refers to a child's ability to control and regulate his own actions, feelings, and thoughts. Choice (a), identification, is the psychoanalytic concept referring to a child's wish to become like his parents and other adults. Choice (c), secure attachment, is the positive attachment classification in which the child will actively explore the environment, accept comfort from a stranger, and be happy upon reuniting with the mother. Choice (d), the concept of goodness of fit, refers to the compatibility between the parents' characteristic ways of behaving and responding and the infant's behaviors and temperament.

9. Choice (a) is correct; identification is the psychoanalytic concept referring to a child's wish to become like his parents and other adults. Choice (b), autonomy, refers to the positive outcome of Erikson's second psychosocial crisis. Securely attached children,, choice (c), will actively explore the environment, accept comfort from a stranger, and be happy to reunite with the mother in the Strange Situation. Choice (d), the concept of goodness of fit, refers to the compatibility between the parents' characteristic ways of behaving and responding and the infant's behaviors and temperament.

10. Choice (d) is correct; social referencing refers to the child's awareness of how parents and other adults are feeling and his ability to use these emotional cues to guide his own emotional responses. Choice (a), observational learning, refers to the child's tendency to observe and imitate the behaviors of parents and other caregivers. Choice (b), self-recognition, is the first point in the development of the self. It refers to the child's ability to recognize physical images of herself on television, in the mirror, and in still photographs. Choice (c), competence, is White's concept of skills and capacity to explore, master, and control one's immediate world.

Multiple-Choice Self-Test / Conceptual Questions

1. Choice (b) is correct; in good infant day care programs, staff turnover is low, and the children have an opportunity to interact with familiar individuals who have learned their temperaments and who have established relationships with them. Choices (a), (c), and (d) are characteristics of good programs.

2. Choice (d) is correct; the expression of fear emerges between five and nine months of age. Choices (a) and (c), the expressions of wariness and surprise, emerge at about four months of age. Choice (b), the expression of shame, emerges at eighteen months of age.

3. Choice (a) is correct; easy babies adapt to new situations easily. Difficult babies, choice (b), are generally highly stressed in new situations. Slow-to-warm-up babies, choice (c), adapt to new situations gradually, in small steps. Choice (d), "impulsive", is not an infant temperament classification.

4. Choice (c) is correct; specific and clear preferences for certain individuals appear in this phase, from seven to twenty-four months of age. In the first phase, choice (a), birth to two months, attachment behaviors are less selective. In the second phase, choice (b), two to seven months, preference is for the most familiar individuals. In the fourth phase, choice (d), twenty-four months onward, attachment relationships are secure and grounded in a sense of basic trust.

5. Choice (c) is correct; infants with an anxious-avoidant attachment are not distressed when separated from the caregiver and tend to ignore the caregiver upon her return. Choice (a), securely attached infants are mildly upset when the caregiver leaves and very happy to see her return. Iinfants with an anxious-resistant attachment, choice (b), are very upset when separated from the caregiver and show ambivalence when reunited with her; they seek closeness to her but they also resist the comfort she offers. Choice (d), disorganized-disoriented attachment style is characterized by high insecurity between infant and parent. When reunited, these infants show contradictory behavior, including unresponsiveness and frozen postures.

6. Choice (d) is correct; parents who display disorganized-disoriented attachment behaviors may alternatively show exaggerated attention to or withdrawal from the child. Choices (a) and (c) are characteristics of securely attached children. Choice (b) is a characteristic of the anxious-resistant attachment style.

7. Choice (b) is correct; the Israeli kibbutz is a residential communal childrearing setting. Choice (a), day care centers, provide part-time child care; they are not residential facilities. The Efe people of Zaire, choice (c), expose their children to multiple relationships with the parents, siblings, and others. An orphanage, choice (d), cares for children without parents; orphanages are typically not segregated by age.

8. Choice (c) is correct. Choice (a) is characteristic of adults classified as *dismissing*. Choices (b) and (d) are characteristic of adults classified as *autonomous*.

9. Choice (b) is correct; identification is the psychoanalytic concept that explains children's wishes to be similar to their parents. Choice (a), autonomy, is the positive outcome of Erikson's second psychosocial crisis. White's concept of competence, choice (c), refers to skillfulness in mastering, controlling, and exploring the environment. Choice (d), social referencing, refers to a child's awareness of the feelings of others, especially parents, and his or her use of this as a guide for his or her own emotional reactions.

10.   Choice (d) is correct; the child interprets a smile as a friendly gesture and replies in kind. Similarly, the child interprets the expression of anger as unfriendly and withdraws. He is *referencing* his own emotional reactions with the emotional expressions of the adults with whom he is interacting. Choice (a), autonomy, is the positive outcome of Erikson's second psychosocial crisis. Choice (b), identification, is the psychoanalytic concept that explains a child's wish to be like parents and other adults. Choice (c), competence, is White's term for explaining skillfulness in exploring, controlling, and mastering the environment.

CHAPTER 6

Physical and Cognitive Development in Early Childhood

Learning Objectives:

1. Describe normal physical development in the preschool years, including the various characteristics, patterns of growth, and genetic influences.
2. Discuss nutritional needs during the preschool years.
3. Discuss the relationship between poverty and the health of preschoolers.
4. Describe the development of bladder control during the preschool period.
5. Identify and describe the development of fundamental motor skills.
6. Differentiate between prerepresentational and representational drawing.
7. Discuss individual differences in physical development during the preschool years, including gender differences.
8. Describe how parents change in response to the child's physical changes and growth, including changes in surveillance and patience.
9. Discuss the effects of different family makeups.
10. Describe Piaget's stage of preoperational thinking.
11. Discuss the development of thought in early childhood, including symbolic and egocentric thought.
12. Describe the work on classification skills and conservation and indicate how extensions of these studies differ from Piaget's original work.
13. Describe how a child's concept of number develops over the preschool period and distinguish between cardinality and ordinality.
14. Define the zone of proximal development (ZPD) and discuss its role in learning.
15. Identify and discuss the changes in Piaget's original ideas that have been proposed by neostructuralists.
16. Describe the basic features of language acquisition during early childhood, with particular focus on the development of syntax.
17. Discuss the roles of reinforcement, imitation, and practice in language acquisition and compare them to innate language acquisition device (LAD).
18. Discuss gender and socioeconomic differences in language.
19. Discuss developmentally appropriate practice in early childhood education.

Chapter Outline

I. Physical development

II. Influences on normal physical development

Physical development in the preschool years is relatively easy to measure. For any preschool child who is reasonably healthy and happy, physical growth is remarkably smooth. Physical growth lacks discrete stages, plateaus, or qualitative changes.

    A. Genetic background

        1. Most dimensions of growth are influenced substantially by heredity.

        2. Both parents contribute equally to growth tendencies.

        3. Races and ethnic groups differ in growth patterns such as height and body shape.

    B. Nutritional needs during the preschool years

        1. The amount of food consumed by preschoolers may be less than that of toddlers.

        2. Eating a variety of foods is important to ensure nutrition.

III. The connection between health and poverty

Children from middle- and high-socioeconomic-status settings are generally very healthy.

    A. About 30 percent of families in the United States have poor access to medical care because of poverty.

    B. Illness and malnourishment put children at risk for additional illnesses.

    C. Strategies can focus on individuals and their communities and on systematic reorganization of the health care system.

    D. Education in health and nutrition can build on the knowledge of low-income parents.

• Focusing On: Reforming children's health care

IV. Bladder and bowel control

Sometime during the preschool years, most children acquire control of their bladders. Daytime control usually precedes nighttime control, sometime before the third birthday. Bladder and bowel control reflects the large advances children make in controlling their bodies.

V. Motor skill development

    A. Fundamental motor skills

    Young children experiment with simple voluntary actions. Older children use action usually as means to other ends.

1. Walking and running. After a year or so of practice, most children can walk without looking at their feet. Their steps are more regular and their feet get closer together. They move to running shortly after walking has smoothed out.

2. Jumping. Early jumping may look like a fast stretch and may improve to the lifting of one foot off the ground. Around age three, efficient arm movement enables the preschooler to gain upward momentum.

3. Throwing and catching. For infants and toddlers, first throws may happen by accident and be followed by more intentional and stereotyped throws. Children proceed through stages in throwing that also appear in catching.

B. Fine motor coordination: The case of drawing skills

Not all motor activities of young children involve strength, agility, and balance of the whole body. Many require **fine motor coordination**. The fine motor skill of drawing serves a number of purposes. There appears to be two overlapping phases of development in drawing.

1. Prerepresentational drawing emerges at the end of infancy, when children begin to scribble. The focus of this activity is initially on the activity itself. Later a child's interest in the results will appear in the patterns she or he imposes on scribbling.

2. Representational drawing emerges as children develop an interest in representing people, objects, and events in their drawings. This interest precedes their ability to do so. Only as children reach school age do their drawings of persons become relatively realistic.

C. Gender differences in physical development

Aside from wide individual differences, preschool boys and girls develop at almost exactly the same average rate. By the time children begin kindergarten at around age five, slight gender differences in physical development and motor skills exist but are noticeable only as averages based on large numbers of children. Gender differences in physical development may be related to social roles.

D. Children show considerable variability in both fundamental and fine motor skill development. These probably result from variations in experience, motivation, and biological endowment.

VI. The impact of children's growth patterns on adults

A. Effects of appearance

1. Having a young-looking face depends on having large features and a large forehead.

2. Younger-looking children are rated as more attractive than older-looking children by both adults and their peers.

3. Adults tend to expect more mature behavior from older-looking children; these children may not be developmentally ready to fulfill these expectations.

B. Effects of motor skills

1. Small children can be handled and carried from place to place. By age five, children have outgrown these physical interactions and must assume more responsibility for themselves. By age five, the child has not only gained in physical growth but has also improved various motor skills and gained increasing physical competence.

2. By the end of the preschool years, minute-by-minute surveillance of children recedes in importance; however, the concern for safety remains and is reflected in rules set by caregivers.

3. During the preschool years, many parents discover a special need for patience in dealing with their children.

4. Effects of differences in families

A child's growth has a different impact on adults depending on the priorities of parents and on the circumstances of the family and the community.

VII. Cognitive development

VIII. Thinking in preschoolers

Preschoolers extend their ability to represent objects and experiences into many new areas of activity and thinking, or cognition.

A. Piaget's preoperational stage

1. According to Piaget, at about age two children enter a new stage of cognitive development.

2. Preoperational children become increasingly proficient at using symbols, recognizing identities, and sensing functional relationships or variations in their environment.

3. Piaget focused on the limitations as well as the achievements of preoperational children.

B. Symbolic thought

1. Probably the most significant achievement of the preoperational stage is the emergence of **symbolic thought**.

2. Symbolic thinking helps children organize and process what they know by providing them with convenient ways of remembering objects and experiences.

3. Symbols help children communicate what they know to others; communication helps them learn from the experiences of others.

C. Egocentrism in preschool children

1. **Egocentrism** is the tendency of a person to confuse his or her own point of view with that of another person.

    2.   Piaget used the three mountains test to assess egocentrism.

    3.   Using more familiar test materials and settings, preschool children can adopt others' spatial perspectives.

    4.   Preschoolers show distinct but incomplete egocentrism in oral communications.

D. Other aspects of children's conceptual development

Preschool children develop specific cognitive skills as a result of their growing symbolic ability.

    1.   **Classification** skills refer to the placement of objects in groups or categories according to some specific standards or criteria. Young preschoolers can reliably classify objects that differ in just one dimension.

    2.   **Reversibility** is the ability to undo a problem mentally and go back to its beginning.

    3.   **Conservation** is the ability to perceive that certain properties of an object remain the same despite changes in the object's appearance; this skill appears around age six.

        a.   Often preschoolers either cannot or do not use reversible thinking, even when the situation calls for it.

        b.   Tasks of conservation are affected by how they are described to the child.

    4.   Children do not fully grasp how the conventional number system works. For the preschooler it is a rote activity. Piaget probably underestimated preschoolers' knowledge of numbers. Young children acquire the notion of numerosity whether or not they can count yet.

E. Cognition as a social activity

Children learn not only from interacting with objects and the physical environment, but also from interacting with adults or others with more experience.

    1.   This kind of thinking is called **situated cognition**--the perspective, social **constructivism**.

    2.   Interactions about the tasks being pursued in common form a context or **activity setting** for learning.

    3.   The gap in difficulty between independent thinking and socially supported thinking is the **zone of proximal development**, the area in which problems are too difficult to solve alone but are solvable with support from more competent individuals. This concept originated with Soviet psychologist Lev Vygotsky. It suggests how stages and skills may emerge and evolve.

F. Neostructuralist theories of cognitive development

1. Much of the research on children's conceptual development does not contradict Piaget's general approach. Other research suggests that Piaget underestimated children's abilities.

2. There is a commitment to keep Piaget's notion of development occurring in stagelike progression but revise the content or details of those stages.

3. This newer view of cognitive stages is sometimes called **neostructuralist** or neo-Piagetian.

4. This view has also paid more attention to how, or by what processes, children acquire new cognitive skills.

IX. Language acquisition in the preschool years

For most children, language expands rapidly after infancy. Dramatic development occurs in syntax--or the way the child organizes utterances. Significant changes also occur in semantics (meaning) and communicative competence.

A. The nature of syntax

1. The **syntax** of language is a group of rules for ordering and relating its elements, or morphemes. Morphemes are the smallest meaningful unit of language.

2. Syntactic rules can change the meaning of sentences.

3. Some syntactic rules have only a small range of application, and others are completely irregular. In acquiring syntax, a child confronts a mixed system of rules.

B. Beyond first words: Semantic and syntactic relations

Before age two, words seem connected by their semantic relations—their intended meanings rather than by syntactic relations—the relations among grammatical classes of words, such as nouns, verbs, and adjectives.

1. Before age two, the child begins forming duos, or linking two words together, when she or he speaks. Leaving out syntactic indicators makes the speech sound stilted and ambiguous; it is therefore also called **telegraphic speech**.

2. After highly individual beginnings, certain aspects of syntax develop in universal and predictable patterns. Sometimes early syntax becomes too regular, and children make **overgeneralizations**.

3. Young children seem to infer grammatical relationships rather than simply copy others' speech.

4. Much syntax must be learned by rote, because rules do not cover many specific cases of language usage. Although children eventually rely on rule-governed syntax, they probably still learn a lot of language by rote, especially idiomatic expressions that bear no logical relation to normal meanings or syntax.

C. Mechanisms of language acquisition

1. One view, the behavioral perspective, is that children learn to speak through reinforcement by caregivers of vocal sounds that approximate genuine words or utterances. Analysis of conversations between parents and children shows that parents are more likely to elaborate on the child's topic if the utterance is a grammatical one.

2. Children must imitate their native language to acquire it. Most children copy only certain selected utterances rather than everything they hear. Imitation may also help children acquire language by initiating playful practice with new expressions.

D. Innate predisposition to acquire language: LAD

1. Some experts conclude that children have an innate predisposition to learn language called the language acquisition device, or LAD.

2. The idea of the LAD is supported by the poverty of content in the speech to which most infants and preschoolers are exposed. Language learned later in life is limited in amount and complexity.

3. Preschoolers do not simply copy their parents' language directly. Certain other experiences with language may be crucial in language development.

4.. Experiences affect the version of language that children acquire, even if they grow up in the same general language community.

5. The fairest conclusion about language acquisition is that children are both predisposed to acquire language and also rely on experiences with it.

E. Parent-child interactions

Certain kinds of verbal interactions apparently help children acquire language sooner and better than other kinds do.

1. **Infant-directed speech,** or "motherese," is a simplified version of language.

2. Recasting a child's utterances is repeating or reflecting on what the child has said. Recasting is a form of scaffolding--providing a temporary structure within which young children can build their own language structures.

X. Language variations

A. Gender differences in language

1. Within any community, girls learn nearly the same syntax as boys but acquire very different ways of using language, which may reflect societal stereotypes.

2. The sexes reinforce their differences in language with certain nonverbal gestures and mannerisms.

3. Gender differences in discourse may contribute to gender segregation.

B. Socioeconomic differences in language

1. Most research has found that low-income children are less verbal than middle- or high-income children.

2. Most tests of language skills favor middle-class versions of English in both vocabulary and style of discourse, or conversational patterns.

3. Low-income children more often lack prior experience with test question exchanges.

C. Language of deaf and hearing-impaired children

1. Children with hearing impairments often do not develop oral language skills as fully as other children do.

2. **American Sign Language (ASL)** is a true language.

3. Children growing up learning ASL experience the same steps in language development that speaking children do.

4. Children learning ASL and English become bilingual.

D. Language deficits or language differences.

Not everyone agrees that variations on language development are equally worthy contributing to the debate over language deficits or language differences.

- Working with Carolyn Eaton, preschool teacher: Introducing sign language to young children

XI. Early childhood education

A. Early education and cognitive theories of development

High-quality early education programs are usually based on some sort of developmental perspective.

B. Effectiveness of early childhood education

1. Staff of program are competent observers of children's educational needs and can make important decisions.

2. Curriculum is an integrated whole rather than independent subject areas.

3. Programs involve parents directly or indirectly.

C. Cultural diversity and best practice in early education

1. **Developmentally appropriate practices** are ways of assisting children's learning that are consistent with developmental needs and abilities.

2. Some developmentally appropriate practices are culture-bound rather than universally beneficial to children.

3. Best practices need to take into account cultural differences and values regarding children's development.

- A Multicultural View: Parents' beliefs about intelligence: A cross-cultural perspective

XII. From preschooler to child

Key Concepts

Directions: Identify each of the key concepts discussed in this chapter.

1. Physical growth of healthy preschoolers is generally _____ and _____, and it does not happen in _____.
2. Children who experience puberty later than average tend to grow _____ than children who experience it early.
3. To assure they receive adequate overall nutrition, preschoolers need _____ in their foods.
4. Preschoolers from low socioeconomic status contract _____ to _____ percent more minor illnesses than preschoolers as a whole. These children are also often _____.
5. Most preschoolers are able to achieve bladder control by age _____. However, _____ control is generally achieved later than _____ control.
6. Coordination of small movements that do not require strength is called _____.
7. Children's earliest drawings are _____; at about age four they begin to _____ in their drawings.
8. At about five years of age _____ are slightly bigger, stronger, and faster than _____. Most differences in motor skills are due to _____ differences and not to _____ differences.
9. _____-looking children tend to be rated as more attractive than _____ children by adults and peers.
10. In Piaget's _____ of cognitive development, preschool children are capable of improved symbolic thinking; however, they cannot think _____.
11. _____ are words or actions that stand for other things. _____ is the ability to think by making one object or action stand for another.
12. Piaget described preschool children as _____, meaning that they could not comprehend the alternative point of view of another person.
13. _____ refers to the placement of objects in groups or categories according to specific criteria. Even three-year-olds can classify objects that differ in _____.
14. The ability to undo a problem mentally and go back to its beginning is called _____.
15. The ability to recognize that certain properties of objects, such as their quantity, remain the same despite changes in the perceived features of the objects, such as their shape, is known as _____.
16. Thinking that occurs jointly with others and is embedded in a particular context or activity setting is called _____.
17. _____ is a theory that views learning as resulting from active dialogue and interaction between an individual and his or her community.
18. Group situations in which a shared focus of attention and shared goals facilitate an individual's learning from others in the group are called _____.
19. According to Vygotsky, the _____ is the difficulty level at which a child can solve problems only with assistance from others with more knowledge.
20. Theories that modify Piaget's stages of cognitive development are called _____.
21. The _____ of a language is a group of rules for ordering and relating its elements. The smallest meaningful units of language are called _____.

22. Children's early one- or two-word utterances that serve to communicate entire sentences are known as _____ or _____ speech.
23. An _____ occurs when a child applies a regular language rule to exceptions that are irregular.
24. According to behaviorist principles, children acquire language through _____ of utterances that approximate genuine words.
25. According to Chomsky, children have an innate tendency to learn language, which he called a _____ ..
26. Infant-directed speech is also called _____ .
27. Boys and girls learn the same _____ but acquire different _____, or discourse patterns.
28. Children from _____ families have difficulty answering questions to which the adult asking the question knows the answer.
29. The language of gestures used by individuals with hearing impairments is known as _____ .
30. The use of methods and goals of teaching considered optimal for young children, given the current knowledge of child development, is called _____ .

Multiple-Choice Self-Test

Factual Questions

1. Most dimensions of growth are influenced substantially by
   a. nutrition.
   b. heredity.
   c. race and ethnicity.
   d. general health status.

2. Ability to achieve nighttime bladder control depends on all of the following *except*
   a. level of anxiety.
   b. quality of deep sleep.
   c. the capacity of the bladder.
   d. not going to the bathroom immediately prior to bedtime.

3. Most children are able to balance on one foot by about _____ years of age.
   a. two
   b. three
   c. four
   d. five

4. Older-looking children
   a. are rated as more attractive by their peers.
   b. are rated as more attractive by adults.
   c. are expected to engage in more mature behavior.
   d. are not treated differently from younger-looking children.

5. Preschool children's tendency to confuse his or her own viewpoint with that of another person is called
   a. egocentrism.
   b. symbolic thought.
   c. reversibility.
   d. conservation.

6. If a child can mentally undo a problem and trace his or her steps back to the original situation he or she is using _____ in thinking.
   a. egocentrism
   b. symbolic thought
   c. reversibility
   d. conservation

7. The smallest meaningful units of language are known as
   a. syntax.
   b. morphemes.
   c. overgeneralizations.
   d. holographic speech.

8. The human predisposition to learn language is called
   a. holographic speech.
   b. telegraphic speech.
   c. the language acquisition device.
   d. infant-directed speech.

9. Boys and girls differ in their acquisition and use of all of the aspects of language *except*
   a. pragmatics.
   b. syntax.
   c. nonverbal gestures.
   d. eye contact.

10. Introducing reading and writing skills by putting them in the context of everyday experiences is called
    a. developmentally appropriate practice.
    b. overgeneralization.
    c. zone of proximal development.
    d. emergent literacy.

Conceptual Questions

1. Lucy's family lives at the poverty level. As a preschooler, Lucy is likely to be
   a. suffering from a major chronic illness.
   b. lacking essential vitamins, such as iron.
   c. suffering from excessive protein intake.
   d. suffering from few minor illnesses.

2. Three-year-old Kinu is drawing a picture. Her work of art probably includes
   a. only scribbles.
   b. scribbles and simple shapes.
   c. representations of real objects.
   d. realistic drawings of people.

3. Of the following skills, which would be most difficult for a three-year-old?
    a. Using a fork
    b. Running in a straight line
    c. Jumping in the air with both feet
    d. Using scissors

4. Monica understands that her dog, which has gained ten pounds within the last year, is still the same dog even though he is now much bigger. Monica has acquired the cognitive skill of
    a. understanding identities.
    b. using symbols.
    c. reversibility.
    d. egocentrism.

5. Pete understands that when his banana is cut into four small pieces, it does not increase in amount. Pete has acquired
    a. symbolic thought.
    b. conservation.
    c. reversibility.
    d. egocentrism.

6. Lila realizes that the candy jar contains as many candies as the number of the last piece of candy she counted. Lila understands the concept of
    a. reversibility.
    b. conservation.
    c. ordinality.
    d. cardinality.

7. Four-year-old Holly is helping her father mow and water the lawn. He has been asking for her help in emptying the bag of the lawn mower and moving the sprinklers. This activity represents learning that occurs in
    a. a social setting.
    b. an activity setting.
    c. the zone of proximal development.
    d. a cognitive setting.

8. Two-year-old Samantha says "juice" to indicate that she spilled her glass of juice on the carpet. Samantha's speech is an example of
    a. an overgeneralization.
    b. infant-directed speech.
    c. telegraphic speech.
    d. developmentally appropriate practice.

9. Tommy says "My feets are wet!" He is using
    a. an overgeneralization.
    b. infant-directed speech.
    c. telegraphic speech.
    d. developmentally appropriate practice.

10. Which question will a child from a low socioeconomic status family be most reluctant to answer?
    a. "What did you do in school today?"
    b. "When is your friend Tina's birthday party?"
    c. "How many days are there in a week?"
    d. "Do you have a spelling test next week?"

Answer Key

Key Concepts

1. smooth; predictable; stages
2. taller
3. variety
4. 25; 50; malnourished
5. three; nighttime; daytime
6. fine motor coordination
7. nonrepresentational; represent objects
8. boys; girls; gender; sex
9. Younger-looking; older
10. preoperational stage; logically
11. Symbols; Symbolic thought
12. egocentric
13. Classification; one dimension
14. reversibility
15. conservation
16. situated cognition
17. Social constructivism
18. activity settings
19. zone of proximal development
20. neostructuralist
21. syntax; morphemes
22. holographic; telegraphic
23. overgeneralization
24. reinforcement
25. language learning device
26. motherese
27. syntax; pragmatics
28. low socioeconomic status
29. American Sign Language
30. developmentally appropriate practice

Multiple-Choice Self-Test / Factual Questions

1. Choice (b) is correct; for example, taller parents tend to have taller children. The effects of nutrition, choice (a), race and ethnicity, choice (c), and general health status, choice (d), on growth are more specific and less substantial.

2. Choice (d) is correct; using the bathroom before bedtime is not reported as a factor contributing to bedwetting. On the other hand, choices (a), (b), and (c) all contribute to a child's difficulties in achieving nighttime bladder control.

3. Choice (d) is correct; ability to balance on one foot generally emerges between 4 2 and 5 2 years of age. Choices (a), (b), and (c) are inaccurate because they are too early for this skill to emerge.

4. Choice (c) is correct; adults expect older-looking children to behave more maturely. Therefore, choice (d) is incorrect. Choices (a) and (b) are incorrect because both peers and adults rate younger-looking children as more attractive.

5. Choice (a) is correct; according to Piaget, preoperational children cannot conceive of alternative points of view. He called this tendency egocentrism. Choice (b), symbolic thought, refers to an ability to think by using symbols. Choice (c), reversibility, refers to the ability to mentally undo a problem. Choice (d), conservation, refers to the understanding that although some features of objects may change, other, more fundamental, qualities will remain constant.

6. Choice (c) is correct; reversibility, or the ability to mentally undo a problem, continues to develop throughout middle childhood. Choice (a), egocentrism, refers to the preschool child's inability to conceive of alternative view-points. Choice (b), symbolic thought, is thinking by use of symbols. Choice (d), conservation, refers to the recognition that although some features of objects may change, other, more fundamental, qualities will remain constant.

7. Choice (b) is correct. Choice (a), syntax, refers to the group of rules for ordering and relating the elements of language. An overgeneralization, choice (c), is applying specific language rules too broadly. Choice (d), holographic speech, is the one- or two-word utterances children make to communicate full sentences when they first begin to use language.

8. Choice (c) is correct; some theorists, such as Chomsky, believe that humans are innately programmed to learn language. This tendency is called the language acquisition device. Choices (a) and (b), holographic and telegraphic speech, are synonymous and refer to the one- or two-word utterances children use to communicate entire sentences when they first begin to speak. Choice (d), infant-directed speech, is another term for motherese.

9. Choice (b) is correct; both boys and girls learn essentially the same syntax. However, girls learn different pragmatics, or discourse patterns, choice (a). For example, girls make requests indirectly, whereas boys make them directly. Also, girls are more likely than boys to use nonverbal gestures, choice (c), and to make more eye contact, choice (d).

10. Choice (d) is correct. Choice (a), developmentally appropriate practice, refers to methods of teaching considered optimal for young children . Choice (b), overgeneralization, refers to applying specific language rules too broadly. Vygotsky used the term zone of proximal development, choice (c), to refer to the difficulty level at which a child needs assistance in order to solve a problem.

Multiple-Choice Self-Test / Conceptual Questions

1. Choice (b) is correct; preschool children living at or near the poverty level are often malnourished and lack important vitamins and proteins; therefore, choice (c) is incorrect. Most children do not suffer from major chronic illnesses, choice (a), unless the malnourishment is very severe and prolonged. Choice (d) is incorrect in that preschool children living in poverty are likely to contract 25 to 50 percent more minor illnesses than preschool children as a whole.

2. Choice (b) is correct; most children begin to scribble and to draw simple shapes and designs between 2 2 and 3 2 years of age. Therefore, choice (a) is incorrect. Choice (c) is incorrect in that children's drawings begin to include object representations at about age four. Choice (d), realistic drawings of people appear at about school age.

3. Choice (d) is correct; use of scissors is possible at about five years of age. Choices (a), (b), and (c) are skills that emerge between 2 2 and 3 2 years of age.

4. Choice (a) is correct; understanding identities refers to the understanding that objects remain constant despite daily changes in appearance. Choice (b), use of symbols, refers to the ability to allow objects, words, and behaviors to stand for something else. Choice (c), reversibility, is the ability to mentally undo a problem and to recreate the original situation. Choice (d), egocentrism, is the preschool child's inability to understand that others have different perspectives than he or she does.

5. Choice (b) is correct; conservation ability is the understanding that fundamental qualities of objects, such as their amount, do not necessarily change when their apparent shape and size changes. Choice (a), symbolic thought, is the ability to think by using symbols. Choice (c), reversibility, is the ability to mentally undo a problem and to recreate the original situation. Choice (d), egocentrism, is the preschool child's inability to understand that others have different perspectives than he does.

6. Choice (d) is correct; cardinality is the idea that a set contains as many items as the last number counted. Choice (a), reversibility, is the ability to mentally undo a problem and to recreate the original situation. Choice (b), conservation ability, is the understanding that fundamental attributes of objects do not necessarily change when their observable attributes change. Choice (c), ordinality, is the concept that numbers always occur in a particular order.

7. Choice (b) is correct; an activity setting is a group situation in which the child learns from others with more knowledge when everyone in the group focuses on the same task. Choices (a) and (d) are not reported as concept labels. Choice (c), the zone of proximal development, describes the difficulty level at which a child can solve a problem with assistance but not individually.

8. Choice (c) is correct; children's one- or two-word utterances that attempt to communicate entire sentences are called telegraphic or holographic speech. Choice (a), an overgeneralization, is the application of a general language rule to cases that are exceptions. Choice (b), infant-directed speech, is synonymous with motherese. Choice (d), developmentally appropriate practice, refers to teaching methods and goals considered optimal for young children.

9. Choice (a) is correct; an overgeneralization is the application of general language rules to exceptional cases. Choice (b), infant-directed speech, is also known as motherese. Choice (c), telegraphic speech, is also known as holographic speech. Choice (d), developmentally

appropriate practice, refers to methods and goals of teaching considered optimal for young children.

10. Choice (c) is correct; children from low socioeconomic status families have difficulty in answering questions to which they believe the person asking the question knows the answer. In these families, parents are less likely to ask "testlike" questions of their children. Choices (a), (b), and (d) are questions to which the adult is unlikely to know the answers.

CHAPTER 7

Psychosocial Development in Early Childhood

Learning Objectives:

1. Summarize the general characteristics of parent-child relationships in early childhood.
2. Discuss the importance of extended-family supports for childrearing.
3. Describe the authoritative style of parenting and discuss the probable outcomes for children.
4. Describe the authoritarian style of parenting and discuss the probable outcomes for children.
5. Describe the indulgent and indifferent permissive styles of parenting and discuss the probable outcomes for children.
6. Describe the nature of the relationship between siblings.
7. Describe the performance of only children.
8. Define empathy and discuss the development of prosocial behavior during the preschool years.
9. Distinguish between overt aggression and relational aggression and describe their appearance in early childhood.
10. Discuss the effects of temperament and parenting styles on aggression.
11. Describe the effects of television on young children's behaviors.
12. Discuss the characteristics of play in the preschool years.
13. Compare and contrast the views of psychoanalytic, learning, ethological, and cognitive theories on play.
14. Identify the four forms of cognitive play exhibited in the preschool years and describe their developmental pattern.
15. Identify and describe Parten's levels of play and indicate the developmental patterns for each.
16. Describe the factors that contribute to the development of play.
17. Describe the development of friendships during the early childhood years.
18. Identify and describe the three steps involved in understanding gender in preschoolers.
19. Describe how parents, peers, and teachers influence gender development.
20. Discuss the various types of child abuse, its causes, and its treatment.

Chapter Outline

I. Relationships with family

   A. Relationships with parents

      1. The child's relationship with his or her parents changes because of verbal and physical development.

2. Family rules pose a challenge to preschoolers. Parents are expected to devise their own standards for rearing children.

3. Enforcing family rules may be less of a problem in cultures that encourage less individualism and stronger interdependence among people.

4. The parent's style of authority is one of the most important aspects of a parent-child relationship.

    a. **Authoritative** parents exert a high degree of control over their children and demand a lot of them, but they are also responsive, child-centered, and respectful of their children's thoughts, feelings, and participation in decision making. Preschool children of authoritative parents tend to be self-reliant, self-controlled, and able to get along well with peers.

    b. **Authoritarian** parents also demand a lot from their children and exert high control, but they tend to be less warm and responsive, arbitrary and undemocratic in decision making, and less sensitive to their children's thoughts and feelings. Children of such parents tend to be relatively distrustful of others and have poorer peer relations, poorer adjustment to school, and lower academic achievement than other children do.

    c. **Permissive** parents show two patterns. **Permissive-indulgent** parents are warm, sensitive, caring, and responsive, but exert low control and make relatively few demands on their children. Their children tend to be less self-reliant and self-controlled and to have lower self-esteem. **Permissive-indifferent** parents are detached and are inconsistent in establishing standards and expectations for their children and in fulfilling their parental responsibilities. Their children tend to be emotionally detached, have a low tolerance for frustration, and experience problems controlling their impulsive and aggressive behavior.

5. Patterns of childrearing also tend to change over time and with changes in family situations; they may be influenced to some degree by particular actions of the child.

- Focusing On: Extended family supports for childrearing

B. Relationships with siblings

    1. Most young children are very interested in babies and their repetitions, explanations, and "language practice" speech are very similar to those of adult caregivers.

    2. Preschoolers often listen to conversations between their parents and older siblings.

    3. Older siblings can be important role models and help young siblings learn social skills and parental expectations.

    4. Older siblings may feel burdened by the care of younger siblings.

    5. While adjustment to the birth of a sibling often leads to increases in behavior problems of older siblings, these tend to be temporary.

6. Only children perform as well or better than children with siblings on several measures.

C. Relationships in an expanding social world

II. In early childhood, the children's social world expands and changes.

A. Empathy and prosocial behavior

1. **Empathy** is the ability to experience vicariously the emotions and feelings of another person. Prosocial behavior refers to positive social actions that benefit others. Altruistic behavior is performed with no expectation of reward.

2. In a variety of situations, preschoolers will respond helpfully to another person's distress.

3. Development of prosocial behavior

a. Prosocial behavior is well established by the preschool years and shows up in many behaviors, such as assisting another child, comforting and protecting another child, and warning another child of danger.

b. Children give increasingly complex reasons for helping and are more strongly influenced by nonaltruistic and altruistic motives as they mature.

4. Sources of prosocial behavior

a. There are many sources of individual differences in prosocial responses. Prosocial behaviors increase due to gains in cognitive functioning, social skills, and moral reasoning.

b. Differences in temperament affect children's prosocial behavior. Easy children tend to display high levels of prosocial behavior.

c. Early exposure to prosocial experiences and parental styles influence prosocial behavior.

d. Both verbal approval for altruistic behavior and an opportunity to discover the benefits of cooperation and helping in play situations have proven successful in increasing altruistic and prosocial behavior among preschoolers.

e. Preschoolers are more willing to help if adults call attention to other children's distress.

B. Conflict and aggression

Conflict over possessions is the most common cause of anger and physical assault is the second most common cause. Children's use of aggressive revenge and tattling are most frequent when their anger is caused by physical assault.

1. **Aggression** refers to actions that are intended to hurt another person or object and can be divided into two types:

    a. Overt aggression harms others through physical damage or the threat of such damage.

    b. Relational aggression harms others through damage or threat of damage to peer relationships.

2. Influences on the development of aggression have been identified.

    a. Temperament differences may contribute to aggression.

    b. Styles of childrearing and the quality of the parent-child relationship influence the use of aggression. A number of childrearing characteristics have been found to contribute to aggressiveness in preschoolers. The quality of the parent-child relationship is the most important factor in the development of aggression.

    c. Peers contribute to aggression by acting in ways that provoke aggressive retaliation.

    d. Watching violence in the media disinhibits, or releases, violent behavior in children already prone to anger and aggression. Most children become desensitized to the pain and hurt that result from aggression. Children have difficulty figuring out the motives of TV characters and the subtleties of plots.

    e. Violent video and computer games pose similar problems for young children and their parents.

3. Responding to aggressive behavior may be necessary since children who have difficulty controlling their aggression experience considerable problems.

    a. In general, preschoolers conform to parental expectations. Children spanked by loving, thoughtful parents rarely have problems as a result of spanking.

    b. Physical punishment may not be effective in the long term for a number of reasons.

    c. The most successful approaches to aggressive behavior involve working with the entire family to observe what triggers and reinforces the aggressive actions.

    d. The most successful methods of intervention involve reinforcement of positive behaviors, assertiveness training for the child, and increasing the predictability and consistency in the child's daily life.

C. The effects of television on preschoolers' development

1. Viewing time increases during the preschool years.

2. The types of programs children prefer watching change with age.

3. Television watching influences children's social development in aggression, prosocial behavior, consumer behavior, and gender stereotypes.

    a. Television programs designed for both children and adults often convey a highly stereotyped and distorted social world that values being male, youthful, beautiful, and white.

    b. Television is also a very useful educational tool for supporting children's intellectual and social development.

4. Differences in family circumstances affect television viewing.

5. Parents attempt to regulate their children's television viewing. Families can be divided into four types.

    a. Laissez-faire parents provide low levels of regulation.

    b. Restrictive parents provide high regulation.

    c. Promotive parents have few regulations and high levels of encouragement.

    d. Selective parents highly regulate their children's television watching and encourage specific types of viewing.

III. Play in early childhood

A. The nature of play

1. Play is intrinsically motivated, because children find it enjoyable and reinforcing.

2. Children are more interested in the process of playing than in the product of play.

3. Play is creative and nonliteral; it resembles real-life activities but is not bound by reality.

4. Play tends to be governed by implicit rules.

5. Play is spontaneous and self-initiated.

6. Play is free from major emotional distress.

B. Theories of play

All theories of play hold that play activities make a major contribution to the development of important social and emotional skills and understandings.

1. Psychoanalytic theory

    a. Psychoanalytic theorists emphasize that play provides an opportunity for children to gain mastery over problems.

   b. Play also allows children to use fantasy to gain satisfaction for wishes and desires and may also provide an opportunity for catharsis of upsetting feelings.

   c. Play allows a child to gain increased power over the environment.

2. Learning theory

   a. Learning theorists view play as an opportunity for children to try out new behaviors and social rules.

   b. Play also exposes the child to adult expectations and practices.

   c. According to learning theory, children learn in three ways: through direct reinforcement for their actions, through vicarious reinforcement, and through cognitive or self-reinforcement.

3. Ethological theory

   Some theorists believe that children's physical activity play has a basis in human evolution and serves several adaptive developmental functions.

4. Cognitive theory

   a. Cognitive theorists identify four major kinds of play.

   b. Play develops sequentially in parallel with major stages of cognitive development.

C. Cognitive levels of play: Developmental trends

1. **Functional play** involves simple, repeated movements and is most common in the sensorimotor period. It requires no symbolic activity.

2. **Constructive play** involves manipulation of physical objects to build or construct something.

3. **Pretend play** substitutes imaginary situations for real ones and dominates the preoperational period.

   a. Family roles and character roles are most likely to be dramatized by preschool children.

   b. Pretend play grows in frequency and complexity during preschool years, but then decreases in later childhood.

   c. This type of play demonstrates how new forms of experience are assimilated into existing schemes of cognitive understanding.

4. **Games with rules** first appear during the concrete operational period.

    a. The rules for many such games apparently develop out of the more flexible, made-up rules of pretend play.

    b. Games with rules can become traditions handed down.

D. Other influences on play and friendship

    1. The composition of children's play is influenced by the range of play opportunities caregivers provide and the types of play they encourage.

    2. The amount of time for play is important especially as it relates to television watching.

    3. Economic, cultural, and situational variables also influence the play of children.

    4. Children use common household objects as props in play.

E. Social levels of play

    1. Play varies according to how social it is and can be described as developing in six levels of sociability.

    2. Changes in age influence social participation in play.

• Working with Javier Hernandez, preschool program coordinator: Play and friendships among preschoolers

F. Play and friendship in early childhood

Children seek intimacy from playing with a familiar friend but also want to play in activities that many different children make possible.

    1. The evolution of friendship

        a. Early friendships tend to be somewhat unstable and may change on a weekly or even daily basis. However, children can have sustaining relationships, which is an important step toward forming more lasting relationships later in childhood.

        b. Early friendships may not be as reciprocal or intimate as adult relationships are.

    2. Conceptions of friendship

        a. Preschoolers' ideas about friendship are based on activity. A friend, for example, is someone who does certain things with you.

        b. As children near school age, more permanent, personal qualities enter into their conceptions, and crucial features of a friend are more often dispositional, or related to how the friend is likely to behave in the future.

    c.   Each child in a friendship is likely to focus primarily on his or her own needs in the relationship.

    d.   Making and keeping friends requires good social skills and is an important indication of good social adjustment.

IV. Gender development

Gender refers to the behaviors and attitudes associated with being male or female. Children go through at least three steps in gender development. Gender identity is one's beliefs about being one sex or the other. Gender preferences are attitudes about which sex one wishes to be. Gender constancy is the belief that sex is biologically determined, permanent, and unchanging. **Gender role stereotypes** are culturally "appropriate" patterns of gender-related behaviors.

A. Learning gender schemata

    1.   From age two onward, preschoolers use gender role stereotypes to guide their behaviors.

    2.   Preschool children develop gender stereotypes about personal qualities relatively slowly.

    3.   Most children acquire gender identity between ages two and three.

    4.   Gender constancy first appears by age four or five.

    5.   A schema is a pattern of beliefs and stereotypes about gender that children use to organize information about gender-related characteristics, experience, and expectations.

        a.   First, children learn which objects are associated with each sex.

        b.   At about age four to six, children make more indirect and complex associations for their own sex.

        c.   At about age eight, children have learned the associations relevant to the opposite sex as well.

B. Influences on gender development

    1.   Parents

        a.   Parents' actions tend to differ from their expressed beliefs in gender equality. Also, parents support their children for sex-stereotyped activities more than for cross-sex activities.

        b.   Chodorow has suggested that the gender differences between girls and boys are related to differences in their experiences of identity formation.

    2.   Peers

        a.   In some ways, peers may shape gender differences more strongly than parents do.

        b.   Peer pressures to practice conventional gender roles are both strong and continual, and they occur even if teachers and other adults try to minimize gender-stereotyped play.

C. Androgyny

    1.   How we choose to define gender can affect our understanding of what it means to be male or female

    2.   **Androgyny** refers to a situation in which sex roles are flexible, allowing all individuals to behave in ways that freely integrate behaviors traditionally thought to belong exclusively to one or the other sex.

    3.   Bem has suggested that androgynous individuals are more flexible and adaptable because they have not formed organized connections between gender and everyday activities.

V. Child maltreatment

Child abuse may be physical, sexual, or emotional; neglect may be physical or emotional.

A. Causes

The causes of child abuse and neglect are best understood within the developmental-ecological contexts in which they occur.

    1.   Parent and child characteristics

        a.   One explanation is that aggressive and antisocial behavior involved in abuse was previously learned through modeling and direct reinforcement by the parent during his or her childhood.

        b.   Personality characteristics may also increase the risk of abuse.

        c.   A child who has a difficult temperament, was premature, has a physical disability, is hyperactive, or has other developmental problems may be at risk for child abuse.

    2.   Parenting and parent-child interactions

        a.   Abusive parents are more likely to use physical punishment and negative control strategies.

        b.   Instrumental aggression is transformed into interpersonal violence.

    3.   Family, community, and cultural factors

Poverty, unemployment, and other factors can increase the risk of child abuse.

- A Multicultural View: The cultural context of child abuse and neglect

B. Consequences

1. Abuse and neglect may interfere with children's physical, intellectual, social, and emotional development.

2. Abused and neglected children may exhibit behavioral problems.

3. Physical abuse in early childhood is linked to aggressive and violent behaviors in adolescents and adults.

4. The most common symptoms of sexual abuse include nightmares, posttraumatic stress disorders, and depression.

C. Treatment and prevention

1. Treatment involves working with parents and children after abuse or the danger of abuse has been discovered. Its goals are to reduce or eliminate the instances of abuse and to provide rehabilitative treatment for the physical and psychological injuries suffered by the child.

2. Intensive professional help, including family counseling and psychotherapy, is often used. Self-help groups such as Parents Anonymous can be helpful. Parent aides, crisis nurseries, foster care, and short-term residential treatment for family members are among the treatment alternatives.

3. Early intervention programs target high-risk families and help parents improve their parenting skills, the family climate, and their ability to better cope with stressful life events and conditions.

4. Social policy efforts include education for parenthood programs and affordable health care.

VI. Looking back/looking forward

A. Continuity within change

B. Lifelong growth

C. Changing meaning and vantage points

D. Developmental diversity

Key Concepts

Directions: Identify each of the key concepts discussed in this chapter.

1. Childrearing practices characterized by a high degree of control, responsiveness to the child's wishes and needs, respectfulness of the child's feelings and thoughts, and demands for maturity are called _____ practices. Preschoolers raised with this style of parenting tend to be _____ and _____.

2. Childrearing practices characterized by a high degree of control and demands, lack of warmth, responsiveness, and nurturance, and arbitrary and undemocratic decision making practices are labeled _____. Preschoolers raised with this style of parenting tend to be _____ of others and _____ with themselves.

3. Childrearing practices characterized by warmth, responsiveness, and nurturance, but lacking in control, limit setting, and demands are called _____. Preschoolers raised with this style of parenting tend to lack _____ and _____ and to have low _____.

4. Childrearing practices characterized by emotional detachment and avoidance of parental responsibilities are labeled _____. Preschoolers raised with this style of parenting tend to lack _____ and _____ and to have low _____.

5. Sibling relationships are important to _____.

6. The ability to vicariously experience the emotions of another person is known as _____.

7. Positive social actions that benefit others are called _____.

8. Actions that are intended to harm other people or objects are called _____. Harm inflicted by physical damage or threat of damage is known as _____. Actions that harm others through damage or threat of damage to peer relationships and friendships is labeled _____.

9. _____ of misbehavior does not have long-term effectiveness, particularly if it is harsh or frequent.

10. Television viewing time _____ from about _____ at two years of age to about _____ at eleven years of age.

11. Parents are classified into four groups based on the extent to which they regulate their children's television watching. These classifications are _____, _____, _____, and _____.

12. Play is _____ motivated, _____ oriented, and _____. Play is also governed by _____ rules, it is _____, and it is free of major _____ distress.

13. According to the psychoanalytic theory, play allows children to gain _____ over problems, to gain satisfaction for_____, and to gain increased power over the _____.

14. The learning theory contends that play affords the opportunity for learning _____ and _____.

15. According to ethological theorists, physical activity play, characterized by vigorous physical activity, has its basis in _____ and serves adaptive developmental functions.

16. _____, a type of play identified by cognitive theorists, involves simple repeated movements focusing on the child's own body.

17. _____, also a type of cognitive play, uses physical objects with the purpose of building something.

18. _____, a third type of cognitive play, involves substituting imaginary situations for real ones. This type of play is also called _____ or _____ play.

19. The final type of play identified by cognitive theorists is _____, which is a more formal type of play.

20. Preschoolers can have peer relationships that last for a _____ or more.

21. Thoughts, feelings, and behaviors associated with being male or female are called _____.

22. _____ or _____ are culturally predetermined behaviors considered appropriate for and expected from males and females.

23.   _____ is a child's ability to correctly label himself or herself as a boy or a girl. _____ refers to the understanding that one's sex is permanent and will never change. The pattern of beliefs and stereotypes about gender that children use to organize information about gender-related characteristics is known as _____.

24.   Socialization of males focuses on _____ and _____, whereas the socialization of females emphasizes _____ and _____.

25.   The tendency to incorporate both masculine and feminine behaviors into one's personality is known as _____.

26.   If mothers who were themselves abused as children nevertheless experienced one close and supportive relationship with an adult, they are much _____ likely to abuse their own children.

27.   Abusive parents are more likely to adopt the _____ parenting style and to use more _____ punishment.

28.   One of the most important treatment aspects of preventing child abuse is to teach parents more adaptive and useful _____ skills.

Multiple-Choice Self-Test

Factual Questions

1.   Warm and responsive parents who make few demands of their children use which parenting style?
    a.   Authoritative
    b.   Authoritarian
    c.   Permissive-indulgent
    d.   Permissive-indifferent

2.   Children whose parents use the _____ style of parenting may turn to their peers for guidance in setting limits.
    a.   authoritative
    b.   authoritarian
    c.   permissive-indulgent
    d.   permissive-indifferent

3.   Positive actions that are meant to help other people are called
    a.   empathy.
    b.   prosocial behaviors.
    c.   rhythmic stereotypes.
    d.   cooperative play.

4.   Which of the following statements is true?
    a.   Boys and girls tend to use similar types of aggression.
    b.   Girls are more likely to use overt aggression.
    c.   Boys are more likely to use relational aggression.
    d.   Boys are more likely to use overt aggression.

5.   Which of the following statements is *false*?
    a.   Children from lower status socioeconomic families watch more television.
    b.   Children who have working mothers and who attend day care watch less television.
    c.   Children with older siblings watch more television.
    d.   Children with younger siblings watch more television.

6. Psychoanalytic theory contends that play provides opportunity for catharsis. This means that
   a. play is not bound by reality.
   b. play allows children to release upsetting feelings they cannot otherwise express.
   c. children choose to play because it is enjoyable.
   d. play is controlled by the child's own free will, not by others.

7. When children play side by side with the same toys without sharing, interacting, or talking,   they are engaging in _____ play.
   a. solitary
   b. onlooker
   c. parallel
   d. associative

8. When children can correctly label themselves and others as male or female they have acquired gender
   a. identity.
   b. constancy.
   c. schema.
   d. preference.

9. Incorporating both masculine and feminine behaviors into one's personality is known as
   a. gender schema.
   b. androgyny.
   c. gender stereotypes.
   d. gender identity.

10. Abusive parents
   a. apply similar punishments to different types of misbehavior.
   b. show fewer threats and less disapproval for misbehavior.
   c. are less likely to be socially isolated.
   d. are not likely to engage in overt aggression.

Conceptual Questions

1. Tamara's parents are sensitive to her needs and always solicit her opinion when making family decisions. The rules they have established for Tamara to follow and the demands they make of her are reasonable and manageable. Which parenting style have Tamara's parents adopted?
   a. Authoritative
   b. Authoritarian
   c. Permissive-indulgent
   d. Permissive-indifferent

2. Danny's parents are permissive-indifferent. Danny is *least* likely to
   a. be aggressive.
   b. have low tolerance for frustration.
   c. have low self-esteem.
   d. be self-reliant.

3. As preschoolers, April and her sister Kim were often jealous of and competed with one another. As early adolescents, their relationship is likely to have
    a. improved and become slightly more positive.
    b. declined in quality and become more negative.
    c. remained relatively stable.
    d. improved dramatically and become very positive.

4. Melody is an only child. In comparison to children with one sibling, her academic performance is probably
    a. slightly better.
    b. slightly worse.
    c. much better.
    d. much worse.

5. When her friend falls and badly injures her arm, five-year-old Sarah cries along with her. Sarah's crying behavior is an example of
    a. prosocial behavior.
    b. empathy.
    c. overt aggression.
    d. relational aggression.

6. Davie's parents frequently use physical punishment in disciplining him. They can expect Davie to
    a. become very dependent on and close to them.
    b. reduce or eliminate his misbehavior permanently.
    c. act aggressively.
    d. act empathetically.

7. Lee's parents don't interfere with her television viewing preferences and encourage television watching. Their behavior can be described as
    a. laissez-faire.
    b. restrictive.
    c. selective.
    d. promoting.

8. Which is the best example of a game with no implicit rules?
    a. Playing house
    b. Playing softball
    c. Playing tennis
    d. Playing hide and seek

9. Sam says that if his hair grows long and he wears a dress he will become a girl. Sam has *not* achieved
    a. gender identity.
    b. gender constancy.
    c. gender preference.
    d. androgyny.

10. Suzy's father is warm and nurturant. Suzy loves watching him gardening and helping him fix the car and cook. She also enjoys seeing her father score a touchdown when he plays football with his friends. Suzy's father has achieved
    a. androgyny.
    b. empathy.
    c. gender schema.
    d. gender preference.

Answer Key

Key Concepts

Directions: Identify each of the key concepts discussed in this chapter.

1. authoritative; self-reliant; self-controlled
2. authoritarian; distrustful; unhappy
3. permissive-indulgent; self-reliance; self-control; self-esteem
4. permissive-indifferent; self-reliance; self-control; self-esteem
5. social development
6. empathy
7. prosocial behavior
8. aggression; overt aggression; relational aggression
9. Physical punishment
10. increases; one-half hour; four hours
11. laissez-faire; restrictive; promotive; selective
12. intrinsically; process; creative/nonliteral; implicit; spontaneous/self-initiated; emotional
13. mastery; wishes and desires; environment
14. adult skills; social roles
15. human evolution
16. Functional play
17. Constructive play
18. Pretend play; fantasy; dramatic
19. games with rules
20. year
21. gender
22. Gender-role stereotypes; sex roles
23. Gender identity; Gender constancy; gender schema
24. autonomy; agency; interpersonal relatedness; emotional expressivity
25. androgyny
26. less
27. authoritarian; physical
28. parenting

Multiple-Choice Self-Test / Factual Questions

1. Choice (c) is correct. Choice (a), authoritative parents, are highly controlling and demanding, as well as responsive and nurturant. Choice (b), authoritarian parents, are highly controlling and demanding but unresponsive and insensitive. Choice (d), permissive-indifferent parents, are detached, unlikely to set limits, and tend to ignore parental responsibilities.

2.   Choice (d) is correct; because the permissive-indifferent parent does not set limits and does not exert any control, the child turns to peers for guidance and learning morality. Choice (a), authoritative parents, set clear and reasonable limits, and their children tend to be self-controlling and self-reliant. Choice (b), authoritarian parents, make arbitrary rules that the child is expected to follow unquestioningly; their children tend to have poor peer relationships. Choice (c), permissive-indulgent parents, do not set limits to guide their children and the children tend to lack self-reliance and have low self-esteem.

3.   Choice (b) is correct. Choice (a), empathy, is the ability to vicariously experience another person's emotions. Choice (c), rhythmic stereotypies, are repetitive movements displayed by infants, such as body rocking. Choice (d), cooperative play, involves a group of children playing together to achieve a goal; in this type of play one or two children typically organize and direct the activity, and the others assume various roles.

4.   Choice (d) is correct; boys use more overt aggression, which hinders the dominance goals of other boys. Girls are more likely to use relational aggression, which hinders the social intimacy goals of other girls. Therefore, choices (a), (b), and (c) are incorrect.

5.   Choice (c) is correct; children with older siblings actually watch less television. The other choices are all correct statements.

6.   Choice (b) is correct. Choice (a), play is not bound by reality, means that play is creative. Choice (c), children play because it is enjoyable, means that play is intrinsically motivated. Choice (d), play is controlled by the child's own free will, means that play is self-initiated and spontaneous.

7.   Choice (c) is correct; parallel play involves almost no interaction between children who play in close proximity to one another and often with the same toys. Choice (a), solitary play, involves a child playing alone without an awareness of or involvement with a playmate. Choice (b), onlooker play, involves a child watching others play without entering into the activity. Choice (d), associative play, occurs when children are involved in a common activity but without clear roles and goals.

8.   Choice (a) is correct. Choice (b), gender constancy, is the understanding that one's sex is biologically determined and will never change. Choice (c), gender schema, are patterns of beliefs and stereotypes of gender that children use to organize information about gender-related characteristics. Choice (d), gender preference, is an attitude about which sex a child wants to be; gender preference may or may not be consistent with gender identity.

9.   Choice (b) is correct. Choice (a), gender schema, are patterns of beliefs and stereotypes of gender that children use to organize information about gender-related characteristics. Choice (c), gender stereotypes, are characteristics attributed to males and females on the basis of sex. Choice (d), gender identity, is the ability to correctly label oneself as either male or female.

10.   Choice (a) is correct; abusive parents do not discriminate the various misbehaviors the child engages in and punish them uniformly, so that the punishment may not fit the crime. Choice (b) is incorrect because abusive parents show more threats and disapproval. Choice (c) is incorrect because abusive parents are more likely to be socially isolated, as well as being unemployed and poor. Choice (d) is incorrect because abusive parents typically rely on overt aggression as a discipline technique.

Multiple-Choice Self-Test / Conceptual Questions

1.   Choice (a) is correct; authoritative parents are warm and responsive, as well as controlling and demanding within reasonable limits that take into account the wishes, needs, and skills of the child. Choice (b), authoritarian parents, are punitive and set unreasonable limits. Choice (c), permissive-indulgent parents, are warm and nurturant but do not set limits to guide the child. Choice (d), permissive-indifferent parents, are emotionally detached and unresponsive and neglect their responsibilities to the child.

2.   Choice (d) is correct. Children of permissive-indifferent parents are often aggressive, choice (a), have a low tolerance for frustration, choice (b), and have low self-esteem, choice (c). Self-reliant children are raised by authoritative parents.

3.   Choice (c) is correct; research indicates that both positive and negative emotions and behaviors between siblings are relatively stable and continuos from early childhood through early adolescence. Consequently, the other choices are not supported by the data.

4.   Choice (a) is correct; research indicates that only children perform as well as or somewhat better than children in two sibling families academically and on measures of achievement motivation and self-esteem. The other choices do are not supported by the data.

5.   Choice (b) is correct; empathy is the ability to vicariously experience another person's emotions. Choice (a), prosocial behavior, refers to positive social acts that intend to help others. Choice (c), overt aggression, employs physical harm or the threat of physical harm. Choice (d), relational aggression, intends to damage peer (social) relationships.

6.   Choice (c) is correct; children who are physically punished often learn to behave aggressively. That is, physical punishment strengthens the very behavior it intends to eliminate. Choice (a) is incorrect in that children who are physically punished often withdraw from and avoid the adult who delivers the punishment. Choice (b) is incorrect in that physical punishment may temporarily eliminate misbehavior but it does not have long-term effectiveness. Choice (d) is incorrect in that physically punished children are more likely to act aggressively and less likely to be empathetic and to engage in prosocial behaviors.

7.   Choice (d) is correct; parents who have few rules regarding television viewing and encourage it are labeled promoting. Choice (a), laissez-faire parents, provide low levels of regulation and encouragement. Choice (b), restrictive parents, strictly regulate television viewing and do not encourage it. Choice (c), selective parents, strictly regulate television viewing and encourage only specific types of viewing.

8.   Choice (a) is correct; when children play house, rules are absent, and children can pretend to be in certain family roles, such as mom or dad. The other choices all refer to games with rules.

9.   Choice (b) is correct; gender constancy is the understanding that one's sex is biologically determined and will never change. Choice (a), gender identity, is the ability to correctly label oneself and others as male or female. Choice (c), gender preference, is an attitude about which sex one wishes to be. Choice (d), androgyny, is incorporating both masculine and feminine behaviors into one's personality.

10.   Choice (a) is correct; androgyny is incorporating both masculine and feminine behaviors into one's personality. Choice (b), empathy, is the ability to be sensitively aware of another person's feelings and to vicariously experience their emotions. Choice (c), gender schema is patterns of belief and stereotypes of gender that children use to organize information about gender-related characteristics. Choice (d), gender preference, is an attitude about which sex one wishes to be.

CHAPTER 8

Physical and Cognitive Development in Middle Childhood

Learning Objectives:

1. Describe the physical growth characteristics of the middle childhood years and compare them with the preschool years.
2. Discuss the social and psychological consequences of obesity during the school years.
3. Discuss both the physical and psychological effects of early athletics.
4. Describe the overall physical health in schoolchildren.
5. Distinguish between acute and chronic illnesses in children during the school years.
6. Describe the effect of socioeconomic status on illness.
7. Identify the characteristics of hyperactivity and attention deficit hyperactivity disorders (ADHD) and discuss possible treatments.
8. Name the main characteristics of Piaget's concrete operational stage and contrast it with the preoperational stage.
9. Describe Piaget's concept of conservation and discuss the results of training studies on conservation.
10. Evaluate Piaget's influence on school curriculum and teaching methods.
11. Describe the changes in short-term and long-term memory during the school years.
12. Discuss learning disabilities during the school years, including their likely causes and treatment.
13. Describe the development of language in the school-age child.
14. Discuss the cognitive and social effects of bilingualism.
15. Define what psychologists generally mean by intelligence.
16. Describe and assess psychometric approaches to intelligence.
17. Present the advantages and disadvantages of gifted education.
18. Discuss the potential biases and misinterpretations associated with intelligence tests.
19. Describe the information-processing approach of Sternberg's triarchic theory of intelligence and Gardner's theory of multiple intelligences.
20. Describe the sociocultural approach to intelligence.
21. Discuss how school characteristics such as participation structures and classroom structures affect children.
22. Discuss gender and race biases in the classroom.
23. Distinguish among assessment by individualized goals, competitive goals, and comparative goals.

Chapter Outline

I. Physical development

Physical growth slows during middle childhood, and practice and instruction help children acquire skills.

II. Trends and variations in height and weight

A. During the middle years, variations in growth among children increase dramatically.

B. Girls tend to become significantly taller than boys of the same age. For boys, a spurt in height tends to follow the other physical changes of adolescence. For girls, a spurt in height usually occurs before the growth of secondary sex characteristics.

C. At least one American child in ten suffers from obesity—weighing more than 130 percent of the normal weight for his or her height and bone size.

D. The dilemma is particularly acute for girls, since cultural norms emphasize physical appearance, especially thinness.

E. The link between weight and health is not simple; heavy weight may be the result, rather than the cause of an ailment.

F. Children must have the full support of parents and siblings to diet and exercise, which may be difficult to sustain over long periods of time.

• A Multicultural View: Dieting in cross-cultural perspective

III. Motor development and athletics in the middle years

A. Fundamental motor skills continue to improve during the school years and gradually become specialized in response to children's particular interests, physical aptitudes, life experiences, and the expectations of others.

B. Children develop the ability to play games with both formal and informal rules. At the same time, their improvements in coordination and timing make performance better in all sports.

C. Physical effects of early athletics

1. The most obvious risks in athletics are sports-related injuries.

2. Injuries usually receive only short-term medical attention, and this may allow minor but long-term disabilities to develop, according to some researchers.

3. Other researchers argue that most children who are injured during sports have relatively minor injuries, and the benefits of participation therefore considerably outweigh the risks.

D. Psychological effects of early athletics

   1. Training in achievement motivation

      a. Most sports provide standards against which children can assess their performance relative to their own scores, those of their peers, or those of top-scoring individuals or teams.

      b. During the school years, however, comparing oneself to standards becomes a prominent concern, which can either motivate some children to better performance or undermine their motivation.

   2. Teamwork and competition

      a. Research on children's teams suggests that children practice teamwork better if their teams tend to win than if they tend to lose. Even the most gracious loser shows noticeable stress due to losing.

      b. Losing teams also show a marked tendency to search for blame by scapegoating individuals or events.

      c. For some children, the path away from losing consists of training harder to win. For others, it consists of learning not to take sports too seriously—to play for social and health reasons rather than for competitive success.

IV. Health and illness in middle childhood

A. During the middle years, children usually are relatively healthy, rarely experiencing serious illnesses or accidents with medical consequences.

B. There is a low **mortality** rate among schoolchildren.

C. Most common childhood diseases are **acute** illnesses, meaning they have a distinct beginning, middle, and end. Most acute illnesses develop from viruses, complex protein molecules that come alive only when they infect a host tissue.

D. Some children develop **chronic** illnesses that persist for many months without significant improvement. The most common chronic illnesses in developed countries are lung and breathing disorders.

E. The seriousness and frequency of illnesses vary according to children's social and economic circumstances.

   1. Low-income families lack money for doctors' visits and access to special child care when the child is sick, and they cannot take time away from work to tend to sick children.

   2. Because of a lack of money, visits to the doctor may occur only when there is a serious illness.

   3. Race and sex are important variables with regard to illness.

F. Attention-deficit hyperactivity disorders

    1. **Hyperactivity**, or **attention-deficit hyperactivity disorder (ADHD)**, makes children extremely active and causes them to have considerable trouble concentrating on any one activity for long.

    2. Most children show excessive activity some of the time.

    3. There are five criteria for deciding when an activity is a problem.

    4. Helping children with ADHD and their families

        a. Although no single strategy exists for treating or dealing with hyperactivity, a group of strategies has proven helpful.

        b. To reduce immediate symptoms, stimulant medication such as Ritalin quiets behavior by making the central nervous system more alert.

        c. **Behavior modification** is a psychotherapeutic technique that identifies unwanted behaviors and uses specific methods for eliminating or reducing them.

        d. Consistency and predictability are important in behavior modification.

        e. About half of all ADHD children eventually outgrow the problem although they often report feeling restless and distractible as adults. The others may be at greater risk as adults for minor antisocial behaviors.

V. Cognitive development

VI. Piaget's theory: Concrete operational skills

A. During the middle years, children become skilled at **concrete operations**, mental activities focused on real objects and events.

B. Concrete operations have three interrelated qualities.

    1. Decentration means attending to more than one feature of a problem at a time.

    2. Sensitivity to transformations combines different perceptions of the same object in logical ways.

    3. Reversibility of thought means understanding that certain logical operations can be reversed by others.

C. **Conservation** refers to the belief that properties of an object remain the same despite changes in the object's appearance. Piaget found that after about age seven, most children can conserve quantity in the water glass experiment.

D. Conservation training

    1. Piaget argued that biological maturation and extensive experience with physical objects having conservation properties lead to the ability to conserve.

2. Many psychologists have tried to teach conservation and have had some success. But children trained in conservation often do not maintain conservation concepts.

E.   Piaget described other forms of knowledge that appear during the middle years.

1. Seriation refers to the ability to put items in sequence according to a specific dimension.

2. Schoolchildren's understanding of the nature of time--or temporal relations, is much better than that of preschoolers.

3. Spatial relations improve during the school years, allowing children to make maps and models of familiar places.

F.   Piaget's influence on education

1. His ideas and approach have significantly influenced educators. The assumption that children develop their own concepts through active engagement with the environment is called constructivist philosophy.

2. Teaching methods

   a. Educators have borrowed Piaget's idea that true knowledge originates from active manipulation of materials.

   b. Activities with tangible materials should be incorporated into learning programs.

3. Curriculum content

   a. Piagetian theory has provided many specific ideas about what cognitive competencies to expect from children of particular ages and developmental levels; these expectations guide the selection and design of appropriate academic experiences.

   b. Piagetian theory has guided many curriculum planners and teachers in the selection and evaluation of academic tasks.

4. Assessment of students' progress

   a. Piaget emphasized the importance of children's actual thought processes and what those processes actually allow children to accomplish, as shown in his emphasis on informal interviews.

   b. Neo-Piagetian revisions to Piaget's theory have focused on how children learn and have proposed more specific stages of cognitive development.

VII. Information-processing skills

During the middle years, children show important changes in how they organize and remember information.

A. Memory capacity

1. Some tasks rely primarily on short-term memory (STM), a feature of thinking that holds information only for short periods. On tasks that emphasize short-term recognition memory, school-age children perform less well than adults do.

2. **Recognition memory** involves comparing an external stimulus or cue with preexisting experiences or knowledge. **Recall memory** involves trying to remember information in the absence of external cues.

3. **Long-term memory** (LTM) is the feature of thinking that holds information for very long periods. This capacity develops slowly, relying on complex storage and retrieval processes.

4. Young children may remember less because they have fewer memorable events, or they use fewer methods of deliberately remembering information and experiences.

5. Children make fewer inferences than adults.

6. A child's memory may affect learning during the school years. Teachers may need to help children see connections among material learned in school.

B. Difficulties with information processing: Learning disabilities

1. About 5 percent of children develop **learning disabilities**, disorders in basic information processing that interfere with understanding or using language, either written or
spoken.

2. Learning disabilities can take many forms, such as dyslexia. There is a diversity of symptoms.

    a. In word blindness, the child can read letters singly but not in combinations that make words.

    b. Some dyslexic children can read words but fail to comprehend them.

    c. Some children with dyslexia can read combinations of digits that make large numbers, but cannot separate out the individual numbers.

3. Causes of learning disabilities

    a. Many learning disabilities may reflect undetected minimal brain damage that occurred during or before birth.

    b. Learning disabilities may result from subtle differences in how the mind organizes and processes information.

    c. Some children with dyslexia show strong perceptual masking.

       4.   Helping children with learning disabilities

           a.   Help consists of a careful diagnosis of which steps in thinking cause difficulty followed by individual instructional plans to strengthen those particular steps.

           b.   Adults can help children by being being optimistic about the child's capacity to learn and supportive of the child's efforts to learn.

- Working with Terry Wharton, special education teacher: Giving children a second chance to learn

VIII. Language development in middle childhood

    A. Although language continues to develop in terms of an expanding vocabulary and increases in complexity and subtlety, children have not necessarily mastered syntax.

    B. Bilingualism and its effects

        A majority of children around the world are bilingual. When children are balanced **bilinguals**, meaning they acquire both languages equally well and the languages are treated with respect by others, their skill benefits their cognitive development.

       1.   Cognitive effects of bilingualism

           a.   Balanced bilingual children show greater cognitive flexibility than children fluent in only one language do.

           b.   Such flexibility shows metalinguistic awareness, the knowledge that language can be an object of thought.

           c.   Unbalanced bilingualism has mixed effects on children's thinking skills.

       2.   Social effects of bilingualism

           a.   When children acquire two languages, one language usually has more prestige than the other.

           b.   Negative attitudes toward non-English languages reduce school performance by making children less willing to use their first language in public and reducing their self-confidence about linguistic skills in general.

           c.   Additive bilingual education programs allow the child to develop skills in both of his or her languages.

    C. Black English

       1.   In the United States, some African Americans use a dialect of English called **Black English**, which differs in several ways from standard English.

       2.   Studies of Black English find it just as complex as other languages and equally capable of expressing the full range of human thought and emotion. Unfortunately, society's attitudes toward it remain rather negative.

IX. Defining and measuring intelligence

    A. **Intelligence** refers to adaptability or a general ability to learn from experience.

    B. **Psychometric approach to intelligence**

Psychometric definitions of intelligence have derived from standardized tests, all of which share three important features. They always contain clearly stated questions with relatively specific answers. They always include clear, standardized procedures for administration and scoring. They allow for comparative evaluation of the performances of particular groups or individuals.

        1. Kinds of standardized tests

            a. Standardized tests can be grouped into **achievement tests**, which measure previously learned skills or knowledge, and **aptitude tests**, which measure ability or try to predict future performance.

            b. Standardized tests, especially achievement tests, can help educators know how well schools or classrooms are functioning.

            c. Standardized tests can help educators to identify students with special academic needs.

        2. Biases of intelligence and general ability tests

            a. Tests often contain biases, such as favoring children who have a good command of language. Intelligence tests measure academic ability better than any other skill.

            b. Tests show their cultural assumptions and biases by including questions that often demand knowledge that can be attained only through immersion in White, middle-class society.

            c. Tests show their cultural assumptions and biases by including conversations that emphasize abstract or general propositions.

• Focusing On: Gifted students: Victims or elite?

    C. Information-processing approaches to intelligence

        1. An approach that draws explicitly on information-processing principles is Sternberg's **triarchic theory** of intelligence. This theory proposes three realms of cognition that contribute to general intelligence: components of thinking, experiences, and context of thinking.

            a. Components of thinking refer to the basic elements of the information-processing model such as coding, representing, and higher-order skills.

            b. Experiences refer to skills with new experiences.

       c.   Context of thinking refers to the extent to which a person can adapt to, select, or alter environments relevant to and supportive of his or her abilities.

    2.   Gardner's theory of **multiple intelligences** proposes that general ability consists of several factors defined in terms of the culture or society of which an individual is a part. These several intelligences include the following skills: language, musical, logical, spatial, kinesthetic, interpersonal, and intrapersonal.

D. Sociocultural approaches to intelligence

    1.   In the **sociocultural perspective**, intelligence is not actually "in" individuals but in the interactions and activities among individuals. Therefore, it is not the individual who adapts to, learns, and modifies knowledge but the person and the environment in combination.

    2.   A key concept in the sociocultural view is Vygotsky's zone of proximal development, or the level of problem solving at which a child cannot solve a problem alone but is able to with the assistance of an adult or a more competent peer.

    3.   This approach assumes that the issue of cultural bias on psychometric tests is an outcome to be expected rather than a problem.

E. The school is probably the single most important influence during middle childhood next to the family.

    1.   Participation structures and classroom discourse. Classrooms provide particular patterns and styles of discourse, or language interaction, which influence how, when, and with whom children can speak.

        a.   Recurring patterns of classroom interaction are sometimes called participation structures.

        b.   Control talk--patterns of speech that remind students that the teacher has power over their behavior and comments--influence classroom interactions.

    2.   Social biases that affect learning. Gender, racial, and ethnic background influence classroom interactions.

    3.   School becomes a primary setting for assessment.

        a.   Individualized goals occur when each student is judged on his or her own performance.

        b.   Competitive goals occur when students are assessed in comparison to each other.

        c.   Cooperative goals occur when students share in rewards and punishments.

X.   The changing child: Physical, cognitive, and social

Key Concepts

Directions: Identify each of the key concepts discussed in this chapter.

1. Middle childhood corresponds to the ages _____ to _____ year. During this time, the rate of physical growth generally _____.
2. For girls, spurt in height typically _____ other physical changes. For boys the spurt in height _____ other physical changes.
3. The condition of being extremely overweight for one's height and bone size is called _____.
4. The most obvious risk of athletics in middle childhood is _____ , and the most obvious benefit is _____.
5. The proportion of persons who die at a certain age is known as _____.
6. Medical conditions that persists for months without significant improvement are known as _____.
7. An excessive level of activity, along with an inability to concentrate for normal periods of time, is called _____ or _____.
8. An umbrella term for techniques based on behaviorism for changing or eliminating selected behaviors is _____.
9. Piaget's _____ stage corresponds to middle childhood. During this stage, children can think logically about _____ or _____ objects and processes.
10. _____ is the ability to focus on multiple features or attributes of a problem simultaneously.
11. The realization that changes in the appearances of objects do not necessarily alter their fundamental qualities is referred to as _____.
12. Piaget's notion that thinking and learning begin with _____ and _____ has been used to advance hands-on learning curricula in many elementary education programs.
13. The _____ is a major alternative to Piaget's theory of cognitive development.
14. _____ memory refers to comparing an external stimulus or a cue to preexisting knowledge or experience, whereas _____ memory is the retrieval of information by using few external cues.
15. When information is held for very long periods or permanently, it is in _____ memory. _____ memory holds information for up to twenty seconds.
16. Difficulties in basic information processing, such as learning reading or arithmetic, are known as _____.
17. During middle childhood, children's primary language deficit is limited _____.
18. A _____ is someone equally fluent in two languages.
19. _____ is the ability to attend to language as an object of thought rather than only to the content or ideas of a language.
20. A dialect of English spoken by many African Americans is called _____.
21. A general ability to learn from experience and to reason abstractly is known as _____.
22. An approach that identifies individual differences in ability through standardized test scores is called the _____.
23. An _____ test measures a person's current state of knowledge, whereas an _____ test estimates future performance in some realm of behavior.
24. According to the _____, developed by _____, intelligence consists of three components. These are _____, _____, and _____.
25. The theory of _____, developed by _____, claims that general ability consists of alternative forms of adaptability or elements.
26. The _____ on intelligence focuses on the social and cultural influences on ability.
27. _____ is extended verbal interaction. _____ are regular patterns of interaction in a classroom regarding when, how, and to whom to speak.

28.   Teachers typically use _____ to indicate their power over activities, discussions, and behavior of students.

29.   The diagnosis of a person's strengths, needs, and qualities is known as _____.

Multiple-Choice Self-Test

Factual Questions

1. Which physical change do girls typically experience first?
    a. Growth of breasts
    b. Pubic hair
    c. Height spurt
    d. Widening of hips

2. Which of the following is not true of early participation in athletics?
    a. Participation encourages achievement motivation.
    b. Participation teaches tolerance for competition.
    c. Participation improves self-esteem.
    d. Participation teaches a true recreational approach to sports.

3. The drug Ritalin is used in the treatment of
    a. obesity.
    b. hyperactivity.
    c. asthma.
    d. chicken pox.

4. When a child can attend to more than one aspect of a problem simultaneously, he has
    a. decentered.
    b. achieved reversibility.
    c. developed an understanding of transformations.
    d. acquired conservation ability.

5. When children are able to make maps and models of places familiar to them, they have achieved an understanding of
    a. seriation.
    b. temporal relations.
    c. spatial relations.
    d. reversibility.

6. When we retrieve information in the absence of cues we rely on
    a. recognition memory.
    b. recall memory.
    c. short-term memory.
    d. long-term memory.

7. A person who is equally fluent in two languages is known as
    a. bilingual.
    b. monolingual.
    c. balanced bilingual.
    d. equally bilingual.

8. A test that estimates future ability is called
   a. an achievement test.
   b. an aptitude test.
   c. a recognition test.
   d. a recall test.

9. Which of the following is *not* one the components of the triarchic theory of intelligence?
   a. Linguistic
   b. Componential
   c. Experiential
   d. Contextual

10. Who developed the multiple intelligences theory?
    a. Robert Sternberg
    b. Jean Piaget
    c. Howard Gardner
    d. Lev Vygotsky

Conceptual Questions

1. Natasha and Lee are both eight years old. Natasha is Russian, and Lee is from South Korea. Who is probably taller?
   a. Natasha is about five inches taller.
   b. Natasha is about an inch or two taller.
   c. Lee is about five inches taller.
   d. Both girls are approximately the same height.

2. Nine-year-old Tim's softball team loses three consecutive games. Which of the following is likely to occur?
   a. Tim and his teammates will try not to miss any future practice games.
   b. Tim and his teammates will miss practice games more frequently.
   c. Tim and his teammates will meet to discuss the details of the games they've lost.
   d. Tim and his teammates will try to avoid being stressed by the losing streak.

3. Ten-year-old Noel is from a low socioeconomic status family, and he has a midgrade fever. Noel's mother is likely to
   a. take him to a private doctor.
   b. keep him at home and in bed.
   c. send him to school.
   d. take him to the emergency room at the hospital.

4. Which of the following children does *not* fit the criteria for a diagnosis of attention deficit hyperactivity disorder?
   a. Latisha, who is overactive while riding in a car
   b. Joey, who does not reduce his activity level even after his teacher has reprimanded him several times
   c. Larry, whose overactivity is accompanied by cognitive disability
   d. Kagan, whose overactivity is accompanied by poor peer relationships and high distractibility

5. Lily understands that a ball of clay weighs the same after it is flattened into a "pancake." Most specifically, Lily has acquired
   a. an understanding of transformations.
   b. reversibility.
   c. an understanding of temporal relations.
   d. conservation of mass.

6. Terry and her sister are watching a video of their previous summer vacation. In remembering the events of their adventures as they watch, they must rely upon
   a. recall memory.
   b. recognition memory.
   c. short-term memory.
   d. working memory.

7. Kevin can read the letters of words but cannot combine the letters to read the entire word. Kevin suffers from
   a. bilingualism.
   b. long-term memory deficits.
   c. mental retardation.
   d. dyslexia.

8. Tina is taking a standardized test. Her score on this test
   a. will be a measure of achievement.
   b. will be a measure of aptitude.
   c. may be a measure of achievement or aptitude.
   d. will indicate her level of intelligence.

9. Eli uses his musical training to understand some of the requirements of his new job as a radio disc jockey. Sternberg would claim that Eli's _____ intelligence is relatively advanced.
   a. componential
   b. experiential
   c. contextual
   d. triarchic

10. Her teacher tells Carmen that her ideas on the topic of human evolution are very pertinent. The teacher's comment is an example of
    a. control talk.
    b. assessment.
    c. discourse.
    d. metalinguistic awareness.

Answer Key

Key Concepts

1. six; twelve; slows down
2. precedes; follows
3. obesity
4. sports-related injuries; better physical fitness

5. mortality
6. chronic illness
7. hyperactivity; attention deficit hyperactivity disorder
8. behavior modification
9. concrete operational; concrete; tangible
10. Decentration
11. conservation
12. manipulation; activity
13. information-processing approach
14. Recognition; recall
15. long-term; Short-term
16. learning disabilities
17. vocabulary
18. balanced bilingual
19. Metalinguistic awareness
20. Black English
21. intelligence
22. psychometric approach
23. achievement; aptitude
24. triarchic theory; Robert Sternberg; componential; experiential; contextual
25. multiple intelligences; Howard Gardner
26. sociocultural perspective
27. Discourse; Participation structures
28. control talk
29. assessment

Multiple-Choice Self-Test / Factual Questions

1. Choice (c) is correct; height spurt in girls generally precedes other forms of physical growth, including growth of breasts, choice (a), pubic hair growth, choice (b), and widening of hips, choice (d).

2. Choice (d) is correct; athletics is historically associated with competition, glory, and "manlinesss." Consequently, it is difficult to teach that athletics is for recreation purposes. Choices (a), (b), and (c) are accomplished with some degree of success when children participate in athletics.

3. Choice (b) is correct; hyperactivity (attention deficit hyperactivity disorder) is associated with difficulties in concentration and very high levels of activity. Ritalin is successful in reducing activity and improving concentration. Obesity, asthma, and chicken pox ,choices (a), (c), and (d) respectively, are not treated with Ritalin.

4. Choice (a) is correct. Choice (b), reversibility, is the ability to mentally undo a problem and recreate the original situation. Choice (c), understanding transformations, refers to having and combining different perspectives of the same object in logical ways. Choice (d), conservation ability, refers to understanding that changes in observable attributes of objects do not necessarily mean that changes in more fundamental attributes have occurred.

5. Choice (c) is correct. Choice (a), seriation, is the ability to arrange objects in sequence according to some dimension. Choice (b), temporal relations, refers to understanding the nature

of time. Choice (d), reversibility, is the ability to mentally undo a problem and recreate the original situation.

6.   Choice (b) is correct. Choice (a), recognition memory, refers to retrieval of information on the basis of cues. Choice (c), short-term memory, holds information for about twenty seconds. Choice (d), long-term memory, is permanent memory.

7.   Choice (c) is correct; balanced bilinguals have certain cognitive advantages over those who speak only one language. Choice (a), a bilingual, is someone who has some degree of proficiency in a second language. Choice (b), a monolingual person, is proficient in one language. Choice (d), equally bilingual is not a recognized concept.

8.   Choice (b) is correct. Choice (a), achievement tests, evaluate current knowledge. An example of a recognition test, choice (c), is a multiple-choice format exam. An example of a recall test, choice (d), is an essay format exam.

9.   Choice (a) is correct. The other choices represent the three components of the triarchic theory.

10.   Choice (c) is correct. Choice (a), Robert Sternberg, developed the triarchic theory of intelligence. Choice (b), Jean Piaget, developed the theory of cognitive development. Choice (d), Lev Vygotsky, advanced the notion of zone of proximal development.

Multiple-Choice Self-Test / Conceptual Questions

1.   Choice (a) is correct; there are height differences among ethnic groups. Research with eight-year-old girls indicates that Russian girls from Moscow are about five to six inches taller than girls from South Korea. Therefore, the other choices are not supported by data.

2.   Choice (b) is correct; sports failures often cause stress for children. One way of avoiding the stress is absenting oneself from the stressful situation by missing practice games. Therefore, choices (a) and (d) are incorrect. Additionally, when children lose at sports, they become less sociable, choice (c).

3.   Choice (c) is correct; in low socioeconomic status families the mother probably works and cannot afford to miss a day of work in order to stay home with a sick child. Therefore, choice (b) is incorrect. The child will also not be taken to the doctor, choice (a), or the hospital, choice (d), because of economic hardships.

4.   Choice (c) is correct; children diagnosed with attention deficit hyperactivity disorder (ADHD) generally do not have other identifiable cognitive disabilities. The other choices are among the criteria for diagnosis with ADHD.

5.   Choice (d) is correct; conservation ability refers to the understanding that changes in the appearances of objects, such as their shape, do not necessarily constitute changes in their fundamental attributes, such as their mass. Choice (a), understanding transformations refers to having and combining different perspectives of the same object in logical ways. This ability is the precursor to conservation skills. Choice (b), reversibility, is the ability to mentally undo a problem and recreate the original situation. Choice (c), temporal relations, refers to understanding the nature of time.

6. Choice (b) is correct; recognition memory involves retrieval of information when aided by cues. In this case, the cues are provided by the content of the video. Choice (a), recall memory, is retrieval of information in the absence of cues. Choice (c), short-term memory, holds information for about twenty seconds. Choice (d), working memory,, is used synonymously with short-term memory in some contexts.

7. Choice (d) is correct; dyslexia is an inability to read. Choice (a), bilingualism, refers to fluency in two languages. Choice (b), long-term memory deficits, are problems with permanent memory, such as amnesia. Choice (c), mental retardation, is typically defined as an intelligence test score (IQ score) of below70. Mentally retarded individuals are no more likely to suffer from reading difficulties than people with average and above average intelligence.

8. Choice (c) is correct; standardized tests may measure current knowledge (achievement) or future ability (aptitude). Therefore, choices (a) and (b) are only partially correct. Choice (d) is incorrect because not all standardized tests are measures of intelligence, although they measure related constructs. For example, the Scholastic Aptitude Test (SAT) is a standardized test.

9. Choice (c) is correct; contextual intelligence involves the application of skills learned in one context to other related contexts. Choices (a) and (b), componential and experiential intelligence, are the other two components of Sternberg's triarchic theory of intelligence, choice (d).

10. Choice (a) is correct; control talk used by teachers indicates their power in the classroom over the students. Choice (b), assessment, refers to diagnosing a person's strengths, needs, and qualities. Choice (c), discourse, is an extended verbal interaction. Choice (d), metalinguistic awareness, refers to relating to language as an object of thought, as balanced bilinguals can do.

CHAPTER 9

Psychosocial Development in Middle Childhood

Learning Objectives:

1. Identify and describe the basic psychosocial challenges of the middle years.
2. Define and describe the development of the self throughout the middle years.
3. Discuss differences in self-descriptions from early childhood through middle childhood.
4. Describe and compare Freud's and Erikson's views of middle childhood.
5. Distinguish between learning orientation/intrinsic motivation and performance orientation/extrinsic motivation.
6. Describe the development of achievement motivation during middle childhood.
7. Examine the role of the child within the family and the changing relationships that occur during middle childhood.
8. Compare short-term and long-term consequences when the focus of the parental concern is the parent, the child, or the relationship.
9. Discuss the impact of divorce and custodial arrangements.
10. Discuss the effects of remarriage and blended families.
11. Describe the effects of maternal employment, paternal unemployment, and child care arrangements.
12. Discuss the effects of siblings on development.
13. Describe Piaget's and Sullivan's views on the impact of peers.
14. Discuss the functions that friends have during middle childhood.
15. Discuss the effects of age, gender, and race or ethnic background on peer group membership.
16. Compare the qualities associated with popularity and unpopularity and distinguish among the types of rejection.
17. Describe the development of aggression over the life course.
18. Discuss the role of peer conformity during middle childhood.
19. Describe the roles school and teachers play during childhood.
20. Discuss the concepts of death, loss, and grieving in children.

Chapter Outline

    I. Psychosocial challenges of middle childhood

    During the middle years, children's psychosocial development involves five major challenges: (1) the challenge of knowing who you are, (2) the challenge to achieve, (3) the challenge of family relationships (4) the challenge of **peers**, and (5) the challenge of school.

II. The sense of self

Throughout their development, children actively develop a **sense of self**, a structure that helps them organize and understand who they are based on others' views, their own experiences, and cultural categories such as gender and race.

    A. The development of self in childhood

        1. **Self-constancy**, a belief that identity remains permanently fixed, does not become firm until the early school years.

        2. The first beliefs in psychological traits

            a. Up to age five or six, children tend to define self in terms of observable features and behaviors.

            b. Around age eight, some children form a more stable sense of self by including psychological traits in their self-descriptions. At first these traits have no reference to others. Often they are contradictory.

            c. By the end of the middle years, fuller integration of contradictory traits occurs, making a more stable sense of self possible. But the middle-years child's consciousness of inner traits still lacks the subtlety and flexibility found in adolescents and adults.

            d. Significant cultural differences exist in how the concept of self is constructed.

    B. Processes in constructing a self

        1. Children in middle childhood develop a sense of identity by developing a social self, which involves awareness of the relationships with others in their lives.

        2. They construct their identities by distinguishing their thoughts and feelings from those expressed by others.

        3. School-age children distinguish between their own emotions and those of others, an accomplishment necessary to develop a mature sense of self.

III. The age of industry and achievement

The years from six to twelve are important to the development of competence.

    A. Latency and the crisis of industry vs. inferiority

        1. Psychodynamic theories explain children's behavior in terms of emotional relationships in early childhood.

        2. Freud emphasized the emotional hardship of preschoolers' disappointment and their consequent repression of their wishes toward their parents.

        3. Because the child's earlier feelings have gone underground, Freud terms this period **latency**.

4. Erikson went beyond Freud's account to stress the positive functions of skill building. Becoming competent helps children be more like adults through identification and recognition from others.

5. Erikson called this process the crisis of **industry versus inferiority**, since children are concerned with the capacity to do good work. Children who do not convince themselves and others of this capacity suffer from feelings of inferiority, or poor self esteem.

B. Achievement motivation

1. **Achievement motivation** is the tendency to show initiative and persistence in goal attainment and increasing competence by successfully meeting standards of excellence.

2. Differences in achievement motivation

a. **Learning orientation** is one type of achievement motivation; it is focused on competence and is intrinsically motivated.

b. **Performance orientation** is extrinsically motivated and may be related to the child's trying to please or satisfy others.

c. Higher levels of intrinsic motivation have been found to be related to an internal sense of control, feelings of enjoyment, and other mastery-related characteristics, including higher academic performance and learning.

3. Achievement motivation in middle childhood

a. During their middle years, children become more performance oriented than in earlier years.

b. A child's belief in his or her ability to achieve depends partly on whether others give him or her credit for having that ability; this belief lies at the core of performance orientation.

c. Successful achievement becomes more complicated in the middle years.

d. Environmental factors, family factors, and cultural and ethnic backgrounds can also influence achievement orientation.

e. Children shift toward a performance orientation and become more similar to adults in their achievement orientation.

IV. Family relationships

A. The quality of parent-child relationships in middle childhood

1. Children gradually learn more about parental attitudes and motivations and the reasons behind family rules, becoming better able to control their own behavior.

2. Parents continue to monitor children's efforts to take care of themselves, but in more indirect ways.

3. If children have become securely attached during the preschool years, they and their parents often enjoy each other's company more than ever during middle childhood.

•Focusing On: The quality of parenting and family life during middle childhood

B. The changing nature of modern families

1. Mothers are working outside the home in increasing numbers.

2. Because approximately two-thirds of divorced parents remarry, it is expected that most children of divorce will live in reconstituted families, consisting of a parent, stepparent, siblings, and stepsiblings.

C. Divorce and its effects on children

1. Most divorcing parents must make adjustments that deeply affect their children.

2. Many divorced mothers must take on new or additional employment, and their standard of living frequently declines. Both custodial and noncustodial fathers are more likely to maintain or improve their standard of living following divorce.

3. The psychological pressures of divorce involve learning to manage a household alone and experiencing isolation from relatives or friends.

4. Even before actual separation and divorce, many families experience long periods of distress, tension, and discord that continue for two or three years following separation.

5. Children face problems of divided loyalties and inconsistent discipline due to poor communication between parents.

6. A study found that ten years following the divorce, children experienced fear of disappointment in love relationships, lowered expectations, and a sense of powerlessness.

7. Divorce has different effects on boys and girls.

   a. Boys tend to express their distress in externalizing ways, such as being more aggressive and willful, and are more frequently victims of power struggles and inconsistencies in matters of discipline.

   b. Some studies suggest that girls become less aggressive after a divorce, tend to worry more about schoolwork, and often take on more household responsibilities. They may be internalizing their stress by acting more responsibly than usual.

   c. Other research suggests that daughters of divorced parents develop a preoccupation with relationships with males.

      d.   Certain factors can help reduce the negative effects of divorce, including parental efforts to reduce conflict and appropriate use of professional help.

   8.   Custody arrangements

      a.   Relationships between parents and children frequently deteriorate during and immediately after a divorce.

      b.   Parents without physical custody of children do not face the same daily hassles custodial parents do, but they report feeling rootless, dissatisfied, and unfairly cut off from their children.

      c.   Fathers often increase time spent with children immediately following divorce, but soon decrease that time to well below what it was before the divorce.

      d.   Sometimes joint custody can alleviate some of these problems.

      e.   For noncustodial fathers and mothers alike, both the quantity and quality of parent-child relationships differ from those of parents who have custody.

   9.   Remarriage and blended families

      a.   Most divorced parents remarry within a few years, creating reconstituted or **blended families**.

      b.   Younger children appear better able than young adolescents to accept a stepparent in a parenting role.

      c.   Daughters, especially those approaching adolescence, appear to have a more intense and sustained negative psychological reaction to their mothers' remarriage and more difficulty accepting and interacting with their new stepfathers.

      d.   Stepmothers are more emotionally involved and take a more active role in discipline than stepfathers do.

      e.   Stepfathers often remain distant and disengaged while conflict and negativity can remain high or increase.

•   A Multicultural View: Parental expectations and academic achievement

V.   Peer relationships

   A.   What theorists say about peer relationships

     1.   Piaget

       a.   Piaget argued that peers help children overcome their egocentrism—their tendency to assume that everyone views the world the same way they do.

       b.   Piaget claimed that parents and other authority figures have limited influence since they cannot behave as true equals with children.

2. Sullivan

    a.   Sullivan also believed peer relationships are fundamentally different than a child's relationships with adults.

    b.   Peers provide a life for children outside their families and thus help correct emotional biases (i.e., warps) imposed on children by their families.

    c.   This form of learning occurs in the **juvenile period**, from about ages five to ten.

    d.   As children near the end of the elementary years, they supposedly focus interest on a few select same-sex friends, or chums.

B. Functions of friends

    1.   During the early middle years, children base friendships on shared interests and activities, exchanges of possessions, and concrete supportive behaviors.

    2.   As children move into later childhood and preadolescence, equality and reciprocity become key elements of friendships.

    3.   Children are increasingly seeing themselves as others view them.

    4.   Better-accepted children are more likely to be involved in friendships that include higher levels of validation and caring, help and guidance, conflict resolution, and intimate exchange and lower levels of conflict and betrayal.

C. Functions of peers

    1.   Peers probably serve several purposes.

        a.   Peers provide a context for sociability, enhancement of relationships, and sense of belongingness.

        b.   Peers promote concern for achievements and a reliable and integrated sense of identity.

        c.   Peers provide opportunities for instruction and learning.

    2.   Children's reliance on peers rather than parents seems to increase with age.

    3.   Although children's relationships with peers show considerable similarities to those with adults, there are several unique features.

        a.   Peer relationships are horizontal and symmetrical.

        b.   The child must act in a way that explicitly supports the relationships.

D. Influences on peer group membership

Peer group formation is influenced by several factors, particularly age, gender, and race or ethnic background.

1. Age

   a. Children play with others of approximately their own age and prefer agemates as friends.

   b. Mixed-age groups have special qualities.

   c. Same-age groups encourage the opposite qualities.

2. Gender

   a. Although mixed-sex play occurs in elementary school, even before school age and as children approach grade five, groups and preferred play partners become increasingly characterized by a single gender.

   b. As children approach middle school and adolescence, the trend reverses.

   c. Gender-based separation emerges primarily in social situations and varies with the gender composition of the groups involved.

   d. Girls' long-term friendships more often tend toward exclusive intimacy than those of boys.

   e. Girls' styles may put them at a disadvantage as children enter adolescence.

   f. Peers exert pressure toward conformity with same-gender friendship patterns.

3. Racial and ethnic background

   a. Prejudice is an attitude toward an individual based solely on the person's membership in a particular group.

   b. Prejudices are often based on stereotypes--patterns of rigid, overly simplified, and generally inaccurate ideas about another group of people.

   c. More research is needed to explore prejudice in middle childhood.

   d. Racial and ethnic prejudice may be reduced by fostering peer interactions, cooperative learning experiences, and multicultural competence.

E. Popularity and rejection

1. Children are generally classified as popular, rejected, controversial, or neglected.

2. The popular child

    a. Easily noticed characteristics are quite important to acceptance in early grades. As children get older, they choose their friends increasingly on the basis of personal qualities such as honesty, kindness, humor, and creativity.

    b. Peers view popular children as confident, good-natured, kind, outgoing, and energetic. Popular children are well liked, easily initiate and maintain social interactions, understand social situations, possess a high degree of interpersonal skills, and behave in ways that are prosocial, cooperative, and in tune with group norms.

    c. Assets such as peer competence and athletic ability remain valuable to children as they move into adolescence.

    d. Because of the importance of peer relationships during the school years, the interpersonal competencies associated with peer acceptance and popularity are likely to have a positive impact not only on a child's current adjustment but on his or her psychological well-being as well.

3. The unpopular child

    a. Peers describe unpopular children as unpleasant, disruptive, selfish, and having few positive characteristics.

    b. Such children are likely to exhibit socially inappropriate aggression, hyper-activity, inattention or immaturity, and experience behavioral and academic problems in school.

4. Aggression

    a. The highest level of aggression is displayed by unpopular-rejected children and is influenced by social context.

    b. Children who are exposed to ongoing violence suffer from emotional distress, learning problems, sleep disturbances, and preoccupation with safety.

    c. Emotional withdrawal may cause problems when these children become parents themselves.

    d. School-based intervention programs help reduce aggression and foster prosocial behavior.

    e. Studies of aggression over the lifespan reveal that some violent adults began to be aggressive as children and became increasingly aggressive with age.

F. Conformity to peers

1. Because peer groups involve social equals, they give children unique opportunities to develop their own beliefs without having parents or older siblings dominate or dismiss them.

2. Peer groups demand conformity to group expectations in return for continued acceptance and prestige.

3. Pressures to conform sometimes lead children to violate personal values or needs or those of parents and other adult authorities. Peer groups can exert positive pressures, too, such as encouraging athletic achievement above and beyond what physical education teachers can produce, and they can create commitments to fairness and reciprocity.

4. Whether pressures are positive or negative, peer groups offer a key setting for acquiring social skills, evaluating and managing personal relationships, and handling competition and cooperation.

G. School influences on peer relations

According to Erikson, school is one of the main arenas in which children resolve the crisis of industry versus inferiority, where they develop cognitive and social skills, gain knowledge about the world, and cultivate peer relationships.

1. School culture

   a. Each school has its own culture including the values, beliefs, traditions, and customary ways of thinking and behaving that makes it unique and distinguishes it from other schools and institutions.

   b. The closer the fit between the school culture and children's values and expectations, the more likely it is that the school's developmental impact will be positive.

   c. Teacher influences

      i. With the exception of their parents, most elementary-school children spend more time with their teachers than with any other adults.

      ii. Effective teachers are able to establish learning environments that are calm, predictable, and engaging; to provide smooth transitions; and to stay on top of the classroom situation.

      iii. Teacher beliefs and expectations can affect students' performance and overall school adjustment by changing students' behavior in the anticipated direction and thereby serving as a self-fulfilling prophecy.

2. The student's experience

   a. In traditional, teacher-centered classrooms students typically experience delay, denial of their desires, distractions, and social disruptions. As a result, many classrooms are organized to minimize these difficulties.

   b. Other classrooms are organized to be academically stimulating and supportive of children's developmental needs.

VI.   Death, loss, and grieving during the school years

    A.   Experiences with death can have a developmental impact throughout the lifespan.

    B.   Loss is being separated from someone to whom one was emotionally attached. Grieving is the emotional, cognitive, and perceptual reactions and experiences that accompany the loss.

    C.   Bereaved children go through three phases of the grieving process.

        1.   Early-phase tasks involve understanding that someone has died, the implications of death, and protecting oneself and one's family from physical and emotional harm.

        2.   Middle-phase tasks consist of grieving, accepting and emotionally acknowledging the reality of loss, exploring one's relationship to the person who died, and experiencing psychological pain.

        3.   Late-phase tasks require the child to consolidate a new sense of personal identity that includes the loss as well as identification with the deceased person.

    D.   Children are faced with the question of why the deceased person had to die and leave them.

    E.   Children between five and seven years old come to understand death as an irreversible, nonfunctional, and universal state. Younger children think death is reversible and think that some people will not die.

    F.   The developmental impact of death is dependent on a number of factors.

    G.   Joining a support group can help children understand and process a death; children in these groups participate in stories, drawings, role playing, and discussion.

VII.   The effects of work on families

    A.   Effects of maternal employment

        1.   Research suggests that maternal employment does no developmental harm to children; what does matter is the woman's choice of whether to work or not.

        2.   Families with working mothers divide household responsibilities and child care more evenly than other families do. Children are often expected to help with household chores and caring for younger siblings.

        3.   The blend of housework and earning money seems to create less stereotyped attitudes in the children of working mothers about the proper roles of mothers and fathers.

        4.   Many working mothers compensate for possible negative effects of their working through more frequent shared activities with their children.

    B.   Involuntary paternal unemployment can create significant economic, social, and psychological disruptions for children and their families.

C. Finding after-school supervision is a concern for many parents.

1. One study found that children attending a formal after-school program had better grades, conduct in schools, emotional adjustment, and peer relations.

2. Formal after-school programs may be less important for children who live in communities that provide safe and constructive after-school experiences.

VIII   Other sources of social support

A. Siblings can provide social support

1. Siblings can help with companionship, friendship, social support, and mentoring.

2. Siblings can transmit customs and family expectations and provide challenges that lead their young sibling to new learning.

3. Young school-age children confer a unique role on their older siblings.

4. Siblings tend to be less domineering and more nurturant in families in which children feel secure and parents get along well together.

B. Children find additional sources of support.

1. Other adults, grandparents, and even family pets can provide support.

2. Children use hobbies to unwind, have special secret hideaways, and seek out peers for activities when they need an emotional lift.

3. This broadening of social support enables them to better manage stresses inside and outside of their families

IX.   Looking back/looking forward

A. Continuity within change

B. Lifelong growth

C. Changing meaning and vantage points

D. Developmental diversity

Key Concepts

Directions: Identify each of the key concepts discussed in this chapter.

1. Individuals who are of approximately the same age and developmental level and share common attitudes and behaviors are called one's _____.

2. Throughout middle childhood, children continue to develop a _____, a structured way of thinking about oneself in order to understand who one is. This development partially depends on the development of _____, the belief that one's identity is fixed and permanent. This understanding emerges after _____ years of age.

3. The Freudian psychosexual stage corresponding to middle childhood is termed _____. During this stage, _____ and _____ lie, dormant and the child focuses on building and mastering new skills.

4. Erikson's fourth psychosocial crisis, _____, corresponds to middle childhood..

5. _____ is behavior that enhances competence or the judgments of competence.

6. When achievement motivation is _____, it comes from the learner and the task. When it is _____, it is stimulated by other individuals who evaluate the learner.

7. Since the mid-1980s, approximately _____ percent of marriages have ended in divorce in the United States.

8. Currently, _____ percent of married women and _____ percent of single women with children under eighteen are employed outside of the home.

9. When parents divorce during the child's school years, the child fares _____ in comparison with children who are either older or younger at the time of the divorce.

10. Boys typically express their distress over parents' divorce by _____ feelings, whereas girls are more likely to _____ feelings.

11. Families consisting of remarried parents and their children are called _____.

12. When mothers feel forced either to work or not to work, they report more _____ relationships with their children.

13. Children often name their _____ and _____ as sources of social support.

14. According to Sullivan, the _____ corresponds to the ages between five and ten, when children are increasingly interested in developing friendships with same-sex peers. Sullivan called these friendships _____.

15. As children move into later childhood, _____ and _____ become important elements of friendship interactions.

16. During middle childhood, children typically prefer to be friends with other children who are the same _____, _____, and _____.

17. _____ that offer specialized programs in science, language, or the arts are successful in attracting students from diverse racial and ethnic backgrounds.

18. Unpopular children occupy one of three statuses: _____, _____, and _____.

19. A _____ is someone whom the child considers a friend but who does not feel the same way about her.

20. A mutual relationship between peers is called a _____.

21. Boys are more likely to exhibit _____ aggression, whereas girls engage more in _____ aggression.

22. Violent individuals are categorized into three developmental types; these are the _____, the _____, and the _____ types.

23. Each school has its own _____, including values, beliefs, and traditions, that influences children.

24. _____ refers to a child's separation from someone to whom he or she was emotionally attached. _____ refers to the complex emotional, cognitive, and perceptual reactions and experiences that accompany it.

25. A child confronting the death of a loved one, such as a parent, must go through a grieving process that is made up of _____, _____, and _____ phases.

Multiple-Choice Self-Test

Factual Questions

1. According to Freud, children's _____ feelings are latent during middle childhood.
   a. mastery
   b. sexual
   c. inferiority
   d. industrious

2. When achievement is intrinsically motivated, it is called
   a. achievement motivation.
   b. performance orientation.
   c. learning orientation.
   d. personal motivation.

3. Following divorce, the most common parenting style of mothers with daughters is
   a. permissive-indifferent.
   b. permissive-indulgent.
   c. authoritarian.
   d. authoritative.

4. During middle childhood, sharing between friends shifts from _____ to _____ reciprocity.
   a. cooperative; symmetrical
   b. symmetrical; cooperative
   c. normative; nonnormative
   d. nonnormative; normative

5. During middle childhood, reliance on peers for support
   a. increases.
   b. decreases somewhat.
   c. decreases significantly.
   d. remains the same.

6. Children classified as _____ receive very few negative and positive evaluations from their peers.
   a. rejected
   b. controversial
   c. neglected
   d. unpopular

7. Popular children are more likely to have
   a. fewer same-age friends.
   b. fewer opposite-sex friends.
   c. more unilateral friends.
   d. more reciprocal friends.

8. Girls are more likely than boys to
    a. engage in overt aggression.
    b. engage in relational aggression.
    c. select girls with a masculine play style as friends.
    d. have primarily opposite-sex friendships.

9. The largest proportion of violent adults are classified as _____ type on their style of aggression.
    a. life-course
    b. limited-duration
    c. late-onset
    d. minimal-harm

10. Emotionally acknowledging the reality of losing a loved one occurs in which phase of the grief process?
    a. Early
    b. Middle
    c. Late
    d. Final

Conceptual Questions

1. When asked if he might enjoy having long hair, Joey says, "No, then I would become a girl." Joey's response indicates that he hasn't yet achieved
    a. reversibility.
    b. egocentrism.
    c. self-recognition.
    d. self-constancy.

2. Minna loves spending time with her dad and often wishes that they could be together more often without the presence of her mother. Freud would describe Minna's feelings as reflective of the _____ conflict.
    a. Oedipus
    b. Electra
    c. Phallic
    d. Latency

3. Natalie is learning to play the piano because she enjoys the sounds this instrument can create. Her achievement motivation is primarily _____ oriented.
    a. learning
    b. performance
    c. power
    d. social

4. Jody is a poor math student; she has difficulty understanding mathematical concepts and often fails math exams. Erikson would predict that this negative experience with math might lead her to have feelings of
    a. industry.
    b. inferiority.
    c. mistrust.
    d. stagnation.

5. Heather's parents divorced when she was seven years old. As an adolescent she is likely to
   a. start dating at a later age.
   b. start dating at an earlier age.
   c. have positive relationships with males.
   d. have a laissez-faire attitude toward relationships with males.

6. Nine-year-old Ahmad attends an after school program. In comparison with children who do not attend such a program,
   a. his school conduct is probably poor.
   b. his grades are probably lower.
   c. his grades are probably higher.
   d. his peer relationships are probably poor.

7. Who is more likely to provide instructional guidance to a younger child?
   a. An older sibling
   b. An older peer
   c. Both older peers and older siblings will provide guidance equally
   d. Neither older peers nor older siblings

8. Libby and Maryann are very interested in having and wearing similar clothing, seeing the same movies, and going to the same birthday parties. Their friendship is characterized by
   a. equality.
   b. reciprocity.
   c. symmetrical reciprocity.
   d. cooperative reciprocity.

9. Carlos, a native Spanish speaker, is not allowed to join a neighborhood soccer game because the other children view him as an outsider because of his heavy accent. Carlos's exclusion from the game is an example of
   a. prejudice.
   b. a stereotype.
   c. discrimination.
   d. neglect.

10. Very few of Ryan's peers say they would choose to play with him, and very few claim to like him. Ryan's popularity classification is most likely to be
   a. neutral.
   b. controversial.
   c. rejected.
   d. neglected.

Answer Key

Key Concepts

1. peers
2. sense of self; self-constancy; six

3. latency; sexual feelings; sexual activities
4. industry versus inferiority
5. Achievement motivation
6. learning oriented; performance oriented
7. 50
8. 69; 60
9. worse
10. externalizing; internalize
11. blended families
12. stressful
13. peers; siblings
14. juvenile period; chum relationships
15. equality; reciprocity
16. age; sex; racial/ethnic background
17. Magnet schools
18. rejected; controversial; neglected
19. unilateral friend
20. reciprocal friendship
21. overt; relational
22. life-course; limited-duration; late-onset
23. culture
24. Loss; Grief
25. early; middle; late

Multiple-Choice Self-Test / Factual Questions

1. Choice (b) is correct; Freud claimed that the sexual conflicts and urges related to the first three stages of psychosexual development remain on hold during the latency stage, when children are in elementary school and mastering new skills and competencies gains priority. Therefore, feelings related to mastery and industry, choices (a) and (d), are active during this time. Choice (c), feelings of inferiority, are not discussed within this context.

2. Choice (c) is correct; learning orientation refers to achievement motivation that comes from the learner and the task. Choice (a), achievement motivation, is an umbrella term that refers to all behaviors that enhance competence or the judgment of competence. Choice (b), performance orientation, refers to achievement motivation stimulated by other individuals. Choice (d), personal motivation, is not a recognized label for a concept.

3. Choice (d) is correct. Mothers with sons tend to adopt permissive, choices (a) and (b), and authoritarian, choice (c), styles of parenting following divorce.

4. Choice (b) is correct; symmetrical sharing involves actually doing the same things and sharing the same objects, whereas cooperative sharing is more mature and based on mutual sharing of assistance and resources. Consequently, choice (a) is incorrect. Choices (c) and (d) are not terms applied to sharing behavior.

5. Choice (a) is correct; research indicates that peers become more important and more frequent sources of support than parents as middle childhood progresses into adolescence. Whereas fourth-graders rate their parents as their most frequent source of support, seventh-graders rate parents and peers equally important, and tenth-graders rate peers as more important than parents. Therefore, the other choices are not supported by the data.

6.   Choice (c) is correct. Choice (a), rejected children, receive few positive and many negative evaluations. Choice (b), controversial children, receive many positive and negative evaluations. Choice (d), unpopular children are divided into the three categories of rejected, neglected, and controversial.

7.   Choice (d) is correct; reciprocal friendships are those in which both individuals recognize the other as a friend. The other choices are characteristics of unpopular children.

8.   Choice (b) is correct; relational aggression attempts to damage peer/social relationships, and girls are more likely than boys to show their aggression in this way. Choices (a) and (c) are characteristics of boys. Data does not indicate quantitative differences in the same-sex and opposite-sex friendships of boys and girls; therefore, choice (d) is incorrect.

9.   Choice (a) is correct; individuals whose aggression is classified as life-course type begin to engage in aggression in childhood and become increasingly more aggressive over time. Individuals classified as limited-duration type, choice (b), outgrow their aggressive tendencies prior to reaching adulthood. Individuals who are classifies as late-onset, choice (c), begin to show aggression in adulthood with no history of earlier aggression. Choice (d), minimal-harm type, is not one of the identified styles of aggression.

10.   Choice (b) is correct; emotionally acknowledging and accepting the loss of a loved one, such as a parent, is one of the middle phase tasks of grieving. Choice (a), early-phase tasks, include understanding that someone has died and the implications of death. Choice (c), late- phase tasks, include developing a new identity that includes the loss as well as identification with the deceased person. Choice (d) is incorrect in that the grief process as identified by Baker and his colleagues includes only three phases, early, middle, and late.

Multiple-Choice Self-Test / Conceptual Questions

1.   Choice (d) is correct; self-constancy is the recognition that the self (identity) is fixed permanently. Choice (a), reversibility, is the ability to mentally undo a problem and to recreate the original situation. Choice (b), egocentrism, is a limitation of the preoperational child in understanding that other people have perspectives different from his own. Choice (c), self-recognition, refers to the ability of young children to recognize physical images of themselves, such as in a photograph.

2.   Choice (b) is correct. According to Freud, during the phallic stage, choice (c), of psychosexual development, children have sexual feelings toward the parent of the opposite sex. He called this conflict the Electra conflict for girls and the Oedipus conflict, choice (a), for boys. Choice (d), latency, is the name of Freud's fourth psychosexual stage, during which sexual feelings, urges, and conflicts of the previous stages are lying dormant and the child is engaged in mastering and learning new skills.

3.   Choice (a) is correct; learning orientation refers to achievement motivation that is self- and task-oriented. Choice (b), performance orientation refers to achievement motivation that is stimulated by others. Achievement motivation is not described as power or social oriented, choices (c) and (d),

4.   Choice (b) is correct; Erikson claims that the task (crisis) of middle childhood is to establish a sense of industry, choice (a), which comes from the recognition that one can do good work. The alternative is a child's failure in being able to accomplish his goals and the consequent feelings

of inadequacy and incompetence, known as inferiority. Choice (c), mistrust, is the negative outcome of the first psychosocial crisis, and choice (d), stagnation, is the negative outcome of the seventh psychosocial crisis.

5.   Choice (b) is correct; females whose parents divorce when they are in middle childhood tend to start dating and having sexual relationships earlier, sometimes before the end of elementary school. Therefore, choice (a) is incorrect. Choices (c) and (d) are incorrect in that these females tend to have negative, conflict-ridden relationships with males and tend to be overly preoccupied with their relationships with males.

6.   Choice (c) is correct; children who attend after-school programs show better academic performance. Therefore, choice (b) is incorrect. Choices (a) and (d) are incorrect in that these children often have better conduct in school, and their peer relationships are more positive.

7.   Choice (a) is correct; older siblings are more likely than older peers to spontaneously provide guidance to younger children. They also provide more explanations and positive feedback in structured teaching situations. Choices (b), (c), and (d) are not supported by the data.

8.   Choice (c) is correct; as children move to later childhood, their friendships shift from being symmetrically reciprocal (sharing objects and activities) to being cooperatively reciprocal (sharing assistance and resources); choice (d). Thus choices (a) and (b), equality and reciprocity, are both characteristic of friendships as children move into later childhood and adolescence.

9.   Choice (c) is correct; discrimination refers to actions against a targeted group, such as mistreatment and exclusion, based on prejudice, choice (a), or attitudes based on group membership. Choice (b), stereotypes, are rigid, simplified, and often inaccurate ideas about members of a particular group. The concept of neglect, choice (d), is not applicable to the described situation.

10.   Choice (d) is correct; neglected children receive few positive or negative evaluations from their peers. Choice (a), neutral, is not a popularity classification. Controversial children, choice (b), receive many positive and negative peer evaluations. Rejected children, choice (c), receive many negative and few positive peer evaluations.

CHAPTER 10

Physical and Cognitive Development in Adolescence

Learning Objectives:

1. Describe the concept of adolescence, explain how it has changed, and cite the factors that have influenced those changes.
2. Discuss adolescence as a period of transitions.
3. Describe the adolescent growth spurt and depict characteristic height and weight changes during adolescence.
4. Define puberty and identify the primary and secondary sex characteristics and how they change during adolescence.
5. Identify and discuss the functions of the major sex hormones in puberty.
6. Describe the effects of early versus late maturing in males and females, including information concerning long-term effects.
7. Characterize the health of adolescents and discuss adolescents' understanding of the relationship between their behavior and their health.
8. Identify and describe common sexually transmitted diseases.
9. Discuss drug, alcohol, and tobacco usage problems in adolescence.
10. Describe nutritional problems and the symptoms and treatment of eating disorders.
11. Discuss the qualities of formal operational thought, including its limitations.
12. Identify and describe Kohlberg's six stages of moral judgment.
13. Describe and discuss Gilligan's ethics of care.
14. Discuss adolescent egocentrism including "imaginary audience" and "personal fable."
15. Discuss the characteristics of experts and the development of expertise.
16. Define critical thinking and discuss its development.
17. Discuss both cognitive and social effects of schooling during adolescence.
18. Discuss concerns about high school dropouts.
19. Discuss the effects of employment on adolescents.

Chapter Outline

I.   The concept of adolescence

Adolescence is a period of transitions leading from childhood to adulthood ranging from about ages ten to twenty-two. Every society uses ceremonies and rituals to signify the transition to adulthood.

A. Adolescence: From idea to social fact

   1. The idea of adolescence was recognized largely as a response to social changes that accompanied U.S. industrial development in the nineteenth century.

   2. Some researchers have proposed that adolescence was defined as a separate stage to prolong the years of childhood.

   3. Compulsory education, child labor laws, and special legal procedures for juveniles together played a role in making adolescence a social reality.

B. Theoretical views of adolescence

   1. One idea holds that adolescence is a time of "storm and stress" when children experience crisis and conflict.

   2. Systematic observation and research suggest that as they pass through adolescence, most individuals adapt quite well to the changes in themselves and to the changing demands and expectations of parents and society.

   3. How negative or positive adolescent changes are depends on the degree of fit between adolescents' developing needs and the opportunities afforded them by their social environments, particularly school and home. The adolescent's subjective construction of his or her environment is also an important variable.

II. Growth in height and weight

A. Rapid change in height and weight is due to a dramatic **growth spurt** preceded and followed by years of comparatively little increase.

   1. The reason for males' greater average height is that boys start their growth spurt two years later than girls do and thus undergo two additional years of childhood growing.

   2. Weight is more strongly influenced by diet, exercise, and lifestyle than height is, and therefore weight changes are less predictable.

B. Adolescents differ greatly in their rate and pattern of growth and its impact on their lives.

C. Society's gender role expectations affect how adolescents view their bodies' changes which in turn affect their health behaviors.

D. The secular trend

   1. The **secular trend** refers to generational differences in direction and magnitude of bodily changes.

   2. The average age at which girls have their first menstrual period has dropped from between fifteen and seventeen to between twelve and fourteen. However, there is no evidence that an earlier onset of puberty is accompanied by an acceleration of the social and emotional development girls need to manage their sexuality.

3. The major reasons for the secular trend are thought to be improvements in health care, diet, and overall living conditions.

- A talk with Jason, age fourteen: Physical development at age fourteen

III. Puberty

Puberty is a set of physical changes that marks the completion of sexuality development or reproductive maturity. **Primary sex characteristics** make reproduction possible. A number of changes in **secondary sex characteristics** also occur.

A. The development of primary sex characteristics

1. The most significant sign of sexual maturation in boys is rapid growth of the penis and scrotum.

a. Enough live sperm are produced during adolescence to allow reproduction.

b. Boys' first ejaculation of **semen** occurs around age twelve.

c. **Nocturnal emissions**, which frequently accompany erotic dreams, usually are experienced one or two years before puberty.

2. For girls, **menarche**, the appearance of the first menstrual period, signals sexual maturity.

a. Menarche is preceded by other physical changes, including enlargement of the breasts.

b. Menstruation involves some inconvenience and discomfort, but also positive feelings.

B. The development of secondary sexual characteristics

Secondary sexual characteristics make both boys and girls more adultlike in appearance and more stereotypically masculine or feminine.

1. Breasts

a. Girls first develop breasts at the beginning of puberty.

b. Breast development is a source of potential concern for girls.

c. Boys also have a small amount of breast development.

2. Body hair

a. Both boys and girls acquire more body hair.

b. **Pubic hair** darkens and becomes coarser, and underarm or **axillary hair** also becomes dark and coarse.

c. Cultural attitudes influence females' feelings about axillary hair.

3. Voice

    a. In both sexes, the voice deepens near the end of puberty and becomes richer in overtones, making it more adultlike.

    b. Social expectations encourage many girls to talk in voices that are higher than is comfortable, necessary, or natural.

C. Hormonal changes: physical and social consequences

    1. Although gender differences in muscularity and other physical changes depend in part on societal expectations and life experiences, the most significant changes are the result of genetic programming.

    2. Hormones are responsible for the typical differences in overall body build between the sexes.

        a. Testosterone stimulates muscle and bone growth in both sexes.

        b. Estrogen stimulates the increased deposits of subcutaneous fat.

    3. Boys tend to keep most of the same amount of fat deposits in adolescence, so the overall proportion of fat tissue to body weight decreases, but girls develop significant new subcutaneous fat deposits.

IV. Psychological effects of physical growth in adolescence

A. Body image and self-esteem

    1. For many adolescents judgments about their physical appearance may be the most important factor in their self-esteem.

    2. Conventional standards of attractiveness, which tend to favor muscular builds in males and a slender figure and curves in females, influence adolescents.

•   Working with Barbara Donohue, nutritionist: Treating nutritional problems and eating disorders during adolescence

B. Timing of puberty

    The timing of puberty can make a lasting difference to the psychological development of an adolescent.

    1. Although *early-maturing boys* are perceived as more mature, self-confident, and competent than others, they are often more somber, less creative, and less spontaneous, due to their need to live up to others' expectations of them. These differences continue into adulthood.

2. *Late-maturing boys* still resemble children physically, sometimes as late as age sixteen, and are judged as impulsive, immature, lacking in self-confidence, and socially inferior. Their physical immaturity may protect them from increasing pressures and allow them freedom to develop their own unique identities.

3. *Early-maturing girls* often feel less attractive and more concerned about their physical appearance, are more awkward in social situations, experience less peer support, and have poorer self-concept.

   a. Because early-maturing girls may be more shapely and sexually mature, they may encounter dating and sexual difficulties that they are not psychologically ready to handle.

   b. After successfully coping with these challenges, early-maturing girls are likely to experience positive effects of maturing early, such as increased status and popularity, and at age 30 report feeling more poised and self-directed.

4. *Late-maturing girls* often experience social advantages, being viewed as attractive and good leaders, but by age 30 report feeling less poised and sure of themselves.

C. Non-normative effects of puberty.

   While the short term effects of nonnormative timing indicate an increase in stress in family relationships, long term effects indicate minimal psychosocial impact.

- A Multicultural View: How do ethnic differences in physical appearance affect social development during adolescence?

V. Health in adolescence

Adolescents experience certain health risks more than either younger children or adults do, even though they may perceive themselves as at less risk than they really are.

A. Continuity with health in childhood

   1. The health and health-care patterns of most individuals show considerable consistency and continuity from early childhood through adolescence.

   2. Factors such as SES and the quality and accessibility of services play a major role in adolescent patterns of use of health and mental health services and their own health-related behaviors.

   3. Adolescents' understanding of the relationship between behavior and health may be inadequate.

   4. Programs to encourage self-care have had significant success, especially when they are based in junior and senior high schools and offer comprehensive health care and family planning to teenagers.

B. Causes of death among adolescents

   1. The death rate during adolescence is one of the highest for all age groups. Risky environments, risk-taking behavior, and adolescents' belief in invulnerability undoubtedly contribute to this fact.

   2. Males are significantly more at risk than females.

   3. Leading causes of deaths are motor vehicle accidents, homicides and other intentional violence, and suicide.

C. Health compromising behaviors

   1. Sexually transmitted diseases are a major problem for adolescents. Risk factors include the increased acceptability of early sexual activity and inadequate use of contraceptives.

   2. AIDS (acquired immune deficiency syndrome) is the best known and most feared sexually transmitted disease.

      a. AIDS is spreading among teenagers.

      b. AIDS destroys the body's ability to maintain its normal immunity to diseases. It is transmitted through introduction of the HIV virus through the body fluids of an infected person.

      c. Formal instruction about AIDS is now given to a growing number of teenagers.

      d. Some sexual practices and behaviors are safer than others.

   3. Drug and alcohol abuse are typical of adolescence and represent a rite of passage. On the other hand, they are associated with leading causes of death and injury among adolescents.

      a. Prolonged or chronic drug abuse is destructive to developmental processes.

      b. Problem drug use is often a symptom rather than a cause of personal and social maladjustment.

   4. Alcohol abuse can lead to severe health problems; alcohol is readily available and is very popular among adolescents. Tobacco use has been advertised as a sign of adulthood.

      a. Patterns of drinking and smoking are strongly influenced by lifestyles of family members and peers and the environment.

      b. Prevention efforts are directed at adolescents and include life skills training, increasing knowledge, and improving confidence and social competence.

5. Nutritional problems occur more often in adolescents any other age group.

    a. Inadequate nutrition can interfere with a teenager's ability to concentrate at school and work and to actively engage in activities with peers.

    b. Obesity can affect a teenager's sense of himself or herself as a physically attractive person and impact overall identity development.

    c. The dominant cultural standard for feminine beauty is a lean body, leading to **anorexia nervosa** and **bulimia** in many adolescent females who desire to achieve this standard.

- Focusing On: Female athletes and eating disorders

VI.   Cognitive development

Cognitive development allows adolescents to imagine situations and events that they have not experienced concretely and to speculate on what might have been. Other abilities that develop during adolescence include the ability to plan ahead, set goals, think logically, and think about thinking.

VII.   Beyond concrete operational thinking

Adolescents acquire formal operational thought.

    A. Possibilities versus realities

       The adolescent can consider possibilities rather than only realities.

    B. Scientific reasoning

       Problems can be reasoned through in a systematic way.

    C. Logical combination of ideas

       1. Several ideas can be kept in mind and combined or integrated in logical ways.

       2. Formal operational thinkers can qualify their opinions better than preformal operational thinkers.

    D. Concrete versus formal thought

       1. Haphazard problem-solving processes mark a child's efforts as concrete operational, still tied closely to the real or concrete.

       2. Formal operational thinking is more systematic, involving developing hypotheses, devising ways to test them, and drawing reasonable conclusions from observations.

E. Cognitive development beyond formal thought

    1. Formal or abstract thought may not be the final cognitive achievement.

    2. Adolescents may overrate their formal reasoning, failing to notice the limits of their logic.

    3. Less systematic reasoning serves as well or better for solving daily problems.

    4. For older adolescents, the cognitive challenge consists of converting formal reasoning from a goal in itself to a tool used for broader purposes and tailored to the problems at hand.

F. Implications of the cognitive development viewpoint

    1. A majority of adolescents (and adults) use formal thinking inconsistently or even fail to use it at all.

    2. One's cognitive performance depends for the most part on how it is observed or measured.

    3. Adolescents use formal operational thought only partially or intermittently.

- Working with Jerry Acton, math and science teacher

VIII. Moral development: Beliefs about justice and care

As adolescents gradually develop formal thought, they also develop their personal morality or sensitivity to and knowledge of what is right and wrong.

A. Kohlberg's six stages of moral judgment

Kohlberg proposed a six-stage process of developing moral judgment, four of those applying to children and adolescents. The stages were developed by presenting children with moral dilemmas.

    1. Earlier stages represent more egocentric and concrete thinking than do later stages.

        a. Stage 1: Children accept the perspectives of authorities.

        b. Stage 2: Children begin to show some ethical reasoning.

        c. Stage 3: Children are concerned chiefly with the opinions of peers.

        d. Stage 4: Children focus on the opinions of community and society.

    2. When thinking about justice, teenagers' ethical judgments are less opportunistic than children's.

3. Adolescents base their evaluations of situations either on principles expressed by peers and relatives or on socially sanctioned rules and principles.

4. A few teenagers and young adults develop postconventional moral judgment (stages 5 and 6), meaning that ethical reasoning goes beyond the judgments society conventionally makes about right and wrong.

B. Issues in the development of moral beliefs about justice

1. Kohlberg's stages describe only the form of thinking, not its content. Studies suggest that ethical thinking probably is not separate from content.

2. Kohlberg's theory does not fully distinguish between social conventions and morality. Social conventions are the arbitrary customs and agreements about behavior that members of society use; morality refers to matters of justice and of right and wrong.

3. Kohlberg's theory may be gender biased.

C. Gilligan's ethics of care

1. According to Gilligan, boys and girls tend to view moral problems differently.

2. Boys learn to think more often in terms of general ethical principles that they can apply to specific moral situations. The principles tend to emphasize independence, autonomy, and rights of others.

3. Girls tend to adopt an ethics of care--a view that integrates principles with the contexts in which judgments must be made. This view grows out of a general concern for the needs of others more than for their own independence.

4. Gilligan argues that Kohlberg's theory underrates the moral development of females.

5. When faced with hypothetical dilemmas, girls show as much capacity as boys to reason in terms of abstract ethical principles. But when faced with real-life dilemmas, girls make
different choices.

D. Ethical beliefs about care in adolescence

1. Adolescents develop somewhat conventional ethical attitudes about caring for others.

2. Egocentrism remains in that teenagers often fail to distinguish between actions that please others and actions that are right in a deeper, ethical sense.

3. A few individuals move beyond the conventional pleasing of others toward integrated care, when they realize that balancing one's own needs and the needs of others is equally important.

IX. The development of social cognition

    A. Most developmental psychologists agree that the new cognitive skills of adolescents have important effects on their social cognition--their knowledge and beliefs about interpersonal and social matters. A special form of self-centeredness, adolescent egocentrism, affects teenagers' reactions to others and their beliefs about themselves.

    B. Egocentrism during adolescence

        1. Adolescents often become overly impressed with the ability to reason abstractly, making them idealistic and keeping them from appreciating the practical limits of logic.

            a. Often teenagers act as though they are performing for an imaginary audience, one that is as concerned with their appearance and behavior as they are themselves.

            b. Teenagers also reveal concern with an imaginary audience through strategic interactions with their peers' encounters that aim to reveal or to conceal personal information. Telephoning often serves as a strategic interaction.

            c. As a result of their egocentrism, teenagers often believe in a personal fable, or the notion that their own lives embody a special story that is heroic and completely unique. Because of this, adolescents fail to realize how other individuals feel about them and have limited empathy.

        2. The relative balance between an accurate awareness of others' opinions about oneself and self-conscious preoccupation with others' opinions depends, among other things, on the supportiveness of parent-adolescent relationships.

- Working with Jerry Acton, math and science teacher

X.   Information-processing features of adolescent thought

    A. Improved capacity to process information

        Typically, an adolescent can deal with, or process, more information than a child can.

- A talk with Joan, age fifteen: Thinking in adolescence

    B. Expertise in specific domains of knowledge

        1. By adolescence, many individuals have become comparative experts in specific domains of knowledge or skill.

        2. Much of this expertise may depend not on generalized development of cognitive structures but on the long, slow acquisition of large amounts of specific knowledge, along with a greater capacity to organize that knowledge.

XI. The influence of school

    School has significant effects on adolescents' lives, both cognitively and socially.

A. Cognitive effects of schooling

   School influences adolescents' thinking through both the formal curriculum, a school's official program, and the informal curriculum, the unplanned activities and relationships which influence students' academic knowledge and motivation to learn

B. The nature of critical thinking

   1. Critical thinking refers to reflection or thought about complex issues, usually to make decisions or take actions.

   2. Critical thinking consists of several elements.

      a. Basic operations of reasoning

      b. Domain-specific knowledge

      c. Metacognitive knowledge

      d. Values, beliefs, and dispositions

•   A Multicultural View: Cross-cultural misunderstandings in the classroom

      3. Programs to foster critical thinking

         a. Programs can differ in a number of ways.

         b. There are several general principles that enhance the quality of critical thinking programs.

            i.   Teaching thinking is best done directly and explicitly

            ii.   Programs offer a lot of practice at solving actual problems.

            iii.   Successful programs create an environment explicitly conducive to critical thinking.

         c. Critical thinking programs are based on Piagetian theory, information-processing theory, and the human context of cognitive development in adolescence.

C. Social effects of schooling

   Graduation from elementary school can be a period of increased social and emotional stress.

   1. Many students report less positive attitudes about school, poorer achievement, and lower levels of participation in extracurricular activities.

   2. A major response to these stresses has been to create middle schools.

3. Dropping out of high school

    a. However defined or measured, high school dropouts continue to constitute a significant social issue.

    b. Resilience in youth, factors that allow individual adolescents to cope with and overcome difficult circumstances, attempts to explain why some students drop out and others don't.

4. Employment

    a. Working during adolescence serves three important functions, providing: a transition from school to work, structure for involvement in other activities, and a context for social experience and material rewards.

    b. Working more than a moderate number of hours may be developmentally unwise.

Key Concepts

Directions: Identify each of the key concepts discussed in this chapter.

1. The period between childhood and adulthood is called _____.
2. The _____ is a rapid change in height and weight that occurs during _____, a time characterized by development of full physical and sexual maturity.
3. _____ sex characteristics are those that make sexual reproduction possible. _____ sex characteristics include the development of characteristics other than the sex organs, such as pubic hair and breasts.
4. The first menstrual period is called the _____.
5. The male sex hormone is called _____; it is a type of androgen. The female sex hormone is known as _____.
6. Early-maturing boys experience _____ as teenagers, whereas early-maturing girls experience _____.
7. The death rate during adolescence is one of the _____ for all age groups. This is due primarily to _____ behaviors associated with adolescence.
8. Since 1986, the overall use of drugs among teenagers has shown a _____. In contrast, the use of _____ has remained stable.
9. Adolescent diet tends to lack _____. Adolescents often consume too many nonnutritious _____, such as from fats and sugars.
10. _____ is a physical and emotional disorder that causes a person to refuse food because of an intense fear of weight gain and an unrealistic view of one's body. _____ individuals consume huge amounts of food and then vomit in order to avoid weight gain. _____ are most often diagnosed with these conditions.
11. According to Piaget, _____ thinking, which emerges in adolescence, is characterized by abstract and hypothetical reasoning.
12. Sensitivity to and knowledge about what is right and wrong is known as _____.
13. According to Kohlberg, moral development progresses through three levels; these are _____, _____, and _____.

14. Arbitrary customs and agreements about behavior that members of a society use are called
     _____.

15. According to Gilligan, female morality progresses through three stages; these are _____, _____,
     and _____.

16. Knowledge and beliefs about interpersonal and social matters are known as _____.

17. The tendency of adolescents to perceive the world and themselves from their own perspective is
     called _____.

18. Young adolescents often act as if they are performing for an audience and believe that others are
     as preoccupied with them as they are with themselves. This tendency is referred to as the
     _____.

19. Adolescents believe in their own uniqueness and that their lives are special and heroic, a notion
     labeled the _____.

20. Specialized experience in specific domains of knowledge that enables effective and efficient
     performance at all ages is called _____.

21. _____ thinking refers to thinking about complex issues, usually to make decisions or to take
     actions.

22. Young adolescents may attend _____, usually spanning the fifth through eighth grades or ages
     ten through thirteen.

23. Some adolescents are _____; they can overcome and even profit from difficult and stressful
     situations.

Multiple-Choice Self-Test

Factual Questions

1. On average, males are taller than females because
   a. boys' growth spurt begins about two years earlier than girls' growth spurt.
   b. boys' growth spurt begins about two years later than girls' growth spurt.
   c. boys add significantly more inches to their height than girls during the growth spurt.
   d. boys tend to eat a more balanced diet than girls during early adolescence, which contributes
      to increased height.

2. Physical characteristics that make reproduction possible are termed
   a. menarche.
   b. puberty.
   c. primary sex characteristics.
   d. secondary sex characteristics.

3. Early-maturing girls tend to experience _____ as a result of the early timing of puberty.
   a. advantages
   b. stresses
   c. pressure to become sexually active
   d. rejection from their peer group

4. Testosterone is present in
   a. males.
   b. females.
   c. both males and females.
   d. males and pregnant females.

5. Which of the following is *not* a leading cause of death during adolescence?
    a. Homicide
    b. Suicide
    c. Motor vehicle accidents
    d. Sexually transmitted diseases

6. In recent years, smoking has increased among
    a. minorities.
    b. males.
    c. females.
    d. minorities and females.

7. Most adolescents reason at which level of Kohlberg's theory of moral development?
    a. Preconventional
    b. Conventional
    c. Postconventional
    d. Heteronomous

8. Adolescents often behave as if they are performing on stage. This tendency is known as
    a. adolescent egocentrism.
    b. the personal fable.
    c. the imaginary audience.
    d. social cognition.

9. The adolescent tendency to view oneself as unique and indestructible is known as
    a. adolescent egocentrism.
    b. the personal fable.
    c. the maginary audience
    d. social cognition

10. Knowledge about how human thinking works is termed
    a. social cognition.
    b. critical thinking.
    c. metacognitive knowledge.
    d. Expertise.

Conceptual Questions

1. Adriana can expect to reach her growth spurt at about age
    a. eleven.
    b. thirteen.
    c. fourteen.
    d. fifteen.

2. Sandy's mother tells her that she has now left girlhood behind and has become a woman. Which of the following is probably true?
   a. It is Sandy's sixteenth birthday.
   b. It is Sandy's eighteenth birthday.
   c. Sandy is experiencing menarche.
   d. Sandy is getting married.

3. Glen was an early-maturing boy. As a young adult, he is likely to be
   a. very relaxed in his peer relationships.
   b. responsible and self-controlled.
   c. irresponsible and lacking self-control.
   d. very open to risk-taking behavior.

4. George has chlamydia. If untreated, the condition can lead to
   a. central nervous system damage.
   b. increased risk of prostate cancer.
   c. sterility.
   d. an acute infection of the liver.

5. Who is most likely to suffer from anorexia?
   a. Jillian, whose parents are professionals
   b. Leanna, whose parents are from the lower class
   c. John, whose parents are professionals
   d. Jay, whose parents are from the lower class

6. Jolene says that she is proud of her perfect math score because her teacher praised her and told her that she is now a member of the math team. Jolene's reasoning reflects
   a. preconventional morality.
   b. conventional morality.
   c. social cognition.
   d. adolescent egocentrism.

7. Erin's friend is upset and depressed about her parents' decision to divorce. According to Gilligan, Erin is most likely to
   a. visit her friend and offer her assistance.
   b. allow her friend privacy so that she may grieve independently and without interference.
   c. suggest that her friend talk with her parents and try to change their minds about divorcing.
   d. suggest that her friend seek help from a mental health professional.

8. Seventeen-year-old Alex doesn't understand why world leaders do not simply distribute food equally throughout the world in order to stop starvation and death. Alex's thinking reflects
   a. social cognition.
   b. adolescent egocentrism.
   c. the personal fable.
   d. the imaginary audience.

9. Julia believes that her relationship with her boyfriend is very similar to the relationship between Romeo and Juliet because her parents do not approve of her boyfriend. Julia's thinking reflects
   a. social cognition.
   b. adolescent egocentrism.
   c. the personal fable.
   d. the imaginary audience.

10. Stan is trying to solve a chemistry problem assigned as a bonus question. In order to solve this problem, Stan must have
   a. social cognition.
   b. metacognitive knowledge.
   c. adolescent egocentrism.
   d. domain-specific knowledge.

Answer Key

Key Concepts

1. adolescence
2. growth spurt; puberty
3. Primary; Secondary
4. menarche
5. testosterone; estrogen
6. advantages; disadvantages or stresses
7. highest; risk-taking
8. decrease; alcohol
9. balance; calories
10. Anorexia nervosa; Bulimic; female adolescents
11. formal operational
12. morality
13. preconventional; conventional; postconventional
14. social conventions
15. survival orientation; conventional care; integrated care
16. social cognition
17. adolescent egocentrism
18. imaginary audience
19. personal fable
20. expertise
21. Critical
22. middle school
23. resilient

Multiple-Choice Self-Test / Factual Questions

1. Choice (b) is correct; boys begin their growth spurt at about thirteen to fourteen years of age, about two years after girls. This gives them two more years of childhood growing and leads to taller eventual height. Therefore, choice (a) is incorrect. Choice (c) is incorrect in that both

boys and girls add about nine or ten inches to their height during the growth spurt. There is no research support for the notion that there are differences between the diets of boys and girls during adolescence, choice (d).

2.   Choice (c) is correct. Choice (a), menarche, is the first menstrual period of females. Choice (b), puberty, is the period of early adolescence characterized by the development of full physical and sexual maturity. Choice (d), secondary sex characteristics, are all physical changes beyond those that lead to sexual maturity.

3.   Choice (b) is correct; early-maturing girls are usually out of step with gender-role expectations for girls. They also experience the close scrutiny of parents and teachers, who monitor their behavior very closely because they appear sexually mature. Therefore, choice (a) is incorrect. Choices (c) and (d) are not reported as disadvantages of early maturity for girls.

4.   Choice (c) is correct; testosterone is present in both males and females, although it is found in higher concentrations in males. Therefore, choices (a) and (b) are partially correct. Choice (d) is inaccurate.

5.   Choice (d) is correct. Choices (a), (b), and (c) are among the leading causes of death in adolescence.

6.   Choice (d) is correct; although the overall use of cigarettes has decreased among adolescents, their use has increased among minorities and females. Therefore, the other choices are inaccurate.

7.   Choice (b) is correct; adolescents, as well as most adults, reason at the conventional level, in which right and good behavior are associated with approval of the peer group (Stage 3) and approval of the larger society (Stage 4). Choice (a), preconventional morality is external morality - goodness is associated with whatever authority figures claim is good, and the individual is motivated to avoid punishment and receive rewards. Choice (c), postconventional morality is related to personal moral principles and ethics of conduct. Choice (d), heteronomous morality, is equivalent to Stage 1 morality.

8.   Choice (c) is correct; the adolescent tendency to behave as if one is performing for an audience is called the imaginary audience. Choice (a), adolescent egocentrism, refers to the tendency to perceive the world and oneself from the adolescent's own perspective. Adolescents often view themselves and their experiences as unique, a tendency termed the personal fable, choice (b). Choice (d), social cognition, is knowledge and beliefs about interpersonal and social matters; adolescent egocentrism, personal fable, and imaginary audience are examples of social cognition.

9.   Choice (b) is correct; adolescents often view themselves and their experiences as unique, a tendency termed the personal fable. Choice (a), adolescent egocentrism, refers to the tendency to perceive the world and oneself from the adolescent's own perspective. The adolescent tendency to behave as if the person is performing for an audience is called imaginary audience, choice (c). Choice (d), social cognition, is knowledge and beliefs about interpersonal and social matters; adolescent egocentrism, personal fable, and imaginary audience are examples of social cognition.

10.   Choice (c) is correct. Choice (a), social cognition, is knowledge and beliefs about interpersonal and social matters; adolescent egocentrism, personal fable, and imaginary audience are examples of social cognition. Choice (b), critical thinking, refers to thinking about complex issues to make a decision or to take action. Choice (d), expertise, is specialized knowledge in specific domains of knowledge.

Multiple-Choice Self-Test / Conceptual Questions

1.   Choice (a) is correct; girls reach their growth spurt at about eleven or twelve years of age. Therefore, the other choices are inaccurate.

2.   Choice (c) is correct; in many cultures the first menstrual period or menarche is considered a passage into womanhood. Age, choices (a) and (b), and marriage, choice (d), are not accurate in this context.

3.   Choice (b) is correct; early-maturing boys experience advantages, such as being responsible and self-controlled. Therefore, choice (c) is incorrect. Choices (a) and (d) are incorrect in that these boys tend to be rigid in their peer relationships and they are unlikely to engage in immature risk taking behaviors.

4.   Choice (c) is correct; if untreated, chlamydia can lead to sterility. Choice (a), central nervous system damage is a danger symptom of syphilis. Sexually transmitted diseases, choice (b), have not been associated with prostate cancer. Choice (d), an acute liver infection, is a result of hepatitis.

5.   Choice (a) is correct; anorexia nervosa is more common among adolescent females from the upper-middle class. It is less likely to be diagnosed in female adolescents from the lower class, choice (b), and in males, choices (c) and (d).

6.   Choice (b) is correct; most youth and young adults reason at the conventional level of morality. They associate goodness with what is approved by their peer group (Stage 3) or what is approved by the larger society (Stage 4). Choice (a), preconventional morality, is external morality; goodness is associated with behaviors that do not receive punishment or alternatively, that bring rewards. Choice (c), social cognition, refers to knowledge and beliefs about interpersonal and social matters. Choice (d), adolescent egocentrism, refers to the adolescent tendency to view the world and themselves from their own perspective.

7.   Choice (a) is correct; according to Gilligan, girls develop an ethic of care that allows them to integrate personal principles with the context in which judgments have to be made. Choice (b), allowing the friend privacy and autonomy, is a reflection of an ethic of justice based on general ethical principles, more common in male morality. Choices (c) and (d) do not reflect Gilligan's claims.

8.   Choice (b) is correct; adolescents often confuse their own thoughts with the thoughts of others, a notion termed adolescent egocentrism. Choice (a), social cognition, is an umbrella term that refers to knowledge and beliefs about interpersonal and social matters. Choice (c), personal fable, refers to the adolescent tendency to view oneself as unique and indestructible. Choice (d), imaginary audience, refers to the adolescent tendency to behave as if performing for an audience on stage, with the related belief system that everyone is as preoccupied with the adolescent as he is himself.

9.   Choice (c) is correct; personal fable refers to the adolescent tendency to view oneself as unique and the belief that one has an extraordinary life story. Choice (a), social cognition, is an umbrella term that refers to knowledge and beliefs about interpersonal and social matters. Adolescents often confuse their own thoughts with the thoughts of others, a notion termed adolescent egocentrism, choice (b). Choice (d), imaginary audience, refers to the adolescent tendency to behave as if performing for an audience on stage, with the related belief system that everyone is as preoccupied with the adolescent as he is himself.

10.   Choice (d) is correct; domain-specific knowledge is an element of critical thinking that refers to content or topic-related knowledge in problem solving. Choice (a), social cognition, is an umbrella term that refers to knowledge and beliefs about interpersonal and social matters. Choice (b), metacognitive knowledge, is knowledge about how human thinking, including one's own, works. Choice (c), adolescent egocentrism, refers to the adolescent tendency to view the world and oneself only from one's own perspective.

CHAPTER 11

Psychosocial Development in Adolescence

Learning Objectives:

1. Discuss the process of identity development from the standpoint of individuation.
2. Describe how Erikson viewed the process of identity development in adolescence.
3. Compare the concepts of the false self and the true self.
4. Identify and describe Marcia's four identity statuses.
5. Discuss gender, social economic status, and ethnic effects on identity development.
6. Discuss the nature of adolescents' relationships with their parents.
7. Identify and describe the various parenting styles and indicate their effect on adolescent development.
8. Discuss short-term and long-term impact of parental marital conflict, divorce, and remarriage on adolescents.
9. Describe the qualities of adolescent friendships, considering both developmental changes in friendships and sex differences in peer relations.
10. Distinguish between the clique and the crowd and discuss the role of the peer group on adolescent development.
11. Discuss parental influences on adolescent peer group choices.
12. Discuss the effects of employment and chores on adolescents.
13. Discuss the nature of sexuality during adolescence, including dating, sexual behavior, and sexual preferences.
14. Describe the impact of dating on adolescent sexuality, including date rate.
15. Discuss effects of sexual orientation on adolescent development.
16. Describe the problem of teenage pregnancy and the likely psychosocial outcomes.
17. Characterize typical parent-teenager communication about sex.
18. Describe the characteristics of teenage depression and suicide.
19. Describe the characteristics of juvenile delinquency and gang involvement during adolescence.

Chapter Outline

I. Theories of identity development

    A. Ruthellen Josselson: Individuation and identity development

        Individuation is the process by which an adolescent develops a unique personal identity or sense of self, distinct and separate from all others. It consists of four distinct, overlapping stages:

1. During differentiation, the early adolescent recognizes being psychologically different from his or her parents.

2. In practice and experimentation, the adolescent believes she or he knows it all and can do no wrong.

3. Rapprochement, which occurs during middle adolescence, is the time when the teenager has achieved a fair degree of separateness from parents and partially but conditionally reaccepts parental authority.

4. During consolidation of self, the adolescent develops a sense of personal identity.

B. Erik Erikson: The crisis of identity versus role confusion

1. Erikson believes the crisis of **identity versus role confusion** occurs during adolescence.

2. During adolescence, teenagers selectively accept or reject the many different aspects of self that were acquired during childhood and form a more coherent sense of identity.

3. Changes in an adolescent's cognitive development and capacity for self-understanding play a central role in identity development.

4. As adolescents experiment with different roles in their search to create a coherent sense of identity, they may experience a sense of false self.

5. According to Erikson, a number of identity outcomes are possible.

    a. **Psychosocial moratorium** is a period during which the individual is free to suspend or delay taking on adult commitments and to explore new social roles.

    b. **dentity diffusion**, or a failure to achieve a relatively coherent, integrated, and stable identity, takes a number of forms, such as avoidance of closeness with others, diffusion of time perspective, diffusion of industry, and **negative identity**.

6. Various historical, cultural, and personal events and experiences may affect how one's identity is resolved.

7. According to Erikson, successful resolution of the crisis of identity versus role confusion prepares one to move on to confront the crisis of intimacy versus isolation that occurs in adulthood.

8. Marcia classified students into four categories of **identity status** based on whether they had gone through an identity crisis and the degree to which they were now committed to an occupational choice and to a set of religious and political values and beliefs.

    a. Identity achievement individuals successfully resolve crises concerning values and life choices and are able to commit to an occupation and to a religious and political ideology.

    b. Identity diffusion individuals, whether or not they have experienced a crisis, show little concern or commitment regarding occupational choice and religious and political beliefs.

    c. Moratorium individuals are presently in crisis, actively making commitments and preoccupied with achieving successful compromises among their parents' wishes, societal demands, and their own capabilities.

    d. Foreclosure individuals prematurely commit to important aspects of identity without experiencing a significant conflict or crisis.

    e. Differences in social class, culture, and ethnicity may also affect identity development.

    f. Both genders are equally represented among the four identity statuses and seem to develop in similar ways.

II. Family relationships during adolescence

  A. Relationships with parents

    1. Most parent-teenager relationships are slightly unstable.

    2. Separation from parents consists of four important accomplishments.

       a. Functional independence is the ability to manage one's own personal and practical affairs with minimal help from one's parents.

       b. Attitudinal independence is a view of oneself as unique and separate from one's parents.

       c. Emotional independence is freedom from being overly dependent on parents for approval, intimacy, and emotional support.

       d. Conflictual independence is freedom from conflict and other negative emotional states.

    3. Leaving home, at least in a psychological sense, is part of becoming self-reliant and achieving an identity.

    4. Parents and teenagers often have a different understanding of and reaction to leaving home, which may lead to conflicts.

    5. The majority of adolescents and parents continue to get along rather well together.

    6. Parents and adolescents most often disagree about matters concerning social life and behavior.

    7. Parents have more influence than peers in basic attitudes and values that guide long-term life choices.

8.   Parenting styles are related to various aspects of adolescent development including personality, academic achievement, and social and emotional adjustment.

9.   A major series of studies of families revealed some important SES and ethnic differences affecting adolescents' development.

  a.   Differences between the values, childrearing practices, and expectations of middle-class parents and those of working- and lower-class parents closely paralleled differences in the nature of their day-to-day work experiences with respect to degree of autonomy versus control.

  b.   Ethnicity and community context also influence family decision making.

• A Multicultural View: Adaptive strategies of families of minority youth.

  B.   Divorce, remarriage, and single parenthood

1.   The impact of separation and divorce on the adolescent depends on a number of factors.

  a.   the individual characteristics of the parents

  b.   the nature of the marital transitions (marriage and remarriage)

  c.   stressful life experiences and economic changes associated with divorce

  d.   the family following divorce or remarriage

  e.   the types and amount of social support available

  f.   the amount of parental distress

  g.   the family process including the nature and quality of the family relationships

  h.   the individual characteristics of the children

  i.   the adjustment of the child

2.   Marital conflict is a source of stress particularly for adolescents struggling to separate from their families in order to establish an independent and autonomous identity.

3.   The impact of divorce and remarriage can be particularly hard for adolescents because of their tendency to disengage from the family as means of avoiding stress.

  a.   Children in divorced families tend to grow up faster.

  b.   Adolescents who grow up in troubled families that remain together are also likely to experience negative developmental consequences.

4.   The effects of divorce and remarriage persist throughout the lifespan putting the individual at risk for academic problems, psychological disorders, lower self-esteem, and problems in their relationships.

III. Social relationships during adolescence

   A. Friendship

      1. Friends offer easier and more immediate acceptance than most adults do.

      2. They offer reassurance, understanding and advice, and emotional and social support in stressful situations.

      3. Friends promote independence by providing knowledge of a world beyond the family.

      4. Friends provide one another with cognitive and social scaffolding that differs from what nonfriends provide.

      5. Qualities of adolescent friendships

         a. There is a trend toward greater mutuality through increased loyalty and intimacy.

         b. There is a recognition of complementary relationships, in which two people with different strengths and abilities cooperate for mutual benefit.

         c. Teenagers gain intimacy in friendships through self-revelation, confidence, and exclusivity.

      6. Gender and friendship

         a. Friendships formed by boys have lower levels of intimacy than those of girls.

         b. Girls tend to develop more intimacy with members of the opposite sex than boys do.

         c. Gender differences may be products of sex role stereotyping or due to the fact that girls tend to have fewer but closer friends than boys, who have many, less intimate acquaintances. Also, adolescent males may equate intimacy exclusively with heterosexual friendships

      7. Interethnic friendships

         a. Friendships between teenagers from different ethnic groups tend to be the exception.

         b. The social contexts in which interactions occur seem to make an important difference in the development of friendships across ethnic groups.

   B. Peer groups

      1. Peer groups play an even greater role in the lives of adolescents than they do for younger children.

      2. Adolescent peer groups frequently include individuals from a relatively wide age range and are much less likely to be all one gender.

3. Peer groups provide a support base outside of the family within which the teenager can more freely try on different identity roles.

4. Adolescent peer groups generally are of two types.

    a. A **clique** is a small, closely knit group of two or more members who are intimately involved in shared purposes and activities and exclude those who are not involved.

    b. A **crowd** is a larger, less cohesive group of between fifteen to thirty adolescents and is composed of from two to four cliques.

5. Advantages of clique membership include security, feelings of importance, and acquisition of socially acceptable behaviors that conform to group norms. However, cliques can suppress individuality, promote snobbishness, intolerance, and other negative values and behaviors, and possibly contribute to adjustment problems.

6. Advantages of crowd membership are opportunities to interact with those from a broad range of backgrounds and experiences. However, crowds can promote snobbishness and pose real or imagined threats to parental and teacher authority.

7. Parents can help adolescents with their friendships and relationships.

•Focusing On: Can parents influence their adolescent's choice of peer group?

  C. Adolescents in the world of work

    1. Work adds the role of employee to the roles an adolescent takes on.

    2. Work both within and outside the family provides a major base for the development of competence and sense of identity and self.

    3. How work influences adolescent development depends on how well it fits the needs of the individual and his or her family.

IV. Sexuality during adolescence.

During adolescence, the expression of sexual urges interacts closely with the need for security, freedom from anxiety, and the need for intimacy.

  A. Sexual fantasies and masturbation

    1. Sexual fantasies about real or imaginary situations often accompany masturbation.

    2. Sexually experienced adolescents tend to masturbate more than those who are less experienced.

    3. Boys tend to give up masturbation when involved in an ongoing sexual relationship, whereas girls tend to masturbate more often.

B. Sexual experience

1. Recent trends in adolescent sexual activity in the U.S. include earlier initiation of intercourse, increased premarital intercourse, and more partners.

2. Timing of first sexual intercourse is related to several factors.

C. Sexual attitudes

1. The "sexual revolution" of the 1960s and 1970s resulted in greater acceptance of premarital intercourse, masturbation, homosexuality, and lesbianism and a decline in the double standard that holds that sexual activity outside of marriage is less acceptable for females than for males.

2. In the 1980s and 1990s, teenagers appear to have had more cautious attitudes concerning sexual activity.

3. Boys tend to be more sexually active and to have more sexual encounters than girls.

4. Girls are more likely to emphasize intimacy and love as a necessary part of sexual activity and less likely to engage in sex merely as a physically pleasurable activity.

5. Males and females differ in reasons for and reactions to first intercourse.

6. Motivations for teenage sex include offering pleasure and confirming masculinity or femininity, affection, rebellion, and other reasons.

D. Dating

1. Dating is a major avenue for exploring sexual activity.

2. Currently, many adolescent girls begin dating at age twelve and boys at age thirteen.

3. Date rape refers to a situation in which a person, usually a female, is forced to have sex with a person she is dating. It typically involves individuals who know each other fairly well. It is likely that cultural expectations and the tendency to place blame on the victim contribute to this problem.

4. Culltural experiences in the U.S. place men at risk for sexually aggressive behavior.

E. Sexual orientations

1. Public acceptance of homosexuality has increased significantly during the past several decades, acknowledging the right of individuals to freely practice their own sexual orientations and lifestyles and to be protected from discrimination.

2. **Homophobia**, the fear or dislike of homosexuals, remains strong among adolescents.

3. Homosexual adolescents are likely to experience feelings of attraction for the same sex for several years before publicly acknowledging their sexual orientation.

4. There is no agreement on the specific pattern of factors that leads to the development of homosexuality.

5. A growing number of researchers are exploring the possibility that biological and familial predispositions may play an interactive causal role.

6. Although achieving a secure sexual identity is a challenging task for most adolescents, it is considerably more difficult for many homosexual adolescents, who may be rejected by parents, peers, schools, churches, and other community institutions.

F. Sex and everyday life

Sexuality does not necessarily dominate the lives of adolescents.

V. Special problems of adolescence

A. Adolescent pregnancy and parenthood

1. The great majority of teenage pregnancies are the result of inadequate or no contraception.

a. Birth control pills are not reliable during the first month of use. Only foam and condoms or a diaphragm and contraceptive jelly are really effective for first intercourse.

b. Irregular use of contraception is correlated with economic disadvantage, poor communication with parents, lack of knowledge about parental contraceptive experience, experiences of friends who became parents, low educational achievements and aspirations, high levels of anxiety, low self-esteem, and feelings of fatalism, powerlessness, and alienation.

c. Parent-teen communication about sexual behavior is often inadequate.

2. Choosing between abortion and parenthood

a. More than 50 percent of teenage mothers who decide to have their babies become increasingly committed to motherhood during the course of the pregnancy.

b. Reactions to an unplanned pregnancy are influenced by feelings about school, relationship with the baby's father, relationship with parents, perceived family support for keeping the child, number of peers who have become parents, and sense of self-esteem.

c. The experience of abortion is psychologically stressful for teenagers.

d. Socioeconomic status, ethnicity, and culture influence teenagers' feelings and attitudes about abortion.

3.   Consequences of teenage parenthood

   a.   Many teenage mothers see having a baby as a way to gain identity and to have a relationship with another person.

   b.   Teenage mothers are less likely to finish high school, find a stable paying job, enter a secure marriage, or achieve equal job status or income in their lifetimes.

   c.   Teenage mothers are more likely to experience complications during pregnancy.

   d.   Children of teenage mothers are also more likely to suffer developmentally, displaying poorer cognitive and social functioning in preschool and elementary school and a higher rate of learning and social adjustment problems as adolescents than are children born to older mothers. Also, they are more likely to become teenage parents themselves.

   e.   Many teenage mothers end up living with their own mothers.

4.   Prevention and support programs

   a.   Prevention programs that appear to be most effective involve teaching abstinence to younger teens and providing contraceptives and information to older teens.

   b.   Effective support programs focus on pre- and postnatal health care, economic support, child care and parenting support, education, and job training.

- Working with Janet Whalen, nurse practitioner: Helping pregnant teenagers

B.   Teenage depression and suicide

1.   Depressive disorders include two major subtypes: major depressive disorder (MDD) and dysthymic disorder (DD).

2.   Depression during childhood and adolescence are nonnormative experiences that interfere with development.

3.   The causes of depression include both environmental and genetic factors.

4.   Suicide is the third leading cause of death for children ages fifteen to nineteen.

5.   Studies have found that many teenagers who attempt suicide have experienced serious family difficulties, and depression often is a factor.

6.   Suicide attempts almost always represent cries for help.

7.   Suicide prevention includes early detection and intervention in family and personal crises, school-based education about depression and suicide risk factors, training in problem-solving and coping skills, crisis counseling, and emergency hotlines.

C. Juvenile delinquency

    1. **Juvenile delinquency** refers to a pattern of destructive or antisocial activities and law-breaking offenses committed by adolescents.

    2. The route to chronic delinquency may follow a predictable developmental sequence of experiences.

        a. The first step involves ineffective parenting and problematic family interaction processes.

        b. The second step involves conduct-disordered behaviors that lead to academic failure and peer rejection.

        c. The third step is increased risk for depression and involvement in a deviant peer group.

    3. A number of factors are associated with delinquency such as parent-child relationships characterized by hostility, lack of affection, underinvolvement, and lack of parental supervision.

    4. Aggression in early childhood may be predictive of some forms of antisocial behavior in adolescence and adulthood.

• A Multicultural View: Differing cultural views of delinquency

    5. Many delinquents belong to gangs, which are highly structured and focused on antisocial activities.

        a. Gangs provide acceptance and social support lacking in families or schools.

        b. Gangs identify with or claim control over territory in the community and engage in violence.

        c. Typically, gangs are formed by individuals from poor and racial or ethnic minority and immigrant backgrounds.

        d. Gangs provide alternative economic opportunities and social support.

    6. Adolescents who are at risk for delinquency can be helped by programs that provide support and opportunities.

    7. Early childhood intervention programs for at-risk preschool children and their families have achieved significant success at reducing delinquency.

VI. Looking Back, Looking Forward

A. Continuity within change

B. Lifelong growth

    C.   Changing meaning, changing vantage points

    D.   Developmental diversity

Key Concepts

Directions: Identify each of the key concepts discussed in this chapter.

1. The process by which an adolescent develops a unique and separate personal identity is known as _____. This process consists of four subphases; they are _____, _____, _____, and _____.
2. Erikson's fifth psychosocial crisis, corresponding to adolescence, is called _____ .
3. Erikson defined _____ as the latency period that precedes puberty and provides a temporary suspension of psychosexual development.
4. When individuals fail to achieve a relatively coherent, integrated, and stable identity, they are said to be _____.
5. A _____ is a form of identity diffusion that involves rejection of the roles preferred by one's family or community in favor of socially undesirable roles.
6. James Marcia identified four identity statuses; these are _____, _____, _____, and _____.
7. Most disagreements between parents and adolescents are related to the adolescents' _____ and _____. In contrast, adolescents tend to agree with their parents on _____ and _____.
8. As in childhood, the _____ style of parenting is also the most effective in adolescence.
9. The acronym _____ stands for _____, also called social class.
10. Experiencing the divorce of parents during adolescence interferes with the normative developmental tasks of adolescence, developing _____ and _____.
11. Women who commit themselves to the roles of wife and mother, then lose these roles as a result of divorce or widowhood and feel unprepared for employment and single parenthood are referred to as _____.
12. Friendships of adolescent girls involve more _____ than the friendships of adolescent boys.
13. Researchers claim that it is developmentally normative for pre- and young adolescents to be _____ in fantasy rather than in reality.
14. Friendships between white and African American teens occur _____.
15. The _____ is a network of social relationships that follow a person over his or her lifetime.
16. A _____ is a small, closely knit peer group of two or three members who are intimately involved. In contrast, a _____ is a large, loosely knit peer group of fifteen to thirty members.
17. The rate of teenage sexual activity in the United States is _____ as in Western European nations.
18. People with a _____ point of view say that their religious beliefs always guide their sexual behavior. People with a _____ point of view say that sex should be a part of a loving relationship. People with a _____ point of view say that sex need not be related to love.
19. When a person, usually a female, is forced to have sex with a person she is dating, it is called _____.
20. Fear, hostility, and prejudice that is directed toward gay and lesbian persons with resultant mistreatment and discrimination is known as _____.
21. Most teenage pregnancies are the result of _____. Approximately _____ percent of these pregnancies end in abortion.
22. _____ is the third leading cause of death among children ages fifteen to nineteen.
23. A pattern of destructive or antisocial activities and lawbreaking offenses committed by adolescents is called _____.

Multiple-Choice Self-Test

Factual Questions

1. In the differentiation subphase of individuation, the adolescent
   a. believes that he or she knows it all.
   b. recognizes that he or she is psychologically different than his or her parents.
   c. has achieved some degree of separateness from the parents.
   d. develops a sense of identity.

2. Adolescents who experience diffusion of industry
   a. are unable to form close relationships with others.
   b. believe that they are out of step with others.
   c. adopt a socially undesirable identity, such as becoming a delinquent.
   d. are unable to concentrate on school- and work-related tasks.

3. Adolescents who are experiencing moratorium
   a. are in a crisis.
   b. have made a commitment.
   c. have borrowed their parents' identities.
   d. show little concern about making commitments.

4. Which of the following shared activities between parents and adolescents does *not* decrease with increasing grade level?
   a. Eating together
   b. Watching television together
   c. Participating in leisure activities together
   d. Talking together

5. Unilateral teens
   a. have permissive parents.
   b. have authoritarian parents.
   c. have decision-making autonomy.
   d. have parents who make all decisions for them.

6. Compared with younger adolescents, high school students
   a. spend more time with their parents.
   b. spend more time with opposite-sex friends.
   c. spend most of their leisure time alone.
   d. spend time equally with parents and peers.

7. A typical clique includes about _____ members.
   a. five
   b. six
   c. three
   d. twenty

8. Sexually experienced adolescents
    a. masturbate more often.
    b. masturbate less often.
    c. do not masturbate at all.
    d. masturbate as frequently as less sexually experienced adolescents.

9. Date rape is more likely
    a. when a woman initiates the date.
    b. when the partners don't know each other well.
    c. when the partners know each other fairly well.
    d. when a woman pays for the date.

10. Which of the following contraceptive methods is *least* reliable and effective for first intercourse?
    a. Condoms
    b. Birth control pills
    c. Foam
    d. Diaphragm and contraceptive jelly

Conceptual Questions

1. Amy is beginning to accept her parents' authority conditionally; sometimes she is argumentative and at other times she is cooperative. Amy is probably about _____ years old.
    a. fourteen
    b. fifteen
    c. seventeen
    d. twenty

2. Jon claims that he is preparing to go to law school because all the men in his family are lawyers. James Marcia would describe Jon's identity status as
    a. achieved.
    b. moratorium.
    c. foreclosed.
    d. diffused.

3. Jim is preoccupied with thoughts of deciding on his college major. He is most likely to follow the opinions of
    a. his friends.
    b. his parents.
    c. his teachers.
    d. No one else; he will probably make the decision on his own.

4. Richard is a very poorly adjusted adolescent. His parents probably use the _____ style of parenting.
    a. authoritative
    b. authoritarian
    c. permissive-indulgent
    d. permissive-indifferent

5. Who is most likely to become a parent during adolescence?
   a. Dana, whose parents recently divorced
   b. Bill, whose parents recently divorced
   c. Dana and Bill equally
   d. Neither Dana nor Bill

6. Which of the following statements is accurate?
   a. Adolescent boys have many intimate friends.
   b. Adolescent girls have many intimate friends.
   c. Adolescent boys have few casual friends.
   d. Adolescent girls have few intimate friends.

7. Which of the following statements is *false*?
   a. Adolescents who live in racially mixed neighborhoods are more likely to have close other-race friends.
   b. Adolescents who have a close other-race school friend are likely to interact with the friend only in the school.
   c. Interethnic friendships are influenced by the attitudes of adolescents toward their own and other ethnic groups.
   d. Interethnic friendships are very common between white and African American adolescents, regardless of the ethnic and racial composition of the neighborhoods they live in.

8. Ryan, Greg, Alex, and Charlie are close friends. They have similar interests and spend most of their free time together. Their group can be considered a
   a. clique.
   b. crowd.
   c. dyad.
   d. triad.

9. Tanner is an African American adolescent; doing household chores will
   a. decrease his self-competence.
   b. increase his self-competence.
   c. not influence his self-competence.
   d. decrease his sense of autonomy.

10 Who is most likely to be better adjusted?
   a. Charisa, who is still a virgin at seventeen years of age
   b. Patricia, who became sexually active at fourteen years of age
   c. Bridget, who became sexually active at fifteen years of age
   d. Jody, who became sexually active at sixteen years of age

Answer Key

Key Concepts

1. individuation; differentiation; practice and experimentation; rapprochement; consolidation-of-self
2. identity versus role confusion
3. moratorium

4.   identity diffused
5.   negative identity
6.   achieved; diffused; moratorium; foreclosed
7.   social life; social behaviors; basic attitudes and values; long-term life choices
8.   authoritative
9.   SES; socioeconomic status
10. intimate relationships; autonomy
11. displaced homemakers
12. intimacy
13. romantically involved
14. rarely
15. social convoy
16. clique; crowd
17. about the same
18. Traditional; Relational; Recreational
19. date rape
20. homophobia
21. inadequate or no use of contraception; 44
22. Suicide
23. juvenile delinquency

Multiple-Choice Self-Test / Factual Questions

1.   Choice (b) is correct. Adolescents believe that they have all the answers to problems, choice (a), and that they can do no wrong in the practice and experimentation subphase of individuation. Some degree of separateness from the parents, choice (c), occurs in the rapprochement subphase of individuation. Choice (d), a sense of identity, is achieved in the final, consolidation-of-self subphase.

2.   Choice (d) is correct. Choice (a), inability to form close interpersonal relationships, is labeled avoidance of closeness. A form of diffusion labeled diffusion of time perspective involves the idea that one is not in step with others, choice (b). Choice (c), a socially undesirable identity, is labeled negative identity.

3.   Choice (a) is correct; moratorium involves an active search through alternatives, a crisis. Choice (b), making a commitment, is characteristic of an achieved identity. Choice (c), a borrowed identity, is a foreclosed identity. Choice (d), little or no concern about making commitments, is characteristic of identity diffusion.

4.   Choice (d) is correct; throughout the period of adolescence, the time parents and their teenagers spend in conversation remains relatively stable. All other choices decrease with increasing grade level.

5.   Choice (c) is correct; these teenagers are left to make all of their own decisions. This concept is not related to parenting styles, choices (a) and (b). Parents who make all the decisions for the adolescent, choice (d), are labeled unilateral parents.

6.   Choice (b) is correct; older adolescents spend more time with their opposite-sex friends, and they also spend more time thinking about opposite-sex friends. Choices (a) and (d) are incorrect in that, as adolescence progresses, children spend less time with their parents and more time

with their friends. Choice (c), time spent alone, is more characteristic of younger than older adolescents.

7. Choice (c) is correct; cliques include two to three members members. When a peer group consists of fifteen to thirty members, it is called a crowd. Therefore, choices (a), (b), and (d) are inaccurate.

8. Choice (a) is correct; sexual experience appears to generally increase levels of masturbation. In general, males give up masturbation when they are involved in an ongoing sexual relationship, whereas females tend to masturbate more often. The other choices are not supported by data.

9. Choice (c) is correct; in most date rape cases, the partners have known each other for about one year. Therefore, choice (b) is incorrect. Date rape is more common when a man initiates the date and pays for it; therefore choices (a) and (d) are incorrect.

10. Choice (b) is correct; birth control pills are not reliable in the first month of use and, therefore, are not an effective form of contraception for first-time intercourse. The other choices are more reliable and effective forms of contraception for first time intercourse.

Multiple-Choice Self-Test / Conceptual Questions

1. Choice (c) is correct; conditional acceptance of parental authority occurs in the rapprochement subphase of individuation, toward the middle of adolescence. Choices (a) and (b) correspond to the practice and experimentation subphase of individuation. Choice (d) corresponds to the final, consolidation-of-self subphase of individuation.

2. Choice (c) is correct; individuals with a foreclosed identity generally follow in their parents' footsteps and adopt their identities without experiencing a crisis. Choice (a), identity-achieved individuals, experience a crisis prior to making a commitment. Choice (b), individuals in moratorium, are going through a crisis. Choice (d), identity-diffused individuals, do not care about experimenting with alternatives and making a commitment.

3. Choice (b) is correct; most adolescents agree with their parents on issues related to long-term life choices, such as their career goals. The other choices are inaccurate.

4. Choice (d) is correct; permissive-indifferent or neglectful parenting leads to the lowest level of adjustment in adolescents. Children of authoritative parents, choice (a), are the best adjusted adolescents. The adjustment levels of adolescents whose parents are authoritarian, choice (b), and permissive-indulgent, choice (c), are average.

5. Choice (c) is correct; boys and girls whose parents divorce when they are in adolescence are equally likely to become parents. Therefore, choices (a) and (b) are only partially correct. Choice (d) is incorrect because parental divorce during adolescence is associated with increased incidence of teenage pregnancy.

6. Choice (d) is correct; adolescent girls tend to have few friends with whom they are intimate, whereas boys have many friends but their friendships are activity-oriented and less intimate. Therefore, the other choices are inaccurate.

7. Choice (d) is correct; research indicates that interethnic friendships are the exception rather than the rule for adolescents. However, living in racially mixed neighborhoods increases the

possibility of having a close other-race friend outside of school. The other choices are accurate and supported by data.

8. Choice (a) is correct; a clique is a closely knit group consisting of an average of six members. Choice (b), a crowd is a loosely knit group of between fifteen to thirty members. Choice (c), a dyad is a two-member group. Choice (d), a triad, is a three-member group.

9. Choice (b) is correct; participation in household chores increases the sense of competence of African American as well as Hispanic boys. Therefore, choices (a) and (c) are inaccurate. Boys' autonomy, choice (d), is not reported to be influenced by doing household chores.

10. Choice (a) is correct; research indicates that adolescents who postpone sexual activity are better adjusted, whereas those who become sexually active at the youngest age show the poorest adjustment when they reach twelfth grade. Therefore, the other choices are not supported by the data.

CHAPTER 12

Physical and Cognitive Development in Early Adulthood

Learning Objectives:

1. Describe the changes in physical growth during the early adulthood period, including changes in strength.
2. Describe the age-related changes in the major body systems.
3. Characterize the health of the young adult.
4. Describe the effects of diet and exercise on early adulthood.
5. Discuss the risk factors for obesity, effects of excess weight on health, and weight loss strategies.
6. Discuss the health-compromising behaviors of having an eating disorder, smoking, drinking alcohol, and using drugs.
7. Identify the risks involved in unsafe sex practices, especially risk for AIDS.
8. Distinguish between eustress and distress, describe Selye's general adaptation syndrome, and differentiate between primary appraisal and secondary appraisal.
9. Define posttraumatic stress disorder and discuss stranger rape and acquaintance rape in this context.
10. Describe the stages of the sexual response cycle.
11. Discuss sexual attitudes and behavior during the young adulthood period.
12. Identify and describe common sexual dysfunctions and issues concerning infertility.
13. Describe the characteristics of postformal thought and compare and contrast the problem-finding, dialectic postformal thought, and intersystematic and autonomous thought.
14. Identify and describe Schaie's stages of adult thinking.
15. Describe Perry's contextual relativism approach to adult cognition.
16. Discuss Kohlberg's theory of moral reasoning and describe the alternatives to and expansions of the theory.
17. Discuss Fowler's stages of faith-knowing.
18. Discuss the effect of college on intellectual development and describe the demographics of college students today.
19. Discuss the role of work and the development of careers during the young adulthood period.
20. Describe workplace differences based on gender, race, and socioeconomic status, including occupational segregation and sexual harassment.

Chapter Outline

I. Physical development

II. Physical functioning

Young adults are at the peak of their physical abilities. Their organs have reached maturity and are at their strongest by the mid-twenties.

A. Growth in height and weight

1. Virtually all people reach their full height by their mid-twenties as a result of ossification.

2. Considerable variables in cessation of growth occur for both women and men.

3. Exercise and good nutrition produce a reservoir of bone and calcium that can alleviate the bone loss associated with aging in later stages of adulthood.

4. Women and men experience weight increases during early adulthood. Increases in percent of body fat occur as the body continues to fill out.

5. Social factors also contribute to adult patterns of weight gain. Society stresses physical attractiveness and being slim.

B. Strength

1. Strength continues to increase after full height is reached and peaks in the early thirties.

2. Organ reserve is the extra capacity each body organ has for responding to very intense or prolonged effort or stress. This extra capacity declines with age after the peak in the thirties.

C. Age-related changes

Appearance changes relatively little during early adulthood, although some individuals may have a few facial creases or a few gray hairs by their late twenties.

1. The cardiovascular system undergoes a steady decline in functioning throughout the adult years.

2. Gradual decreases in respiratory efficiency start at about age twenty-five, and noticeable decreases appear by age forty, although it is difficult to distinguish between normal aging of the lungs and aging due to damage caused by environmental factors.

3. Peak central nervous system functioning occurs in early adulthood.

a. The senses vary in the degree of age-related changes.

b. The changes in senses are slight and usually do not concern young adults.

III.   Health in early adulthood

Typically, young adults are healthy and even when ill do not experience symptoms. Young adults with poor health habits are not yet likely to suffer from the negative effects, although damage is occurring in their bodies.

A. Health behaviors

Adopting healthy behaviors and avoiding health-compromising behaviors promote better health.

1. Many of the losses in functioning associated with aging are the result of illness, abnormality, genetic factors, or exposure to unhealthy environments. This is called pathological aging.

2. Health-compromising behaviors can lead to pathological aging as well as to illness.

3. Diet plays a significant role in cardiovascular disease and contributes to the development of cancer.

    a. A healthy diet is one low in cholesterol, fats, calories, and additives and high in fiber, fruits, and vegetables.

    b. This diet is not typical of most Americans. Both poor eating habits acquired in childhood and poor attitudes influence one's eating behavior.

4. Exercise. Physical activity is associated with staying healthy.

    a. Exercise is beneficial to the cardiovascular system. It reduces or controls hypertension and improves cholesterol levels.

    b. Exercise can also improve mood and self-esteem and reduce the chance of engaging in health-compromising behaviors.

5. Weight control

Obesity is a major health problem and is associated with a number of medical problems such as heart disease.

    a. Normal body weight is determined by a person's body mass index (BMI).

    b. Fifty-five percent of the adult population is overweight or obese, and the percentage has been increasing since 1960.

    c. There are several factors that increase the risk of obesity: genetic predisposition, childhood patterns of eating and exercise, and socioeconomic status.

    d. The best strategies for weight loss are exercise and a healthy diet.

B. Health-compromising behaviors

Many of the behaviors that put individuals at risk in adolescence persist among young adults.

1. Eating disorders

Eating disorders begun in adolescence frequently persist into adulthood.

a. Eating disorders are equally prevalent across race, ethnic, and SES groups.

b. New research suggests promising treatments for eating disorders.

2. Smoking is responsible for more preventable illnesses and deaths than any other single health-compromising behavior. Although smoking rates have declined overall, smoking among adolescents has increased 73% since 1988.

a. Passive smoking increases the health risks to nonsmokers who are subjected to air contaminated by smokers.

b. Smoking-related illnesses take years to develop. This permits smokers to deny or ignore the threat to their health.

c. Smoking is influenced if parents, older siblings, best friends, or peers smoke; socioeconomic status also plays a role.

d. There are racial/ethnic differences in smoking patterns and attitudes.

e. People who suffer from multiple addictions report that smoking is harder to stop than taking drugs or drinking alcohol.

f. Smoking prevention is particularly important because nicotine may serve as an entry-level drug that makes one more likely to use other drugs in the future.

3. Alcohol consumption can affect health in many ways, such as increasing the risk of some cancers and cirrhosis of the liver.

a. For some, one or two drinks a day may be too much.

b. Alcohol abuse can damage nearly every organ and function of the body.

c. Problem drinking and alcoholism can result from heavy drinking.

d. Drinking and heavy drinking are more common among younger adults than older adults.

4. Unsafe sex creates risk for STDs and HIV infection.

a. Adolescents and young adults are at greater risk than other age groups because they have more sex partners.

b. AIDS is the most feared sexually transmitted disease because it is fatal.

    c.   Young adults often do not consider the consequences of unsafe sex, forget about them when under the influence of alcohol or drugs, or protect themselves from AIDS but not from other STDs.

    d.   The risk for AIDS has been greatest for homosexual men, intravenous drug users, and minority populations, but the number of affected women is growing.

- Working with Daniel Longram, care manager: Helping families cope with AIDS

IV. Stress

Stress is the arousal of the mind and body in response to demands made on them by unsettling conditions or experiences. Stress can be positive (eustress) or negative (distress). Selye developed the general adaptation syndrome to describe the pattern of physical response to stress; the syndrome consists of three stages: alarm, resistance, and exhaustion.

A. Stress and health

    1.   Stress can have a direct effect by increasing wear and tear on the physiological system and causing physical changes that can lead to illness.

    2.   Some people have personalities or health conditions that predispose them to stress. People with negative affectivity may be prone to disease.

B. The experience of stress

    1.   Lazarus identified a two-step process that people go through when faced with a stressor.

        a.   In primary appraisal, the person determines if the stressor is positive, neutral, or negative. If negative, the person assesses its potential for harm, threat, or challenge.

        b.   The person's assessment of whether he or she has sufficient coping strategies to the negative stressor is called secondary appraisal.

        c.   Negative, uncontrollable, ambiguous, or overwhelming events are perceived as more stressful than positive, controllable, clear-cut, or manageable ones.

    2.   Posttraumatic stress disorder (PTSD) describes the physical and psychological symptoms of a person who has been the victim of a highly stressful event.

    Rape is one traumatic event very likely to result in PTSD.

- Focusing On: How does stress relate to women's employment?

V. Sexuality and reproduction

A. The sexual response cycle

    1.   Masters and Johnson studied women's and men's physiological response in sexual activity.

    a.   Healthy individuals go through the same physiological processes.

    b.   Male and female sexual responses are much more similar than different.

2.   There are five physiological stages in the human sexual response cycle.

    a.   In the desire stage, physiology and emotion contribute to sexual arousal.

    b.   The first sign of arousal occurs in the excitement stage and includes vasocongestion.

    c.   When the changes of the excitement stage reach a high state and then level off, the plateau stage has been reached.

    d.   Orgasm releases the buildup of muscular tension and vasocongestion and involves involuntary, rhythmic contractions of the muscles of the pelvis.

    e.   The resolution stage is characterized by the body's return to a nonaroused state.

B. Sexual attitudes and behaviors

Sexual attitudes fall into three broad categories—traditional, relational, and recreational.

1.   For traditional people, their religious beliefs serve as a guide for sexual behavior.

2.   Relational people say that sex is a part of a loving relationship but is not limited to marriage.

3.   Sex and love are not necessarily related for recreational people.

4.   There is a relationship between attitudinal groups and behavior.

C. Sexual dysfunction is an inability to function adequately in or enjoy sexual activities and has been experienced by a large percentage of both wives and husbands.

1.   Low sexual desire is a common complaint of women and men and can be caused by a variety of physical factors.

2.   Orgasmic problems in females can take the form of primary orgasmic dysfunction, where a woman never experiences an orgasm, and it may be related to psychological and physiological problems.

3.   The most common male sexual dysfunction is premature ejaculation.

4.   Erectile dysfunction is when a man is generally unable to get or keep a firm enough erection to have intercourse. One popular treatment option is Viagra.

D. Infertility

Infertility refers to a couple's inability to conceive a pregnancy after one year of sexual relations without contraception. Infertility has become a more frequent problem in the last twenty-five years. There are several suspected causes, including sexually transmitted diseases, environmental hazards, and limited access to medical care.

1. The two major causes of female infertility are failure to ovulate and blockage of the fallopian tubes.

2. Male infertility may be due to low sperm count, low sperm mobility, poor semen quality, or blockage of the ducts of the reproductive tract.

3. Psychological reactions to infertility include five common emotional responses, and people often initially respond to the diagnosis of infertility with shock or denial.

4. Many new reproductive technologies have been developed, but they can be expensive and are not always successful.

VI. Adult choices

Major life decisions made during early adulthood can have significant implications for development.

VII. Cognitive development

Some cognitive theorists believe that we reach higher levels of cognitive development than described by Piaget.

A. Postformal thought

Formal operations is the final Piagetian stage of cognitive development; it represents a generalized orientation toward problem solving.

1. Critiques of formal operations

Several researchers have criticized formal operations and suggest postformal thought.

a. Postformal thinkers understand that knowledge is relative and nonabsolute.

b. Postformal thinkers accept contradiction as a basic aspect of reality.

c. Postformal thinkers can synthesize contradictions into coherent wholes.

2. Is there a fifth stage of cognitive development?

a. Problem finding involves generating new questions about oneself, one's work, or one's surroundings.

b. Some researchers have proposed a fifth stage of cognitive development and include problem finding, dialectical postformal thought, intrasystemic and intersystemic thought, and autonomous thought.

B. Development of contextual thinking

Schaie conducted longitudinal research and proposes three or four stages of adult thought.

1. Schaie's stages of adult thinking

   a. Childhood and adolescence constitute the period of acquisition, when a person builds basic skills and abilities.

   b. Young adults are in the achieving stage and move toward specific goals while considering contexts and consequences.

   c. In middle adulthood, people enter the responsible stage and strive to meet personal goals and consider their responsibilities to others.

   d. Some middle-aged people who have more complex responsibilities are in the executive stage, requiring the application of postformal thinking to practical problems.

   e. People in late adulthood are in the reintegrative stage, when they have fewer long-range plans and fewer responsibilities to job and family.

2. Contextual relativism

   Perry studied how students at Harvard University progressed through the college years.

   a. Freshmen had a **basic dualism** perspective: they saw things in terms of right or wrong, good or bad.

   b. In the **contextual relativism stage**, students began to see truth as relative—that meaning depended on context and who was trying to understand the event.

   c. Perry's sample did not represent all adults or even all college students, and no female responses were used.

   d. Perry's work has been broadened by Belenky et al. in their interview of 135 women. Their study revealed other responses:

      i. Silent knowing involves seeing authorities as all-powerful.

      ii. Received knowing consists of receiving the truth from others.

      iii. Individuals in subjective knowing are less concerned about persuading others; they distrust logic, analysis, and abstraction, and use inward listening and watching to learn.

      iv. Procedural knowing is based on abstract reasoning and is a shift from subjective opinions to reasoned arguments.

      v. Constructed knowing consists of integrating subjective and objective knowing.

VIII. Adult moral reasoning

   Kohlberg's theory focused on the abstract ethic of justice, while Gilligan's argued that empathy is a primary motivator for moral reasoning and ethical behavior.

A. Context and moral orientation

Research has shown that individuals used both a care orientation and a justice orientation.

B. Gender and moral voice

1. Studies of adult moral development have found the use of feminine and masculine themes in both males and females.

2. Most adults use more than one moral orientation, and many studies show that there appear to be no gender differences in moral orientation.

• A Multicultural View: Moral orientation in the United States and China

IX. Development of faith

A. As young adults begin to think from different ethical perspectives they may also develop a more complex sense of faith which may or may not evolve within a religious context.

B. James Fowler's stages of the development of faith range from self-centered and one-sided to more complex, other-centered, and multi-sided levels of understanding.

X. College

College cultivates intellectual development and fosters a progression in ways of thinking. The United States has the most educated population, although there are ethnic differences in completion rates. Most studies have shown that the benefits of college can be realized at any type of school. Faculty-student contact is an important variable in cognitive growth.

A. Who attends college?

1. The rate of college enrollment for younger students has grown substantially, but the number of older students has been growing even more rapidly.

2. Students attend college for many reasons, including to obtain an education and to satisfy parental expectations.

B. Women and racial/ethnic minorities

1. Women are more likely than men to attend college and to complete it within four years of starting.

2. Although no differences between men and women were found in the cognitive structures or learning styles, there is a difference in how they view acquisition of knowledge.

3. The college student body has become more racially and ethnically diverse in the last two decades.

4. There are differences between African Americans and White students in terms of attrition rates, overall progression rates, and other variables, although these differences disappear when other variables are controlled.

5. Higher dropout rates among ethnic minorities may be due to inhospitable climate on most predominantly White college campuses.

XI. Work

Work is a major social role of adult life and forms a critical part of one's identity. Occupation refers to all forms of work, whereas career usually refers to professional occupations.

A. Career stages

1. Greenhaus proposed a five-stage ladder of career development, with each stage consisting of an approximate age range and a set of major tasks. Three of those stages are relevant in early adulthood.

a. Preparation for work includes self-exploration to discover interests, talents, and preferences.

b. Organizational entry involves finding a job.

c. The early career stage involves gaining competence on the job as well as developing balance between fitting into the organization and learning about other options and directions for one's career.

2. It is important to develop a balance between work and nonwork commitments.

B. Gender, race, and SES in the workplace

1. Gender, race, and socioeconomic status affect which jobs people attain. **Discrimination** is the valuation by the labor market of personal characteristics of a worker that are not related to productivity.

2. Most jobs are held almost exclusively by men or women; this is called **occupational segregation**. Few jobs are truly integrated.

3. Occupations that depend on education have been more receptive to women than occupations that require physical strength and skill.

4. Females' aspirations toward gender-appropriate occupations are influenced by many variables.

5. The primary sector includes high-wage jobs that provide good benefits, job security, and advancement opportunities. The secondary sector includes low-wage jobs with few fringe benefits.

a.   Many ethnic and racial minorities are employed in the secondary sector.

b.   There are more gender similarities than differences between male and female African American youth in the school-to-work transition.

6. Sexual harassment

Sexual harassment limits women at work. It can include physical or verbal abuse or unwelcome sexual advances or a hostile work environment.

XII.   Growth and change

Key Concepts

Directions: Identify each of the key concepts discussed in this chapter.

1. Early adulthood generally spans the years between ages _____ and _____.

2. The main tasks of early adulthood include establishing oneself in _____ and forming _____ with another person.

3. _____ refers to the extra capacity of major organs of the body to function under unusually prolonged and intense stressful events.

4. _____ is caused by illness, genetic factors, abnormality, or exposure to unhealthy environments.

5. Smoking, unsafe sex, and drug use are examples of _____.

6. Poor diet contributes to _____ disease and the development of _____.

7. People who exercise regularly maintain higher levels of _____ functioning.

8. Excessive accumulation of energy in the form of body fat is the definition of _____.

9. Studies indicate that patterns of eating disorders differ in various American subcultures. _____ is more common among white women, and _____ is more common among African American women.

10. _____ is responsible for more preventable illnesses and deaths than any other single health-compromising behavior.

11. Breathing in of secondhand smoke from other people's cigarettes is the definition of _____.

12. Moderate alcohol consumption is defined as _____ drinks per day for men and _____ drinks per day for women. This type of drinking may _____ longevity.

13. Drinking and heavy drinking are more common among _____ adults than _____ adults.

14. _____ may cause low-grade inflammations in both men and women that lead to _____.

15. Risk for AIDS is greatest for _____, _____, and _____.

16. Hans Selye's identifies the three stages of _____, _____, and _____ as a pattern of physical responses to stress.

17. _____ describes the physical and psychological symptoms of a person who has been the victim of a highly stressful event, such as war or earthquake.

18. Rape is categorized as either _____ or _____ rape. While most people believe the opposite, _____ rape is more common.

19. The sexual response cycle was studied most intensively by _____ and _____. These researches identified four stages of the cycle. These stages are _____, _____, _____, and _____.

20. An often temporary inability to function adequately in or enjoy sexual activities is the definition of _____.

21. About _____ percent of _____ cases are due to female causes and about _____ percent are due to male causes. The remaining _____ percent are due to immunity or incompatibility of man's sperm and woman's egg or to unknown causes.

22. Various reproductive technologies, such as artificial insemination and in vitro fertilization, have drawbacks; they tend to be _____, and they carry _____.

23. Thought that is characterized by relative and nonabsolute thinking that accepts and synthesizes contradiction is described as _____.

24. The practice of aiming at the truth by using conversation involving question and answer to understand contradictions is the definition of _____.

25. Theories that propose a _____ of cognitive development emphasize the increasingly pragmatic, relative, and changing nature of adult knowledge.

26. Schaie's model of adult thinking is based on _____ research. He measured the _____ of the same individuals over many years.

27. According to Perry, as individuals become gradually aware of the diversity of opinions, _____ is replaced by _____. Finally, _____ is reached when individuals begin to see that truth is relative, and that the meaning of an event depends on its context and on the framework of the knower who is trying to understand the event.

28. _____ and others have criticized Kohlberg's theory of moral development because it emphasizes _____ as the primary motivator of moral judgment. The critics argue that for females, _____ is the primary motivator.

29. Galotti's research found that moral orientations of men and women are _____.

30. According to Fowler, _____ develops through a series of _____ stages and its growth depends on the development of _____.

34. Studies indicate that young adults who attend college grow in _____ compared to those who did not attend college and that women are _____ likely to attend college than men.

35. Higher college dropout rates of African American, Hispanic, and Native American students may be due to _____ on college campuses.

36. _____ refers to all forms of work, whereas _____ usually refers to professional occupations, such doctor and lawyer.

37. The five-stage _____ladder was proposed by _____.

38. _____ refers to the reality that most job categories in the United States are dominated by either men (e.g., architects) or women (e.g., nurses); few are truly integrated.

39. Unwelcome behavior that limits the victim's ability to function effectively on the job is the definition of _____.

Multiple-Choice Self-Test

Factual Questions

1. Both men and women achieve maximum bone mass by age
   a. eighteen.
   b. twenty.
   c. twenty-five.
   d. thirty.

2. Gradual decreases in respiratory efficiency start at about age
   a. eighteen.
   b. twenty.
   c. twenty-five.
   d. thirty.

3. Aging that occurs due to illness, genetic factors, or unhealthy environments is referred to as
   a. pathological aging.
   b. normal aging.
   c. abnormal aging.
   d. genetic aging.

4. Royce and her associates found that _____ make up the highest proportion of those who want to quit smoking.
   a. white men
   b. white women
   c. African American men
   d. African American women

5. According to Selye, which of the following happens in the alarm stage of the general adaptation syndrome?
   a. The body mobilizes to cope with the stressor.
   b. The body actually works to cope with the threat.
   c. The person becomes depleted of energy, and illness onset occurs.
   d. The sympathetic nervous system and the adrenal glands decrease the production of hormones.

6. During which stage of the sexual response cycle does vasocongestion occur?
   a. Excitement stage
   b. Plateau stage
   c. Orgasm
   d. Resolution stage

7. Which of the following conditions is the most common cause of infertility in females?
   a. Ovulatory problems
   b. Previous miscarriages
   c. Reproductive tract infections
   d. Sexually transmitted diseases

8. According to Arlin, problem finding refers to
   a. abstract problem solving.
   b. generating questions related to oneself, one's work, and one's surroundings.
   c. a search for truth through analysis of relations among systems.
   d. objective thought.

9. In Schaie's model of adult thinking, the achieving stage is related to
   a. building basic skills.
   b. integrating responsibility for others with personal goals.
   c. meeting personal goals.
   d. meeting the needs of the larger society.

10. Compared with jobs in the primary sector, jobs in the secondary sector provide
    a. good wages.
    b. job security.
    c. advancement opportunities.
    d. few fringe benefits.

Conceptual Questions

1. Carol and Rick are both seventeen years old. Which of the following statements is true about their physical growth?
   a. Rick will reach his maximum height earlier than Carol.
   b. Rick has a higher proportion of body fat than Carol.
   c. Carol has a higher proportion of body fat than Rick.
   d. Rick will achieve maximum bone mass earlier than Carol.

2. Steven is thirty-seven years old, and he does not smoke. Which experience is he most likely to have?
    a. He notices a need for reading glasses.
    b. He quickly feels out of breath while playing soccer.
    c. He notices that he does not hear as well as he used to.
    d. His sense of touch is not as sensitive as it was just a few years ago.

3. Which of the following seventeen-year-old teenagers is most likely to be suffering from anorexia?
    a. Nora, who is African American and on the volleyball team at her high school
    b. Tracy, who is African American and had been sexually abused as a child
    c. Kelly, who is white and had been obese as a child
    d. Amanda, who is white and had a chronic illness during childhood.

4. Tom and Lilly both consume six glasses of wine during a dinner party. At the end of the evening, who is more likely to be intoxicated?
    a. Lilly and Tom will be equally intoxicated.
    b. Tom will be more intoxicated.
    c. Lilly will be more intoxicated.
    d. The person who consumes the wine in the shortest amount of time will be more intoxicated.

5. Which of the following is an example of eustress?
    a. Lisa is planning her wedding.
    b. David is making arrangements for his dad's funeral.
    c. Sally and Ron are involved in an auto accident.
    d. Chris has received a demotion at his job.

6. John and Jane are both in their early fifties, and they have been married for twenty-four years. Which statement best reflects their sexual attitudes/behaviors?
    a. They believe sex and love are separate and that sex without love is possible.
    b. They believe sex should be a part of a loving relationship.
    c. They have sex more frequently now than they did when they first married.
    d. They have sex more often than other married couples who have been married as long but are younger.

7. Sam and Donna have been trying to conceive for the past two years. Who is more likely to seek infertility treatment?
    a. Sam
    b. Donna
    c. Both will seek treatment
    d. Neither will seek treatment

8. Janet and Bob are jurors in a murder case in which the accused is a twenty-nine-year-old woman. After hearing all the testimony, they both decide that the woman is guilty. However, Janet is concerned for the welfare of the women's 3 children, who will be placed in foster homes if the mother goes to jail, whereas Bob feels that consideration for the children is beyond the limits of their duty as jurors. Gilligan would claim that Janet is using the _____ approach and Bob is using the _____ approach in attempting to resolve this dilemma.
    a. mythical-literal; synthetic-conventional
    b. synthetic-conventional; mythical-literal
    c. justice; care
    d. care; justice

9. Who is more likely to graduate from a four-year college: Michael, who has been attending a four-year college since graduating from highschool, or Jason, who transferred to the same institution from a community college?
    a. Michael.
    b. Jason.
    c. Both equally
    d. Neither

10. Which of the following statements is true?
    a. Men have been entering traditionally female jobs over the past three decades.
    b. Women have been entering traditionally male jobs over the past three decades.
    c. Women have more success entering male-dominated blue-collar jobs.
    d. Women try job training and job changes more often than men.

Answer Key

Key Concepts

1. twenty; forty
2. work; intimate connections with another person
3. Organ reserve
4. Pathological aging
5. Health-compromising behaviors
6. cardiovascular; cancer
7. cardiac
8. obesity
9. Anorexia; binge eating
10. Smoking
11. passive smoking
12. two; one; decrease
13. younger; older
14. STDs; infertility
15. homosexual men; intravenous drug users; minority populations.
16. general adaptation syndrome; alarm; resistance; exhaustion
17. Posttraumatic stress syndrome
18. stranger; acquaintance; acquaintance
19. Masters; Johnson; excitement; plateau; orgasm; resolution
20. sexual dysfunction

21.   40; infertility; 40; 20
22.   expensive; risks
23.   postformal thought
24.   dialectical thinking
25.   fifth stage
26.   longitudinal; intellectual development
27.   dualism; multiplicity; contextual relativism
28.   Gilligan; justice; care
29.   similar
30.   faith; six; cognitive skills
31.   intellectual capacity; more
32.   inhospitable climate
33.   Occupation; career
34.   career; Greenhaus
35.   Occupational segregation
36.   sexual harassment

Multiple-Choice Self-Test / Factual Questions

1.   Choice (d) is correct. Both sexes achieve maximum bone mass by their late twenties and early thirties. The other choices are all too early.

2.   Choice (c) is correct. Respiratory decline starts at about age twenty-five and becomes noticeable by age forty. Choices (a) and (b) are too early and choice (d) is too late – it has already started.

3.   Choice (a) is correct. Pathological aging results from factors other than the normal aging process. Choice (b), the process of normal aging, does not involve illness, damage caused by unhealthy environments, or genetic predisposition. Choices (c) and (d), abnormal and genetic aging, are not applicable terms.

4.   Choice (d) is correct. Research indicated that in general African Americans wanted to quit smoking more than whites and that more African American women had made an attempt to quit smoking within the last year. Choices (a) and (b), whites, wanted to quit less than African Americans did. African American women wanted to quit more than African American men, choice (c).

5.   Choice (b) is correct. During the alarm stage, the person becomes aware of the stressor and mobilizes into action. Choice (a), coping, occurs during the resistance stage. Choice (c), illness, may occur during the exhaustion stage. The sympathetic nervous system and adrenal glands *increase* the production of hormones during stressful encounters; therefore choice (d) is incorrect.

6.   Choice (a) is correct; vasocongestion is the first sign of physiological arousal during the initial excitement stage of the sexual response cycle. Choices (b), (c), and (d) are the remaining three stages of the sexual response cycle.

7.   Choice (a) is correct; ovulatory problems are one of the two major causes of infertility in females. Choices (b), (c), and (d) may lead to infertility, but the likelihood of this is smaller.

8. Choice (b) is correct. Choices (a), abstract problem solving and choice (d), objective thought, are related to Piaget's ideas on formal operational thinking. Choice (c) is the definition of dialectical thinking.

9. Choice (c) is correct. Choice (a), building skills, occurs during the acquisitive stage. Choices (b) and (d), integrating responsibility with goals and meeting the needs of the larger society, occur during the executive stage.

10. Choice (d) is correct. Choices (a), (b), and (c) are characteristic of primary-sector jobs.

Multiple-Choice Self-Test / Conceptual Questions

1. Choice (c) is correct; women have a higher proportion of body fat than men. It is believed that this is probably related to sex-specific reproductive functions. For this reason, choice (b) is incorrect. Choice (a) is incorrect in that women reach their maximum height earlier than men. Choice (d) is incorrect in that both sexes reach their maximum bone mass at about thirty years of age.

2. Choice (b) is correct; normal respiratory decline begins at about age twenty-five. Vision remains intact until about age fifty (middle adulthood); therefore choice (a) is incorrect. Hearing loss during young adulthood is too minor to notice and sensitivity to touch improves until age forty-five. Therefore choices (c) and (d) are incorrect.

3. Choice (c) is correct; anorexia is more common among whites and those who had been previously obese. Choices (a) and (b) are incorrect in that binge eating rather than anorexia is more common among the African American population. Choice (d) is incorrect in that childhood chronic illnesses do not appear to be related to incidence of eating disorders.

4. Choice (c) is correct; women become more intoxicated than men do from the same amount of alcohol because they have more fatty tissue, which retains alcohol, and less body water, which dilutes it. For these reasons, choices (a), (b), and (d) are incorrect.

5. Choice (a) is correct; eustress is positive stress. Choices (b), (c), and (d) are all examples of negative stress.

6. Choice (b) is correct; research indicates that older married people have more traditional views of sex. More liberal attitudes toward sex, choice (a), are more common among younger individuals. Choices (c) and (d) are incorrect in that younger people have sex more frequently than older people.

7. Choice (b) is correct; women are more likely to seek treatment if a couple is having difficulty in achieving pregnancy. Research does not support the accuracy of the other choices.

8. Choice (d) is correct; Gilligan argues that female morality is motivated by an ethic of care, which allows the individual to feel compassion toward others and to make moral   judgments by considering the social and emotional aspects of a moral dilemma. Therefore choice (c) is incorrect. Choices (a) and (b) are stages 2 and 3 of Fowler's faith-knowing system.

9. Choice (c) is correct; data indicate that transferring to a four-year college from a community college and attending a four-year college directly after high school both lead to similarly positive graduation outcomes from the four-year institution. The other choices are incorrect.

10. Choice (b) is correct; for the past three decades women have been more successful in entering traditionally male jobs than men have been in entering traditionally female jobs. Therefore, choice (a) is incorrect. Choice (c) is incorrect in that women have had more success entering male dominated professions than blue-collar jobs. Blue-collar jobs often require physical strength and skill and most women cannot fulfill these requirements. Choice (d) is incorrect in that research indicates that women receive job training and change jobs less often than men.

CHAPTER 13

Psychosocial Development in Early Adulthood

Learning Objectives:

1. Compare timing of events and normative crisis-theories of psychosocial development.
2. Compare the normative crisis theories of Grant and Valliant and Levinson.
3. Describe Erikson's intimacy versus isolation stage of early adulthood.
4. Discuss the primary ideas of relational theory.
5. Discuss the development of intimacy during adulthood.
6. Identify the characteristics and benefits of friendships.
7. Compare male friendships and female friendships.
8. Describe the three components in Sternberg's triangular theory of love.
9. Identify and define the seven types of love.
10. Discuss gender effects on love.
11. Discuss the process of mate selection and the relevant variables.
12. Identify and describe the different types of marriage and explain how they affect marital equality and satisfaction.
13. Discuss the relationship between marital status and happiness and well-being.
14. Discuss cross-cultural similarities in spousal abuse.
15. Discuss alternatives to marriage, including singlehood and heterosexual cohabitation.
16. Discuss current attitudes toward homosexuality, lesbian/gay cohabitation, and lesbian/gay parenting.
17. Discuss the effects of divorce and remarriage on the family.
18. Identify the challenges that come with parenthood and indicate how having children might alter marital relationships.
19. Discuss the effects of single parenthood.
20. Discuss the effects of stepparents and blended families.
21. Discuss the consequences of not having children for long-term marital relationships.

Chapter Outline

I. Theories of adult development

Adulthood development has less to do with biology and more to do with cultural, social, and personal factors. As a result there is more diversity in adult development than in child or adolescent development.

A. Timing of events: Social clocks

1.   This approach focuses on the importance of the developmental context.

2.   The developmental context is described by a **social clock** that tells us whether we are "on time" in following an age-appropriate social timetable.

   a.   These social norms dictate when certain life transitions should occur.

   b.   People who follow this expected pattern experience fewer difficulties than people who deviate from it.

3.   Society has become less rigid in its expectations of when significant life events should occur. But these age-graded roles have not disappeared.

4.   Timing of events theories are better than normative-crisis theories to explain dissimilarities among groups.

B.   Crisis theory: Vaillant and the Grant study

1.   Vaillant studied 204 white men in a longitudinal study and came to several conclusions.

   a.   Growth and development are a lifelong process.

   b.   Isolated events rarely mold individual lives. What is more important are the relationships with others.

   c.   **Adaptive mechanisms**, or coping styles, determine individuals' level of mental health. Vaillant found four types of adaptive mechanisms—mature, immature, psychotic, and neurotic.

2.   Vaillant found that individuals were more likely to use one adaptive mechanism over another at certain ages. Some subjects made maturational shifts in adaptive styles. Several variables were associated with this shift.

   a.   A healthy brain leads to mature adaptive mechanisms. Injuries and alcoholism lead to less mature mechanisms.

   b.   Sustained loving relationships lead to mature adaptive mechanisms. Close, loving relationships provide models for coping with life events.

3.   During **career consolidation**, between the twenties and forties, men tended to work hard, devote themselves to career achievement, and sacrifice play.

4.   Career consolidation for women

   a.   Women were not part of the Grant study; it would appear that the study's findings would not apply as consistently to them because of cohort gender roles.

   b.   Contemporary women and men are both less likely to follow the patterns described by Vaillant.

C.   Crisis theory: Levinson's seasons of adult lives

1. Levinson used the **biographical method** to learn about his subjects' lives. The method involves reconstructing the life course through interviewing and using other sources.

2. Levinson identified three eras, or seasons, in the adult male life, two of which occur in early adulthood; during each era, a man builds a life structure. It is then followed by a transition, and then he builds a new life structure.

   a. The novice phase is characterized by exploration of the possibilities of adult life, testing of some initial choices, and creating a provisional entry life structure. The age thirty transition allows reassessment and improvement to this first adult life structure. The phase has four major tasks: forming a Dream, forming mentoring relationships, developing an occupation, and establishing intimate relationships and finding the special woman.

   b. In the second phase, the culminating phase, the young man establishes occupational goals and makes plans for advancing them. He is settling down and is more independent and self-sufficient. Around forty, the man enters midlife transition.

3. Because Levinson excluded women from the study, there is some question about their course of development. Levinson later reported that his formulations fit women too.

   a. The Dreams of women may differ from those of men.

   b. Women were also unlikely to have had mentors.

   c. Integrating career and family was difficult for women for several reasons, including their husbands' expectations that their wives would support their own Dreams.

   d. Women also did not have "a special man" to help them pursue their Dreams.

D. Crisis theory: Erikson's intimacy versus isolation

   1. In **intimacy versus isolation**, the crisis of early adulthood builds on Erikson's earlier stages of ego development.

      a. During this stage, the individual must develop the ability to establish close, committed relationships and to tolerate the threat of fusion and loss of identity that intense intimacy raises.

      b. The avoidance of intimacy leads to isolation and self-absorption.

   2. Critics have suggested that identity and intimacy develop simultaneously.

   3. Relational theories of women's development suggest that socialization experiences result in gender-differentiated personalities in which women typically have a more relational way of being and men have a more autonomous way of being.

II.   Intimate relationships

During early adulthood, attachment to friends and lovers increases while attachment to family decreases. Although family members continue to be important in young adults' lives, they are not as important as they were during earlier life stages.

A.   Friendship

1.   Friendships are particularly important during early adulthood, since young adults rely increasingly on friends for intimacy and support.

2.   The essential elements of friendship include its voluntary nature and its ability to provide many important forms of support, such as validation and acceptance.

3.   In other cultures, friendships are often based on more basic survival needs.

4.   Friendships provide many mental and physical health benefits.

5.   Men and women tend to have different styles of friendships.

a.   Women tend to talk with their friends in more deep and more self-revealing ways and to define friendships in terms of emotional sharing of confidences.

b.   Men tend to define friendships in terms of proximity and shared activities and interests.

c.   Gender differences may be related to issues of power and control.

d.   Recent studies indicate more commonalities in men's and women's friendships than previously thought.

6.   Single adults have more cross-gender friendships than any other group.

•   Working with Marilyn Kline, suicide hot line worker: Helping individuals through crises

B.   Love

1.   Since young adults are waiting longer to marry, they experience more love relationships. Each of these relationships is likely to reflect **serial monogamy**.

2.   Sternberg developed a triangular theory of love and argued that love has three essential components: intimacy, passion, and decision/commitment.

a.   The three components have different properties and vary in different kinds of love relationships.

b.   According to Sternberg, there are seven combinations of these three components.

3.   Men and women place different values on the instrumental and expressive aspects of love.

       a.   Women report significantly higher confidence in expressing liking, love, and affection to men than men do for women. Women also place more emphasis on expressive qualities like emotional involvement and verbal self-disclosure.

       b.   Men consider practical help, sharing physical activities, spending time together, and sex more important.

  C. Mate selection

      1.   Most people's partners are like them in race/ethnicity, age, and educational level.

      2.   Most people meet their partners in conventional ways in familiar places like school, work, a private party, or a religious institution.

      3.   People are more vulnerable to falling in love when their life is in turbulence.

      4.   Getting to know someone as a friend is more likely to lead to a long-term relationship than responding to passion first and then trying to build emotional intimacy.

III. Marriage, Divorce, and Remarriage

During early adulthood, almost everybody finds a marriage partner. Marriage is the socially sanctioned union of a man and a woman that, to some extent, symbolizes being an adult.

  A. Marriage types

      1.   The **equal-partner relationship** is characterized by negotiating about shared concerns and responsibilities. Everything is open for renegotiation. This pattern is quite rare.

      2.   **Conventional relationship** describes a marriage in which the man is the head of the household and sole economic provider, and the woman is the mother and the homemaker.

      3.   The **junior partner relationship** has elements of both equal-partnership and conventional relationships.

  B. Marital equality

      1.   Many women work the second shift, meaning that they work the first shift at work and the second shift in the family.

      2.   Family size, social class, ethnicity, husband's income, and wife's employment are associated with the degree of the husband's dominance in the marriage.

•   A Multicultural View: Cross-cultural similarities in wife abuse

  C. Marital satisfaction

      1.   Different types of marriages are related to different levels of satisfaction with marriage.

   a. Both spouses in equal partnerships express the highest levels of marital satisfaction and psychological well-being.

   b. Equality is a desirable basis for marriage and is related to greater marital happiness and lower marital conflict and aggression.

2. Married people fare better than unmarried people with regard to mortality, morbidity, mental health, and more general measures of psychological well-being.

   a. Formerly married people have the lowest levels of well-being of all types, and never-married people have intermediate levels.

   b. Men seem to benefit more from marriage than women.

   c. The marriage-happiness relationship appears to be consistent across cultures.

   d. Differences in personal happiness between married and never-married individuals have decreased in recent years.

D. Divorce

   1. About 50 percent of first marriages and 40 percent of all marriages end in divorce.

      a. Most divorces occur during early adulthood.

      b. The age at which people divorce has been rising since the mid-1970s.

      c. The probability of marital success dropped between 1970 and 1990.

   2. Two social changes have contributed to the rising divorce rates.

      a. There are increased expectations of marriage, coupled with a breakdown of consensus about marital and gender roles and the issue of equality within marriage.

      b. There has been a decline in the belief that marriage really means "until death do us part." Many young adults witnessed their mothers becoming **displaced homemakers** and thus fear becoming fully committed to marriage.

      c. The long-term effects of divorce on adult children indicate no serious negative consequences; however, as adolescents they exhibit behavioral unrest.

E. Remarriage

   1. People remarry at about the same rate at which they marry; 72 percent of divorced people remarry, with divorced young adults remarrying at the highest rates.

   2. About half of these remarriages will end in divorce.

   3. People who have divorced and remarried several times report less happiness.

4. There is a relationship between the types of relationships marriage partners have with ex-spouses and the quality of their current marriages.

5. Relationships with ex-spouses that are low in conflict and low in emotional attachment have the best outcome for the new marriage.

6. Some individuals choose not to remarry because of a redefinition of their sexuality from heterosexual to homosexual.

IV. Alternative lifestyles

Some adults spend significant portions of their lives as singles, and some never marry.

A. Singlehood

1. Singles are not a homogeneous group.

2. One-third of the men and one-fifth of the women are single by choice.

B. Heterosexual cohabitation

1. The trend toward **cohabitation** is replacing early marriage. Since couples are marrying later, the majority of young adults now cohabit before marriage.

2. Cohabitation can serve many purposes.

    a. It can be perceived as part of the courtship process.

    b. Living together can be seen as a temporary arrangement prior to marriage.

    c. It may be a good way to test for compatibility before marriage.

3. Heterosexual cohabitation typically does not last long. Within a few years, most relationships have either broken up or ended in marriage.

4. The research on the influence of cohabitation on the quality of marriage is inconclusive. Some studies suggest that cohabitation makes no difference in level of satisfaction with marriage; others suggest that it can have a negative effect.

C. Lesbian/gay sexual preference

1. **Homophobia** discourages many gay men and lesbians from making their sexual identity public.

2. The percentages of gay men and lesbians are small, but they still represent a great many individuals.

3. Most gay men and lesbians live in larger cities and the surrounding suburbs.

D. Lesbian/gay cohabitation

1. It is estimated that one-half of gay male couples and three-quarters of lesbian couples live together.

2. Most couples form equal partnerships and share household tasks and decision making.

3. Gay male couples do not differ from heterosexual men in their levels of relationship satisfaction, and lesbians do not differ from wives in their levels of relationship satisfaction.

V. Parenthood

People have children for different reasons. Whatever the reason, pregnancy and childbirth are major life experiences.

A. Transition to parenthood

1. There is less preparation for the parenting role than for any other role in early adulthood.

2. Both fathers and mothers feel the strain of new parenthood, but mothers feel it more fully.

3. The gap between the mother's expectations of fulfillment and the realities of exhaustion and distraction is often enormous.

4. Expecting a baby arouses anxieties in men about their capacity to provide.

5. Employment outside the home may cause problems since women still carry 90 percent of the responsibility for the children, leaving mothers with the heavy demands of two jobs.

6. Marital satisfaction declines before and after the birth of the first child.

a. Having a baby does not bring couples with distressed marriages closer together.

b. Couples may regain satisfaction by successfully negotiating how they will divide the new family responsibilities.

B. Single parenthood

1. There is a rise in the number of single parents due to increasing numbers of couples divorcing and delayed marriages.

2. Many children of single parents live in poverty, making it difficult to separate the effects of single parenting from the effects of poverty.

3. The problems of single parenting are particularly acute for African American families.

  4. Extended families provide many single parents with support systems.

  5. Many single parents successfully raise happy and healthy children despite the particular difficulties they face.

- Focusing On: The effects of growing up in a lesbian or gay family

 C. Stepparent/blended families

  1. A blended family results when remarriage reconstitutes a single-parent family into a family with a stepparent.

  2. Blended families show the highest number of within-family problems.

  3. The complexity of the relationships in these families is significant.

  4. Adults in stepfamilies have more difficulty than children do in coping with stepsibling relationships.

   a. Being a stepparent is an ambiguous role.

   b. Men generally have an easier time being stepfathers than women do being stepmothers.

   c. Stepmothers tend to be more involved with their stepchildren than are stepfathers, but neither is as involved as the biological parent.

 D. Child free

  1. Only about 5 percent of married couples choose not to have children.

  2. People who choose not to have children pay a social price.

  3. In couples who choose to forgo parenthood, the woman almost always makes the initial decision and remains more committed to the decision than the man.

   a. An **early articulator** is someone who knew from childhood that she or he did not want children.

   b. A **postponer** is likely to be less definite about whether he or she wants children.

  4. Women who complete their education, postpone marriage, and hold jobs outside their home tend to have higher childlessness rates.

  5. Many women on the career path feel ambivalence about childbearing.

  6. Couples with no children tend to have a slightly higher degree of overall satisfaction and closeness than couples with children.

VI.   Looking back/looking forward

    A.   Continuity within change

    B.   Lifelong growth

    C.   Changing meaning and vantage points

    D.   Developmental diversity

Key Concepts

Directions: Identify each of the key concepts discussed in this chapter.

1.   The _____ allows us to time our major life events and tells if we are "on time" in following the age-appropriate timetable of our social group.

2.   Vaillant's _____ suggest that the coping styles people use in adjusting to major life events reflect their levels of mental health.

3.   According to Vaillant's research with men, _____ involves working hard and devoting oneself to career advancement.

4.   Levinson identified the _____ as corresponding to the first three periods of early adulthood for men. This phase includes four main tasks: _____, _____, _____, and _____.

5.   Levinson's research with females revealed that for most women the Dream is split between _____ and _____.

6.   According to Erikson, during the stage of _____, young adults focus on _____ while at the same time experiencing anxiety over _____ in relationships.

7.   In same-sex friendships, young adult men associate intimacy with ----- and -----. Women's same-sex friendships define intimacy as _____ of confidences.

8.   A series of exclusive, intimate, and sexual relationships with one person at a time is called _____.

9.   In Sternberg's_____ theory of love, three components of love are outlined. These are _____, _____, and _____.

10.   Women place greater emphasis on the _____ of love, such as _____ and _____, than men do.

11.   Most people partner with those who are _____ to themselves.

12.   In a _____, responsibilities are divided in a gender-stereotyped fashion.

13.   The concept of the _____ refers to the notion that women who work outside of the home are also responsible for most of the household chores.

14.   The term _____ refers to a woman who is unprepared for employment and single parenthood following a divorce or widowhood.

15.   People who remarry and divorce a second time report less _____ and more frequent _____ than people who divorce only once.

16.   Singles report that the best part of being single is _____ and the worst part is _____.

17. _____ refers to unrelated adults living together and sharing a sexual relationship.

18. Prejudice that is directed toward gay people and that results in mistreatment and discrimination is called _____.

19. The level of relationship satisfaction in homosexual partnerships is _____ to the level of satisfaction in heterosexual partnerships.

20. Women who score higher on _____ report a greater sense of well-being one year after the birth of a child than women who score higher on _____.

21. Most couples find parenthood _____.

22. _____ percent of single parents are mothers and these families often live in _____.

23. A _____ is one which both husband and wife have children from previous relationships.

24. About _____ percent of married couples choose not to have children.

25. Veevers used the term _____ to identify people who were uncertain about having children and who delayed childbearing, initially for a definite period of time and later for an indefinite period of time.

26. People who are certain from childhood that they want to remain childless throughout their lifetimes are called _____.

Multiple-Choice Self-Test

Factual Questions

1. Most theories of adult development do not consider individual differences such as
    a. gender, race/ethnicity, and socioeconomic status.
    b. inner needs and impulses of the individual.
    c. the importance of developmental context.
    d. diversity of developmental paths during adulthood.

2. The concept of a "social clock" was proposed by
    a. Daniel Levinson.
    b. George Vaillant.
    c. Bernice Neugarten.
    d. Carol Gilligan.

3. Which of the following is an example of an immature adaptive mechanism?
    a. Repression
    b. Sublimation
    c. Irrational fears
    d. Hypochondria

4. Which method of data collection did Levinson use?
   a. Cross-sectional
   b. Longitudinal
   c. Biographical
   d. Correlational

5. According to Erikson, young adults who avoid intimacy will
   a. achieve autonomy.
   b. become isolated and self-absorbed.
   c. develop a gender-differentiated personality.
   d. never develop a "dream."

6. Companionate love includes
   a. intimacy.
   b. intimacy and commitment.
   c. passion and commitment.
   d. intimacy, passion, and commitment.

7. In a junior partnership relationship;
   a. the man is the head of the household and the woman is the homemaker.
   b. the couple negotiates responsibilities and shared concerns.
   c. the junior partner is usually the woman, and she brings in some of the family income.
   d. the husband takes on all of the household responsibilities in addition to working outside the home.

8. Which of the following does *not* contribute to rising divorce rates?
   a. Discord over financial issues within a marriage
   b. Lack of consensus about gender and marital roles
   c. Increased expectations of marriage
   d. The tendency for today's younger generation to marry at a very young age

9. Which of the following is a common characteristic of women who choose cohabitation?
   a. They tend to be less educated.
   b. They tend to be African American or Hispanic.
   c. They tend to view themselves as dependent and nonassertive.
   d. They tend to live in small towns.

10. In comparison with white single mothers, Mexican American single mothers
    a. are more upset and depressed.
    b. receive more support from their extended families.
    c. encounter more problems during the first year of single parenthood.
    d. are older.

Conceptual Questions

1. Jack is well established in a career in a law firm. He has also traveled frequently and feels that he has done the most he can as a single individual. Lately, he has been paying a lot of attention to the lives of his married friends. Jack's feelings and actions are most consistent with
    a. the Eriksonian theory.
    b. normative-crisis theory.
    c. timing of events theory.
    d. Levinson's theory.

2. Twenty-two-year-old Don envisions himself as the CEO of the large electronics firm he works in parttime as a clerk. He reasons that after finishing graduate school he can advance up the career ladder and eventually reach the top.   Levinson would describe Don's vision as
    a. neurotic.
    b. an adaptive mechanism.
    c. the Dream.
    d. a transition.

3. Debby married at age twenty-three and raised two children. During young adulthood she remained very close to her own parents and siblings and to her husband's family. Now, at age fifty-four, she is caring for elderly parents. Relational theory would claim that Debby has well established her
    a. kinkeeping skills.
    b. gender-differentiated personality.
    c. intimacy skills.
    d. friendship skills.

4. Lee and Marvin have been married for nineteen years and they have two teenage sons. They were married very traditionally, by arrangement of their parents. They are committed to each other and to their children; however, they have no passion and intimacy in their marriage. Sternberg would describe their marriage as
    a. liking.
    b. empty love.
    c. companionate love.
    d. consummate love.

5. Ana and Joe have one child, and both work full-time outside the home. When she comes home from work, Ana is responsible for cooking dinner, doing the laundry, and all other household chores. This demonstrates the concept of
    a. a junior partnership.
    b. a conventional partnership.
    c. an equal partnership.
    d. the second shift.

6. Which of the following statements is true?
    a. Premarital cohabitation does not influence quality of marriage for white couples.
    b. Premarital cohabitation has a positive impact on the marriages of African American couples.
    c. Couples who cohabit prior to marriage report more commitment to their marriages.
    d. Premarital cohabitation reduces the risk for divorce.

7. David and Karen recently became parents for the first time. What is likely to happen to their level of marital satisfaction?
    a. It will remain the same.
    b. It will increase temporarily.
    c. It will increase permanently.
    d. It will decrease.

8. Pat is a never-married single mother. She is most likely to be
    a. African American.
    b. Hispanic.
    c. Asian.
    d. white.

9. Dan and Denise married and created a stepfamily. Which of the following is most likely to occur in this family?
    a. Dan and Denise discipline both their own and each other's children.
    b. Dan does not have biological children; he disciplines Denise's children.
    c. They discipline their own biological children only.
    d. Denise has an easier time adjusting to stepparenthood than Dan.

10. Gene and his wife have been married for twelve years, and they are voluntarily child-free. Which is true about their level of satisfaction?
    a. They are happier than couples with children in their marriage.
    b. They are not as happy as couples with children in their marriage.
    c. In general, they are slightly more satisfied than couples with children.
    d. In general, they are slightly less satisfied than couples with children.

Answer Key

Key Concepts

1. social clock
2. adaptive mechanisms
3. career consolidation
4. novice phase; forming a Dream; forming mentor relationships; developing an occupation; finding the special woman
5. achievement; relationships
6. intimacy versus isolation; developing intimate relationships; loss of identity
7. proximity; shared activities and interests; emotional sharing
8. serial monogamy
9. triangular; intimacy; passion; commitment
10. expressive qualities; emotional involvement; verbal self-disclosure
11. similar
12. conventional relationship
13. second shift
14. displaced homemaker
15. happiness; depression
16. freedom; loneliness
17. Cohabitation

18. homophobia
19. similar
20. autonomy; affiliation
21. rewarding
22. Eighty-five; poverty
23. blended family
24. 5
25. postponers
26. early articulators

Multiple-Choice Self-Test / Factual Questions

1. Choice (a) is correct. Normative crisis theories focus on the inner crises of individuals, choice (b). Timing of events theories focus on developmental context, choice (c). Choice (d) is incorrect in that all theories examine developmental diversity.

2. Choice (c) is correct. According to Neugarten, people strive to time their major life events to match societal expectations. The other choices are incorrect.

3. Choice (d), hypochondria, is correct. Choices (a), repression, and (c), irrational fears, are examples of neurotic mechanisms; choice (b), sublimation, is an example of a mature mechanism.

4. Choice (c) is correct. This method involves interviews with and visits to the home and workplace of the subject in order to gather data. Cross sectional research, choice (a), involves testing various age-groups of participants at one time. Longitudinal research, choice (b), involves testing one cohort at various intervals over time. Correlational research, choice (d), involves analyzing the relationship between two variables.

5. Choice (b) is correct. Choice (a), autonomy is a positive outcome for Erikson's second stage of development; choice (c), gender-differentiated personalities, refers to a part of the self that has internalized the socially prescribed meanings of gender; choice (d), the "dream," is a concept developed by Levinson, not Erikson.

6. Choice (b) is correct. Choice (a) describes liking; choice (c) describes fatuous love; choice describes consummate love.

7. Choice (c) is correct. Choice (a) describes a conventional relationship; choice (b) describes an equal partnership; choice (d) is incorrect because such a relationship has not been identified.

8. Choice (d) is correct. Contemporary men and women have been marrying later than previous cohorts. The other choices all contribute to rising divorce rates.

9. Choice (a) is correct. Choices (b), (c), and (d) are incorrect in that most tend to be white, to view themselves as independent and assertive and to live in large metropolitan areas.

10. Choice (b) is correct. Choices (a), (c), and (d) all describe white single mothers – they tend to be upset and depressed, tend to encounter more problems during the first year of single parenthood, and they tend to be older.

Multiple-Choice Self-Test / Conceptual Questions

1. Choice (b) is correct; normative-crisis theory focuses on the stirrings and impulses within an individual. Erikson, choice (a), examined the intimacy needs of young adulthood and how the failure to form intimate relationships leads to isolation. Choice (c), timing of events theories, focus on the influence of social expectations and culturally shared ideas about the timing of major life events. Choice (d), Levinson's theory, is an example of normative- crisis theory.

2. Choice (c) is correct; Levinson describes the formation of the Dream as one of the tasks of the novice phase. The dream may be realistic or unrealistic - either way it represents a vision that provides motivation to move forward in the adult world. Choice (a) is incorrect in that although this type of vision may be unrealistic, it is not evidence of neuroticism. The concept of adaptive mechanisms, choice (b), was advanced by George Vaillant. Transitional periods, choice (d), in Levinson's theory represent temporary restructuring as the person moves from one phase of development into the other.

3. Choice (a) is correct; kinkeeping skills, skills essential for establishing and maintaining relationships, are described by the relational theory of women's development. Choice (b), gender-differentiated personality, refers to internalized meanings of maleness and femaleness as described by cultures. Choices (c) and (d) are not applicable terms.

4. Choice (b) is correct; empty love does not involve passion and intimacy. Choice (a), liking includes intimacy only. Choice (c), companionate love, includes intimacy and commitment. Choice (d), consummate love, includes intimacy, passion, and commitment.

5. Choice (d) is correct; the concept of the second shift refers to the woman working the first shift at her job and the second shift in her family. Choices (a), (b), and (c) describe different types of partnerships with respect to the relative responsibilities and contributions of the partners to earning an income and taking care of the household and in decision making.

6. Choice (a) is correct; in one study, researchers found no differences in level of marriage satisfaction between couples who had and who had not cohabited prior to marriage. Choices (b), (c), and (d) are false statements; in each case, the opposite is true.

7. Choice (d) is correct; research indicates that marital satisfaction declines after the birth of the first child. The arrival of the baby initially brings change and disorganization, and the leading topic of conflict is the sharing of family responsibilities. If differences are resolved successfully, the couple will regain equilibrium. The other choices are incorrect.

8. Choice (a) is correct; research indicates that the majority of never-married mothers are African American. Therefore the other choices are incorrect.

9. Choice (b) is correct; in a stepfamily only one marriage partner has children from a previous marriage. Choices (a) and (c) are incorrect because they are examples of blended families in which both partners have children from previous marriages. Choice (d) is incorrect because in general, females have a harder time adjusting to stepparenthood than men.

10. Choice (c) is correct; research indicates that couples without children show a slightly higher degree of overall satisfaction and closeness. For this reason, choice (d) is incorrect. Choices (a) and (b) are incorrect; research does not indicate differences in the level of satisfaction with marriage between couples with children and those voluntarily child-free.

CHAPTER 14

Physical and Cognitive Development in Middle Adulthood

Learning Objectives

1. Explain how life expectancy and cultural views influence the concept of middle age.
2. Distinguish between primary aging and secondary aging.
3. Describe the major physical changes associated with middle age, including strength and appearance.
4. Characterize the major changes in the various body systems (cardiovascular, respiratory, and sensory) associated with middle age.
5. Discuss healthy and health-compromising behaviors and their effects during middle adulthood.
6. Describe and discuss breast cancer and prostate cancer.
7. Identify the changes in female reproduction during middle age, defining menopause and discussing potential treatment.
8. Define the male climacteric and discuss the changes in male reproduction during middle age.
9. Describe the changes in sexuality and sexual functioning during middle age.
10. Describe the findings about intelligence from early cross-sectional and longitudinal studies.
11. Describe and evaluate Schaie's sequential studies of intelligence.
12. List and explain factors that maintain good cognitive functioning in later life.
13. Distinguish between fluid and crystallized intelligence and describe the changes in each across adulthood.
14. Distinguish between practical intelligence and expertise.
15. Discuss the effects of aging on expertise knowledge.
16. Describe the adult learner and differentiate between the skills needed for independent learning and those needed for organized instruction.
17. Discuss why some individuals return to college during adulthood.
18. Discuss changes in work and job satisfaction during the middle adulthood years. including race and gender influences on these changes.
19. Describe the effects of unemployment on middle-aged individuals.

Chapter Outline

Expectations of middle age have become more diverse as the line between young adulthood and middle adulthood has become less distinct.

I. Physical development

II. Changing images of middle adulthood

A. Changes in appearance and functioning of the body characterize middle adulthood, which spans roughly ages forty to sixty.

B. The timing of middle adulthood depends on **life expectancy**.

C. The changes in middle adulthood are due to **primary aging** and **secondary aging**.

    1. Primary aging refers to the normal, age-related changes that everyone experiences.

    2. Secondary aging refers to pathological aging, and it shows more variability.

III. Physical functioning in middle adulthood

Most adults do not feel the impact of the decline before age fifty, and some do so much later than that.

A. Strength

    1. Strength slowly but steadily declines after peaking in early adulthood, but people differ in the amount of strength lost.

    2. Expending maximum effort only at the exact moment it is required helps to conserve energy and makes the decline barely noticeable to most people.

B. External and internal age-related changes

    1. Changes in skin, hair color, and body build result from a combination of primary and secondary aging.

    2. People tend to gain weight through the mid- to late fifties as fatty tissue and muscle are redistributed throughout the body. The "middle-age spread" is not inevitable with regular exercise and proper diet.

    3. Cardiovascular system changes

        a. The cardiovascular system continues the changes begun during early adulthood.

        b. Continuous and regular exercise helps to counteract these changes.

    4. Respiratory system changes

        a. The breathing apparatus and tissues of the lungs change due to primary aging.

        b. The amount of oxygen in the blood after passing through the lungs decreases with age.

        c. Getting regular exercise and avoiding environmental pollutants and smoking can reduce the effects of respiratory system changes.

5. Sensory system changes

    a. By age fifty, most people require reading glasses or bifocals if they already wear glasses as the lens of the eye continually grows fibers without shedding the old ones. This results in the lens thickening and gradually losing its capacity to accommodate.

    b. Hearing loss begins gradually in early adulthood and progresses until the eighties.

    c. Taste and smell sensitivity also decrease.

    d. Most adults are able to function normally despite these losses.

IV. Health in middle adulthood

Adults become more aware of health issues than when they were younger. They pay more attention to body monitoring, reflecting the realities of chronic disease and the effects of lifelong behaviors taking their toll. **Morbidity** refers to the number of cases of disease, while **mortality** refers to the number of deaths. Most middle-aged adults are not much different in physical health than young adults.

A. Health and health-compromising behaviors

    1. Behaviors at younger ages lay the groundwork for health and well-being in later life.

    2. Health-promoting behaviors positively affect health in several ways.

        a. The cardiovascular and respiratory systems benefit.

        b. Weight is controlled.

        c. Exercise enhances the ability to cope with psychosocial stressors.

    3. Health-compromising behaviors are often linked; for example, individuals who smoke heavily are also likely to drink heavily.

    4. Research has shown that drinking to "drown sorrows" is more of a risk factor for cancer and coronary heart disease than "pleasure" drinking.

• Focusing On: The gender gap in life expectancy

B. Breast cancer

    1. Lifestyle factors play a role in breast cancer.

    2. More new cases of breast cancer than lung cancer are diagnosed each year.

    3. The overall incidence of breast cancer is higher for White women than for African American women, but the death rate is greater for African Americans and may be related to socioeconomic factors.

4. Cultural factors may also be important in breast cancer screening and seeking and following medical care.

C. Prostate cancer

1. Prostate cancer is the most common cancer in men, and its incidence has increased since 1968.

2. Causes of prostate cancer are unknown but may be related to family history, ethnicity, socioeconomic status, diet, and environmental factors.

3. Prostate cancer is slow-growing and unlikely to produce symptoms.

a. It is typically discovered during surgery, digital exam, or a blood test.

b. There is no standard recommended treatment for prostate cancer. Some treatments may include removal of the prostate and/or radiation.

D. Health and inequality

Greater health problems and earlier deaths are experienced by disadvantaged ethnic minorities who may have less access to health care and beliefs and behaviors that have an impact on health care.

V. Reproductive change and sexuality

The gradual reduction in sex hormone production is called the **climacteric**; it is more noticeable in women than in men.

A. Menopause

1. When a previously menstruating woman has an entire year without a menstrual period, she has reached **menopause**.

2. Attitudes regarding menopause are generally negative, but not all cultures share this view of menopause.

3. Decreased ovarian functioning causes menopause, which ultimately leads to reduced levels of estrogen and progesterone.

4. The menopausal process occurs in three stages.

a. Premenopause is characterized by the ovaries gradually reducing hormone production.

b. Menopause is the second stage of the female climacteric.

c. Postmenopause, the third stage, occurs when hormonal levels stabilize and menopausal signs subside.

5. The most common physical sign of menopause is the hot flash. Vaginal changes are another common sign of menopause. Only about 10 percent of women experience severe symptoms.

6. The surgical removal of the uterus, called **hysterectomy**, is performed as a treatment for cancer and can cause sudden onset of menopause. **Oophorectomy**, which is the surgical removal of the ovaries, always triggers menopause.

7. **Estrogen replacement therapy (ERT)** and **hormone replacement therapy (HRT)** are options to alleviate menopausal symptoms by replacing the natural decrease in hormones.

    a. These replacement therapies can increase the risk for cancer.

    b. In combination with exercise and diet, they can help prevent **osteoporosis**.

    c. Women who take hormones are generally more affluent and healthier than those who do not and would have lower rates of disease anyway.

•   A Multicultural View: Japanese and North American attitudes toward menopause

B. The male climacteric

   1. Unlike menopause, the male climacteric does not lead to sterility.

   2. Decreased testicular functioning characterizes the male climacteric, causing a reduction in the number and vitality of sperm and a gradual reduction in testosterone production.

   3. The most notable changes affect the prostate gland, with **hypertrophy** occurring, causing pressure on the urethra and restricting and eventually blocking urine flow.

   4. Many signs of the male climacteric are similar to those attributed to menopause.

C. Sexuality in middle adulthood

   The changes in the reproductive systems of men and women have implications for sexual functioning which are not always perceived negatively.

   1. Female sexuality

      a. Many women find that the hormonal changes of menopause affect their sexual responsiveness.

      b. The cycles of sexual response continue, but with diminished speed and intensity.

      c. A reduction of vaginal lubrication can cause irritation or pain during intercourse.

      d. There is no evidence of decline in postmenopausal women's physical capacity for sex.

2. Male sexuality

    a. Erections take longer to obtain and are not as hard as they were earlier in life.

    b. Changes in orgasm are also experienced by aging men, with a reduction in intensity and an increase in the refractory period.

VI. Cognitive development

VII. Intelligence in middle adulthood

Conflicting ideas about the intellectual capacities in middle adulthood include being at one's "intellectual peak" or "over the hill."

A. Does intelligence decline with age?

It is difficult to determine the course of cognitive competence or intelligence over the adult years due to several factors.

1. Early negative studies

    a. Early studies suggested that intellectual decline begins in the teenage years.

    b. Later studies suggest that the decline occurs in early adulthood.

    c. More recent research has studied whether the differences in performance are due to age-related declines or to other variables.

2. Cross-sectional versus longitudinal studies

    a. Cross-sectional studies assume that the older subjects perform at the same level as the younger subjects did when they were young. However, cohort differences may challenge this assumption.

    b. Cross-sectional studies may "create" age decline because they confound cohort differences with age.

    c. Longitudinal studies measure intelligence across adulthood and minimize negative age patterns.

    d. Longitudinal studies may be biased in a positive direction since people who perform poorly are less likely to be available for retesting.

    e. In contrast to cross-sectional studies, longitudinal studies suggest a more positive view of intellectual competence in middle adulthood.

B. Schaie's sequential studies

1. Schaie began a longitudinal study of a cross-sectional sample that resulted in a sequential study. The study assessed the mental abilities of more than five thousand adults.

2. The SLS used the Primary Mental Abilities battery and assessed a number of abilities.

3. The results indicate no uniform pattern of age-related changes in adulthood across all intellectual abilities. Abilities tend to peak at different ages, change at different rates, and differ systematically for women and men.

4. Age-related changes in word fluency were found. All abilities showed some decline by age sixty-seven, but the declines were modest until the eighties.

5. Research also revealed that age-related declines depend on the ability being measured.

6. Individual performance varied widely, with some showing stability and some showing decline. Schaie identified seven factors that reduce the risk of cognitive decline in old age.

7. Age-related decline in intellectual abilities is multifaceted and multidimensional.

    a. The onset and rate of decline differ for the various abilities and with gender.

    b. Number skills show the sharpest decline overall, and word fluency begins to decline the soonest.

    c. Environmental and personality factors account for the large differences in how long individuals maintain their mental abilities.

C. Fluid and crystallized intelligence

Horn studied fluid and crystallized intelligence, two general types of abilities, both of which are influenced by hereditary and environmental factors.

1. Two types of intelligence

    a. **Crystallized intelligence** refers to learned cognitive processes and primary abilities.

    b. **Fluid intelligence** is the ability to process new information in novel situations. It depends more on neurological development and less on education.

    c. Each type changes differently with age.

        i.   Crystallized intelligence improves or stabilizes with age.

        ii. Fluid intelligence peaks in late adolescence and declines rapidly from early adulthood to old age.

2. Negative assessment

    a. Fluid intelligence is seen as the most salient indicator of intellectual capacities since it allows a person to understand relations, comprehend implications, and draw inferences, and it is independent of cultural and experiential influences.

    b. Age-related declines in fluid intelligence result from accumulations of small losses of brain function.

    c. Conflicting views

        i. Horn's theory has been criticized on several grounds, primarily because it is based on cross-sectional research and confounds cohort differences with age differences.

        ii. Longitudinal research is criticized for painting a falsely positive picture.

        iii. Different patterns of age-related declines may be due to speed rather than to fluid-crystallized differences.

D. Practical intelligence and expertise

Performance on traditional laboratory problem-solving tasks decreases during the adult years, while performance in the real world increases at least through middle age. Traditional laboratory problem-solving tasks have limited value testing intellectual development in middle adulthood. **Practical intelligence** involves the application of intellectual skills to everyday activities, whereas **expertise** and **wisdom** refer to behaviors that require intelligence as well as specialized experience in specific domains.

1. Solving real world problems

    a. Performance on more practical problem-solving tasks increases from age twenty to age fifty and then declines after that.

    b. These findings are consistent with real-life experience, in which middle-aged adults typically are more knowledgeable than young adults.

2. Becoming an expert

    a. Experience is highly relevant to competence and much less relevant to abstract assessment of cognitive abilities.

    b. This explains why older adults hold many of the most responsible and challenging leadership positions in society but perform at lower levels on conventional psychometric and abstract problem-solving tasks than younger adults do.

    c. Despite declining fluid abilities, older adults continue to function efficiently when given tasks that allow them to use their expert knowledge.

    d. Skill appears to matter more than age in domain-specific tasks, whereas age is important in general, abstract tasks.

    e. Aging appears to lead to poorer performance in nonpracticed tasks and slower acquisition of new skills, particularly those that depend on new types of knowledge.

VIII. The adult learner

Adults have a variety of motivations for adult learning, including job or occupation, managing home and family, hobby or leisure time activity, and curiosity.

A. Adult education

   1. Adult education refers to all non-full-time educational activities.

   2. Most of the learning done by adults is self-planned, and these activities are very important to them.

   3. Life changes, or transitions, are often the impetus for adult learning.

   4. Triggers, a specific life event that generates the decision to learn at that time, often precipitate a transition.

   5. Career transitions are the most common trigger for men and women. Family is more often the trigger for women than for men.

   6. Family may also serve as a barrier to women pursuing adult education.

B. Returning to college

   1. Adults have been returning to college in record numbers.

   2. Typically adults return to college because they are dissatisfied with their lives and regard finishing their education as a way to improve themselves.

   3. Older students experience cognitive gains in critical thinking.

   4. Career development is the most frequent reason for returning to college in the middle years.

• Working with Carol Singer, associate dean of continuing education: Counseling students returning to college

IX. Work in middle adulthood

Midlife workers are confronted with fear of job loss and **plateauing**, which is reaching a point of constricted occupational opportunity. Mid-to-late-career stages are often accompanied by negative emotions and feelings of personal failure. Some workers experience **burnout**, disillusionment and exhaustion on the job.

A. Age and job satisfaction

   1. Older people are more satisfied with their jobs than younger people are.

   2. There appear to be distinctly different age satisfaction curves among nonprofessionals, elite professionals, and ordinary professionals.

B. Racial and ethnic minorities

    1. Racial and ethnic minorities are more likely to plateau or reach a glass ceiling before they reach their corporate dream.

    2. As minorities climb the corporate ladder, they become more isolated from same-sex or same-race superiors or peers. Their status becomes more obviously "token," and they are more likely to feel alienated.

    3. Minorities and women face problems that do not affect White males. As a result they must meet higher performance standards than White men, with fewer resources and more barriers.

C. Gender

    1. Men constitute the majority of full-time workers age fifty and older, and women comprise the majority of part-time workers.

    2. New family issues, like providing care for aging parents, may put pressure on midlife women's employment.

    3. Caregivers are more likely than other employees to report conflicts between work and family responsibilities and are more likely to miss work.

D. Unemployment

    1. Unemployed workers feel as if they are without part of themselves, since work is an important aspect of one's identity.

    2. Responses to job loss follow the stages of initial shock, relief/relaxation, efforts to become reemployed, frustration, and resignation to being out of work.

    3. Unemployment has a negative impact on physical, mental, and social well being.

    4. The psychological impact of unemployment may be greater for male workers than for female workers.

X. Change and growth

Key Concepts

Directions: Identify each of the key concepts discussed in this chapter.

1. _____, the statistically estimated number of years remaining in the life of an individual, has increased dramatically from 1900 to 1990.

2. _____ is normal aging, whereas _____ is due to pathological conditions, such as illness and disease.

3. Continuous and regular _____ counteracts the decline of cardiovascular functioning.

4. Strength peaks in _____ and then declines very slowly but steadily until about age fifty.

5. The ability of the lens of the eye to _____, or to change its shape to focus on things close by, declines by age fifty, when most people need _____.

6. ----- refers to the number of cases of a disease; _____ refers to the number of deaths.

7. The overall incidence of breast cancer is higher for _____ women than for _____ women. The death rate is greater for _____.

8. The most common type of cancer in men is _____. Mortality rate from this disease is higher among _____.

9. _____ is the gradual reduction of hormone production that leads to _____ in women and to _____ in men.

10. When the ovaries no longer produce eggs, hormone production is reduced, and menstruation ends, the female has reached _____.

11. _____ is the surgical removal of the ovaries. The surgical removal of the uterus is called _____.

12. Menopausal symptoms may be alleviated by _____, taking replacement estrogen in combination with progestin.

13. About one-third of postmenopausal women suffer from _____, the degeneration of bone.

14. One of the physical changes of the male climacteric is _____, the overgrowth of tissue in the prostate gland that may interfere with urine flow.

15. Research indicates that menopause does not significantly affect _____, which depends on androgens, not _____.

16. The most apparent physical change in male sexuality is the longer time required to attain _____.

17. _____ that compare groups of people of different ages at the same time often yield results that indicate intellectual _____ with increased age.

18. _____ that test the same participants periodically over an extended period of time often yield a _____ view of intellectual competence in middle adulthood.

19. Schaie's _____ indicate that _____ and _____ factors account for the large differences in how long individuals maintain their mental abilities .

20. _____ intelligence refers to abilities that are strongly influenced by formal education, such as vocabulary. In contrast, _____ intelligence represents abilities influenced by neurological development, such as reasoning. The latter skills _____ with age.

21. When we apply intellectual skills to everyday activities we are using _____. In contrast, _____ and _____ require intelligence and specialized experience in specific domains.

22. Research indicates that the most frequent reason adults to return to school is _____. In addition, women also report _____ -related reasons for seeking education.

23. _____ is reaching a point of constricted occupational opportunity, usually in mid-career. _____ occurs when workers become disillusioned and exhausted on the job.

24. The _____ is an invisible barrier that women and minorities confront as they approach the top of the corporate hierarchy.

25. The majority of full-time workers age fifty and older are _____. Most part-time workers in this age group are _____.

26. The initial reaction to job loss is often _____ followed by _____. Finally, _____ and _____ set in if the person is unsuccessful in becoming reemployed.

Multiple-Choice Self-Test

Factual Questions

1. The timing of middle adulthood depends on
    a. primary aging.
    b. secondary aging.
    c. life expectancy.
    d. organ reserve capacity.

2. Which of the following statements is *true*?
    a. The percentage of cigarettes smoked increases as alcohol consumption increases.
    b. The percentage of cigarettes smoked decreases as alcohol consumption increases.
    c. Smoking and alcohol consumption are not associated with one another.
    d. Alcoholic beverage preference is not related to smoking.

3. The incidence of breast cancer for women under age seventy is
    a. one in eight women.
    b. one in fourteen women.
    c. one in twelve women
    d. one in five women.

4. In a study examining the differences in the hypertension levels of black versus white Cuban participants, results indicated that the variable responsible for differences was
    a. Socioeconomic status.
    b. type of diet.
    c. race/ethnicity.
    d. geographic region.

5. In general, the most common sign of menopause is considered to be
    a. ceasing of menstruation.
    b. moodiness.
    c. the hot flash.
    d. depression.

6. Surgical removal of the ovaries is called
    a. hysterectomy.
    b. oophorectomy.
    c. hypertrophy.
    d. osteoporosis.

7. Cross-sectional studies may "create" age declines in intellectual performance because they
    a. confound cohort differences with age.
    b. confound neurological functioning with age.
    c. require multiple testing of individuals, which leads to fatigue and lowered performance.
    d. confound socioeconomic status with age.

8. According to Schaie's research, which primary ability is the only one to decline significantly by age fifty?
    a. Number skill
    b. Inductive reasoning
    c. Spatial orientation
    d. Word fluency

9. Which of the following statements is *true*?
    a. Fluid intelligence improves with age.
    b. Crystallized intelligence improves with age.
    c. Fluid and crystallized intelligence are not affected by age.
    d. Crystallized intelligence declines with age.

10. Which of the following is *not* a characteristic of the typical adult education participant?
    a. Being well educated
    b. Having a good income
    c. Living in the suburbs
    d. Holding a blue-collar job

Conceptual Questions

1. The year is 1910, Carla is forty-five years old, and she is white. Which stage of the life span is she in?
    a. Young adulthood
    b. Middle adulthood
    c. Late adulthood
    d. Carla was probably not alive because the life expectancy for females during the early part of the century was thirty-five years.

2. Which of the following physical changes is *not* normal in middle adulthood?
    a. Weight gain
    b. Changes in hair color
    c. Lowered amount of blood pumped with each heartbeat
    d. Loss of ability to lose body fat

3. Who is *most* likely to prefer liquor?
    a. Women
    b. Young men
    c. Middle-aged or older men
    d. Nonsmokers

4. Who is *least* likely to suffer from prostate cancer?
    a. Asian Americans
    b. African Americans
    c. Whites
    d. Native Americans

5. Nora is experiencing sleep disturbances, sudden hot flashes, and alterations in her menstrual cycle. Her doctor tells her she is experiencing the symptoms of menopause. Which doctor is *least* likely to prescribe replacement hormones for her?
    a.   A doctor educated in the United States
    b.   A doctor educated in Japan
    c.   A doctor educated in Canada
    d.   All of the above doctors are equally likely to prescribe medication

6. Rita recently had a hysterectomy. Which experience is she likely to have?
    a.   She now definitely has menopause.
    b.   She may or may not have menopause.
    c.   She must now be on estrogen replacement therapy.
    d.   She must now be on hormone replacement therapy.

7. Dave is unable to determine the best route to his destination even though he is reading a map. Which skill is he limited in?
    a.   Inductive reasoning
    b.   Verbal meaning
    c.   Spatial orientation
    d.   Number skill

8. Tom is a sixty-one year old mechanical engineer. He is currently installing a sophisticated sprinkler system in his garden.   We can say that Tom is using
    a.   practical intelligence.
    b.   fluid intelligence.
    c.   crystallized intelligence.
    d.   expertise.

9. A group of surgical nurses is asked to perform a medical procedure. Who is likely to perform better?
    a.   Older nurses
    b.   Younger nurses
    c.   Expert nurses
    d.   Novice nurses

10. Who is *most* likely to participate in adult education?
    a.   A forty year old woman
    b.   A sixty-two year old man
    c.   A sixty-two year old woman
    d.   Men in general

Answer Key

Key Concepts

1.   Life expectancy
2.   Primary aging; secondary aging
3.   exercise
4.   early adulthood

5.   accommodate; reading glasses
6.   Morbidity; mortality
7.   white; African American; African Americans
8.   prostate; African American men
9.   Climacteric; menopause; decreased fertility
10.   menopause
11.   Oophorectomy; hysterectomy
12.   hormone replacement therapy
13.   osteoporosis
14.   hypertrophy
15.   sexual drive; estrogen
16.   an erection
17.   Cross-sectional studies; decline
18.   Longitudinal studies; positive
19.   sequential studies; environmental; personality
20.   Crystallized; fluid; decline
21.   practical intelligence; expertise; wisdom
22.   career development/transitions; family
23.   Plateauing; Burnout
24.   glass ceiling
25.   men; women
26.   shock/anger/disbelief; relief/relaxation; frustration; resignation

Multiple-Choice Self-Test / Factual Questions

1.   Choice (c) is correct; life expectancy is the statistically estimated probable number of years remaining in the life of an individual based on a probability that members of his or her cohort will die at particular ages. Choice (a), primary aging, is normal aging. Choice (b), secondary aging, is pathological aging. Choice (d), organ reserve, is the extra capacity of various organs of the body to respond to stressful situations.

2.   Choice (a) is correct; research indicates a positive correlation between smoking and alcohol consumption. Consequently, choices (b) and (c) are incorrect. Choice (d) is incorrect; alcoholic beverage preference is related to smoking in that liquor drinkers smoke most and wine drinkers smoke least.

3.   Choice (b) is correct, threfore choices (c) and (d) are incorrect. Choice (a), the incidence is one in eight for women who live to be ninety-five.

4.   Choice (a) is correct; research results indicate that inequality leads to higher levels of hypertension partially because it limits access to better quality health care and leads to more health-compromising behaviors. Choice (c) is incorrect in that results did not support the hypothesis that race/ethnicity is responsible for differences in levels of hypertension. Choices (b) and (d) are incorrect in that the study did not examine the influences of diet and area of residence on hypertension.

5.   Choice (c) is correct; the hot flash is a sensation of internally generated heat beginning in the chest and moving to the face and the rest of the body; 50 to 75 percent of Western women experience the hot flash for about two to three years. Choice (a), the ceasing of menstruation, is one of the defining properties of menopause and generally occurs some time after the hot

flashes have started. Choices (b) and (d), moodiness and depression in mid-life women are not supported by data.

6. Choice (b) is correct. Choice (a), hysterectomy, is the surgical removal of the uterus. Choice (c), hypertrophy, is the overgrowth of tissue in the prostate gland. Choice (d), osteoporosis, is the degeneration of bone.

7. Choice (a) is correct; a cohort is an age group whose members experience major world events at about the same age. Data collected via the cross-sectional design may represent the influences of cohort rather than chronological age. Choices (b) and (d), neurological functioning and socioeconomic status are not related to the cross-sectional design in any way. Choice (c), multiple testing of subjects is a characteristic of the longitudinal design, not the cross-sectional design.

8. Choice (d) is correct; word fluency is the only primary ability that clearly decreased in middle adulthood. Choices (a), (b), and (c) showed modest decline by age 67.

9. Choice (b) is correct; crystallized intelligence is influenced by experience and formal education and increases with age. Therefore, choices (c) and (d) are incorrect. Choice (a), fluid intelligence, peaks during adolescence and decreases with age.

10. Choice (d) is correct; most adult education participants hold white-collar jobs. Choices (a), (b), and (c) are characteristic of adult education participants.

Multiple-Choice Self-Test / Conceptual Questions

1. Choice (c) is correct; in the year 1900 the life expectancy for white females was 48.7 years. Consequently, 45 years of age corresponded to late adulthood. The other choices are incorrect.

2. Choice (d) is correct; regular endurance-type exercise leads to loss of body fat in middle and late adulthood as it does in younger years. Choices (a), (b), and (c) represent normal physical changes of middle adulthood.

3. Choice (c) is correct; liquor drinkers tend to be middle-aged and older men. Choices (a) and (d), women and nonsmokers, tend to prefer wine. Choice (b) is incorrect in that young men tend to prefer beer.

4. Choice (d) is correct; research indicates that the incidence of prostate cancer is lowest among Native Americans. The highest incidence is found among African Americans, choice (b), followed by whites, choice (c), and Asian Americans, choice (a).

5. Choice (b) is correct; research indicates that Japanese doctors prescribe medication and surgery very infrequently in order to treat the symptoms of menopause. Therefore, choice (d) is incorrect. In contrast, North American doctors, choices (a) and (c), are most likely to view menopause as an illness and to treat its symptoms with medication.

6. Choice (b) is correct; hysterectomy sometimes triggers menopause. Choice (a), surgical removal of the ovaries (oophorectomy), always triggers menopause. Choices (c) and (d), hormone therapy, may or may not be prescribed to menopausal women depending upon the nature and extent of their symptoms and their doctor's training.

7. Choice (c) is correct; people with limitations in spatial orientation skills may have difficulty in reading a map. Choice (a), inductive reasoning, is the ability to follow logical rules in decision making. Choice (b), verbal meaning, is understanding word and sentence meanings. Choice (d), number skill, is the ability to use numbers in simple arithmetic.

8. Choice (d) is correct; expertise refers to behaviors that require intelligence as well as specialized experience in specific domains. In this case, specialized knowledge in engineering is providing Tom with task-specific skills. Choice (a), practical intelligence, is applying intelligence to everyday problems and activities. Choice (b), fluid intelligence, is the ability to deal with new, never-before-encountered information. Choice (c), crystallized intelligence is the knowledge of world facts and general information.

9. Choice (c) is correct; research indicates that experience and skills override age in influencing performance ability. Consequently, choices (a), (b), and (d) are incorrect.

10. Choice (c) is correct; older women are more likely to participate in adult learning than middle-aged women, who are often pressured by employment, child rearing, and homemaking responsibilities. Also, women are more likely than men to seek education in adulthood. Consequently, choices (a), (b), and (d) are incorrect.

CHAPTER 15

Psychosocial Development in Middle Adulthood

Learning Objectives

1. Describe people's conceptions about stability and change in personality during the adult years.
2. Summarize Jung's view of personality and middle-age development.
3. Define social-clock projects, normative life events, and nonnormative life events.
4. Describe Erikson's generativity versus stagnation stage.
5. Compare and contrast the views that support the notion of a midlife crisis, no midlife crisis, and normative personality change.
6. Discuss the stability of personality in adulthood in relationship to the Big Five dimensions of personality.
7. Discuss the usefulness of the Mills College study in understanding female adult development.
8. Explain how identity status is related to midlife adaptations.
9. Describe the characteristics of successful long-term marriages.
10. Discuss marital satisfaction during the family life cycle.
11. Discuss the impact of divorce during middle adulthood.
12. Compare the effects of adolescent children and young adult children on parents.
13. Describe and compare the empty nest and the multigenerational household.
14. Discuss the role of grandparents in middle-age adulthood, including off-time grandparenthood and grandparents as surrogate parents.
15. Discuss the changing relationship between middle-aged adults and their aging parents.
16. Describe middle-aged sibling relationships, including how siblings might deal with a family crisis.
17. Discuss middle-aged adults' responses to parental death.
18. Discuss leisure activities across the lifespan and identify the variables that influence leisure-time activities.
19. Distinguish between wills and advance directives and discuss the role of long-term planning in the middle adult years.

Chapter Outline

I. A multiplicity of images of middle age

   A. Many images, often contradictory, exist of middle age. Like early adulthood, there is much variability to middle adulthood.

   B. People tend to believe that following an increase in desirable traits in early adulthood, there is a moderate decrease in middle age, paralleling an increase in undesirable traits in old age.

C. Perceptions of life periods vary by social class, gender, and age.

II. Crisis or no crisis?

  A. Developmental theories reveal differing perspectives on the experience of midlife.

    1. Carl Jung identified the midlife years as the time when men and women become more balanced in terms of their nurturant and assertive tendencies.

    2. Helson takes a normative perspective of adult development whereby the social clock regulates appropriateness of the timing of life events.

    3. Erikson believed that middle-aged individuals experience a normative crisis in the task of generativity versus stagnation. Some researchers question whether Erikson's theory applies well to women.

    4. Stage theories of adult development focus on midlife crisis as a normal component of midlife. A **midlife crisis** refers to the radical changes within the personality associated with the adult's reexamination of goals, priorities, and life accomplishments in middle age.

  B. Normative-crisis models: Midlife crisis

    1. Gould found the transformation of middle adulthood to be the most significant one in adulthood.

      a. Individuals begin to confront the long-held assumption of immortality resulting in a need to question and reassess priorities.

      b. How an individual negotiates the midlife crisis determines the individual's adaptation to old age.

    2. Vaillant argues that midlife brings forth a sense of life's limits and a need to use time wisely.

      a. Pain during the forties is seen as preparation for entering a new stage.

      b. A heightened self-awareness results and leads to further growth and opens the way for a sense of generativity.

    3. Using the biographical method, Levinson found that men come to terms with the Dream and how it didn't come to fruition; based on this, men revise the Dream and make changes in lifestyle.

      a. Drastic changes are made by some men; for others, the change is still important though less obvious.

      b. Men struggle within the self and the external world, and if this struggle is not experienced, a later developmental crisis is likely to occur.

    4.   Women may experience a midlife reappraisal but Levinson provides little evidence of crisis.

        a.   Women tend to experience nurturance and investment in relationships rather than a normative midlife crisis.

        b.   Women's lives include developmental tensions throughout adulthood rather than a predictable crisis at midlife.

        c.   Issues of identity, intimacy, and generativity typically occur simultaneously rather than sequentially.

C. No crisis

    1.   The evidence for midlife crisis comes from clinical impressions from people seeking help dealing with issues related to their stage of life or from nonrandomly selected samples.

    2.   The frequency of midlife crisis is overestimated by clinicians.

    3.   When middle-aged individuals are randomly selected, they rarely report a crisis.

    4.   Costa and McCrea argue that roles change with age, but roles are not personality. Rather they focus on the **trait** as a dimension of psychological functioning.

        a.   Traits contribute to the person's basic tendencies.

        b.   Specific behaviors may change, but basic tendencies do not.

    5.   Cross-sectional studies show little consistency of traits.

        a.   Longitudinal studies show that personality is quite stable after about age thirty.

        b.   Since personality is highly predictable over long periods of time, it enables individuals to prepare for successful aging.

D. Normative personality change

    1.   Another position, a timing of events approach, found considerable stability from early through middle adulthood.

    2.   They also found evidence for normative personality change, change in the same direction in accordance with the social expectations of their cohort.

    3.   Changes associated with roles were often related to issues of identity and intimacy.

    4.   Change associated with personality types was related to the four statuses of identity formation: foreclosed, diffused, moratorium, and achieved.

III. Marriage and divorce

A. Long-term marriage

1. Research reveals that in discussing pleasant topics, elderly couples were more affectionate than middle-aged couples, while middle-aged couples displayed more interest, humor, anger, and disgust.

2. When discussing conflict in their relationship, older couples managed to express higher levels of affection and lower levels of negative feelings toward their partners.

3. Positive emotions are more likely to emerge in happy marriages than in unhappy marriages, even when discussing marital conflict.

4. Wives show more emotion and a greater range of emotions than husbands, while husbands show more defensiveness.

5. Husbands and wives mention very similar qualities to which they attribute long-term marriage.

B. The family life cycle

1. The **family life cycle** is a series of predictable stages through which families pass.

2. Families are placed into stages based on the ages of the children and the age of the wife.

3. The different stages of the family life cycle are associated with different levels of marital satisfaction.

4. Gender role attitudes correlated with household involvement of husbands and wives.

a. More stage I and II families were characterized by equal partnerships.

b. In stage III and IV families, the wives were likely to be modern and the husband traditional.

5. Gender role attitudes are correlated with employment of stage I and II wives; when husbands and wives were both traditional, the young wife was unlikely to be employed.

6. Wives reported distress when their husbands experienced competing demands, and the husbands reported distress when their wives spent large amounts of time at work.

7. Family life stage was highly correlated with strain for dual-earner families.

a. Younger dual-earner husbands experienced more strain than older ones.

b. Younger families experience higher role strain between occupational and family demands than middle-aged and older couples.

c.   The husband's role strain differentiates the harried families from the calmer ones.

8.   Middle-aged families are happier than those in the earlier stages.

a.   Marital satisfaction follows a curvilinear path over the family life cycle.

b.   The presence of younger children creates demand, lowering marital interaction and happiness.

c.   In long-term marriages, marital satisfaction dips during the childrearing years.

d.   Children are rated as the largest source of marital conflict for middle-aged couples.

• Focusing On: The effects of middle-aged adult children's problems on older parents

C.   Midlife divorce

1.   Most divorces occur before middle age.

2.   Divorce during middle adulthood has a significant impact on women, men, and their children.

a.   Divorce can represent entry into a lifetime single status.

b.   For wives, separation and divorce usually lower the standard of living significantly.

c.   For husbands, divorce or separation usually means that they see their children far less often, since custody of young children is frequently awarded to mothers. This has implications for the father-child relations and the well-being of men after age fifty.

d.   For young adult children, divorce can have significant effects depending in part upon the levels of predivorce marital conflict.

e.   Recent parental divorce is associated with reduced intimacy and contact between fathers and their children.

f.   Lack of contact between fathers and children of recent divorce may be due to lack of interest on the part of the father, ongoing conflict with the ex-wife, forcing children to take sides, personal problems, and geographic distance.

3.   Fathers may lack kinkeeping skills, which are skills that keep the individual in touch with other family members.

4.   Parental divorce does not influence the amount of contact between young adults and their grandparents.

IV. Family relationships

Middle-aged adults have been called the **sandwich generation**; they are caught between the needs of adjacent generations.

    A. Delayed parenthood. For many reasons, couples may delay starting a family. These older parents may be better prepared and adapt more easily to parenthood.

    B. Adolescent children

        1. Adolescent children have the most detrimental impact on marital satisfaction.

        2. An authoritative parenting style promotes adolescent development.

        3. Having an adolescent may cause an adult to reassess his or her own self and goals, and this may cause crises.

        4. For some families, adolescence is characterized by reduced interaction and closeness with families; this may not be true for all families, especially African American families, where the family represents a safe haven and where higher levels of parental control and family intimacy are reported.

        5. Research reveals that there is conflict over control in every culture and in every historical period.

    C. Young adult children

        1. The parent-child relationship changes when the child becomes an adult.

        2. Young adult children do not necessarily become fully independent and may rely on their parents for financial and emotional support, and they may return home for holidays, summer vacations, and whenever they feel the need.

        3. When children are in their forties and their parents in their seventies, the support tends to shift from parent to child to child to parent, although ethnicity and family income may influence the flow of money between generations.

        4. An "empty nest" generally results in improved marital satisfaction and opportunities for self-development and autonomy and even employment for wives.

        5. Wives appear to benefit more than husbands from the empty nest.

        6. Multigenerational households. Many young adults never leave home or return one or more times to the parental household.

            a. Children's marital status is the best predictor of coresiding.

            b. All racial and ethnic minorities are more likely than Whites to live in multigenerational households.

            c. Coresiding adults and their parents influence each other and monitor each other. This can lead to conflict.

d. Coresidence works best when young adult children are mature, employed, or in school.

• Working with Joan Stone, victim advocate: Helping victims of abusive family relationships

D. Grandparenting

1. In general, couples become grandparents in their late forties and early fifties, and the role of grandparenting is likely to last three or four decades.

2. Timing affects how people experience the transition to grandparenting.

a. "Right time" grandparenting is in late middle age and can be a positive experience. Very early "off-time" grandparenting can be very distressing.

b. Social class influences timing of grandparenthood.

3. Grandparents are generally viewed as a valuable resource. The way that resource is used depends on the family's circumstances.

a. Grandparents can provide a sense of family continuity and family history.

b. Grandparents can provide substantial assistance to their adult children and grandchildren.

4. Some gender differences exist in how grandparents view their relationships with their grandchildren.

a. Grandmothers report greater satisfaction from relationships with their grandchildren than grandfathers.

b. Grandfathers place greater stress on generational extension of the family and indulging grandchildren.

5. Sometimes grandparents are called on to become surrogate parents.

a. Some reasons for grandparents parenting their grandchildren are teenage mothers, parental joblessness, drug addiction, emotional problems, mental problems, incarceration, and AIDS.

b. The role is associated with both challenges and rewards.

6. Effectiveness of grandparents. Research suggests possible racial and ethnic differences in self-perceptions among grandparents and perceptions of grandchildren. Social class, unemployment, moving away from home, and marital status are confounding variables.

• A Multicultural View: Diversity in intergenerational families

E. Aging parents

    1. As middle-aged adults become grandparents, their own parents are likely to be reaching late adulthood; middle-aged adults and their aging parents report high levels of regard, closeness, warmth, and satisfaction.

    2. Still-healthy aging parents tend to provide the most financial and emotional support to their children. Parents seem to give to their children in one way or another for as long as they are able.

    3. Young-old parents tend to give more aid, while old-old parents tend to receive more aid.

    4. Middle-aged adult children are second only to spouses in providing care to frail, aging parents. Daughters tend to be the principal caregivers, with sons tending to do more home repair and maintenance tasks; when acting as primary caregivers, sons tend to be managers rather than direct providers of care.

F. Siblings

    1. Sibling relationships are among age peers and therefore last longer, are more egalitarian, more sociable, and more like friendships than other family relationships.

    2. Sometimes siblings increase contact and get closer in middle adulthood as they face family crises and transitions.

    3. Marriage separates siblings and reduces contact.

    4. Helping aging parents is a new developmental task for middle-age siblings.

        a. Siblings go through a series of stages as they face this challenge.

        b. Parental caregiving arrangements can be a source of conflict for middle-aged siblings.

V. Bereavement

A parent's death involves many emotions because of the intensity and uniqueness of the parent-child relationship. **Bereavement** is the process of getting over another person's death.

A. Mourning for one's parents

    1. Three tasks are evident as middle-aged children mourn the death of parents. Each task focuses on a different aspect of the child's relationship to the deceased parent.

        a. Stocktaking involves the exploration of changes.

        b. The reminiscence task involves recalling harsh and meaningful memories.

        c. Internalization and passage involve discussion about the present without denying the past.

B. Bereavement and growth

1. Bereavement for a parent during middle age may promote personal growth and maturity and help to resolve developmental tasks.

2. Research reveals that after the parent's death, there is a time of upheaval and a change in outlook on life.

C. Reactions to grief

1. Increased psychological distress and reduced sense of personal mastery are initial reactions to parental death.

2. Unresolved grief reactions include depression, thoughts of suicide, and other psychiatric symptoms.

3. Initial and residual grief is influenced by the expectedness of the parent's death, the extent of filial autonomy, age, and gender.

4. Many middle-aged adults deny the impact of the loss and express their feelings of pain through physical symptoms more than younger or older adults do.

a. Younger adults may be protected by their greater physical capacities and sense of invulnerability, which act as buffers against the strain of readjustment.

b. Older adults are better prepared for the death of another, as they are preparing for their own deaths.

c. The deaths of spouses and siblings are most likely to affect middle-aged adults because they are members of the same generation.

VI. Leisure

A. Because of the many changes in midlife, adults often feel less constrained.

B. **Leisure** is choosing whatever activities one enjoys and participating in them at one's own pace.

C. The same activities can have different meanings for different individuals.

D. As people enter middle age, their view of leisure shifts.

1. Validation and gratification may come from leisure activities.

2. A shift occurs from activities requiring physical exertion and high-intensity involvement to more sedentary, moderate-intensity activities.

3. There is also some continuity in level and types of leisure activities over the life course.

E. Higher socioeconomic status is associated with greater leisure involvement.

F. Racial and ethnic minorities have more limited leisure options.

G. Gender affects the leisure activities people choose.

1. Women tend to engage in social and home-based activities and in cultural activities.

2. Men are more likely to be involved in exercise and outdoor recreation, to attend spectator sports, and to travel.

H. Involvement in leisure activities seems to promote psychological well-being.

1. The degree of satisfaction is more important than the number and types of activities.

2. Pursuing satisfying leisure activities is good preparation for the life changes associated with late adulthood.

VII. Preparing for late adulthood

A. Aging changes activities and perspectives in predictable ways. Taking more responsibility for one's own life increases one's sense of mortality.

B. A will is important even if the person does not have property; a will can describe after-death choices.

1. An **advance directive** is a legal document specifying what medical care can be given in the event the person becomes unable to make or communicate his or her decisions. There are two types of advance directives.

a. A **living will** notifies the person's physician of his or her wishes regarding the withdrawal of life-sustaining equipment even if the result is death.

b. A **durable power of attorney for health care** designates a person to make medical decisions on your behalf other than the withdrawal of life-support systems.

2. Middle age is the optimal time to make decisions about long-term care.

3. Planning for retirement financially and psychologically is another developmental task of middle age.

VIII. Looking back/looking forward

A. Continuity within change

B. Lifelong growth

C. Changing meaning and vantage points

D. Developmental diversity

Key Concepts

Directions: Identify each of the key concepts discussed in this chapter.

1. Age-related expectations about one's goals and activities, such as marriage and career development, are termed _____.

2. Retirement, which is a life event associated with chronological age, is an example of a _____ life event.

3. _____ occur in the lives of some but not all people, and they are not associated with a particular age or life period.

4. Erikson's seventh psychosocial stage is termed _____.

5. When mid-life adults reexamine their goals, priorities, and accomplishments with resultant changes within their personalities, they are said to be going through a _____.

6. When we view developmental change as a series of distinct periods that are influenced by physical and cognitive performance, we are using the _____.

7. A _____ is a relatively enduring disposition of the individual.

8. The _____ is a series of predictable stages that families experience based on the age of the children.

9. Marital satisfaction follows a _____ path; it is high before _____ and _____, and it is at its lowest when the children are _____.

10. Remarriage is most likely for women who are _____ and have _____ children.

11. Middle-aged adults have been called the _____ because they are caught between the needs of their aging parents and their children.

12. Middle-aged parents with children in college live in what is called _____ because children return for holidays, summer vacations, and whenever they feel the need.

13. Early _____ grandparenthood may be caused by teenage pregnancy.

14. A family structure that has more generations but fewer people in each generation is referred to as the _____ family structure.

15. When aging parents need care, _____ are more likely to provide care than _____, regardless of the gender composition of the sibling group.

16. Siblings have _____ emotional ties, such as loyalty, that are triggered by _____.

17. _____ is the process of getting over another person's death.

18. Because our society does not support overreacting to loss of loved ones, many people express feelings of grief of losing a parent through _____.

19. Activities chosen freely and enjoyed at one's own pace are called _____ activities.

20. A legal document specifying what medical care can be given in the event the person becomes unable to make or communicate decisions is called a(n) _____.

21. A _____ is a legal document that informs doctors of a person's wishes regarding the withdrawal of life-sustaining equipment even if the result is death.

22.   A legal document designating someone to make medical decisions on another person's behalf other than the withdrawal of life support systems is called a(n) _____.

Multiple-Choice Self-Test

Factual Questions

1.   Having experienced the Great Depression when one was in his or her 40s is an example of
    a.   a normative life event.
    b.   a nonnormative life event.
    c.   an instance of generativity.
    d.   an instance of stagnation.

2.   Who conducted the UCLA study on the psychosocial development of adult males?
    a.   George Vaillant
    b.   Daniel Levinson
    c.   Erik Erikson
    d.   Roger Gould

3.   The difference between cross-sectional and longitudinal data on the stability of traits is that
    a.   cross-sectional data indicates stability.
    b.   longitudinal data indicates stability.
    c.   longitudinal data indicates large-age related changes.
    d.   longitudinal data is inconsistent.

4.   Who were the primary participants of the Mills Longitudinal Study?
    a.   Middle-aged males and females.
    b.   Middle-aged females.
    c.   Middle-aged males.
    d.   Females of an average age of twenty-one.

5.   Which of the following is a reported by wives but not husbands as a perceived reason for successful long-term marriages?
    a.   Liking one's mate as a person
    b.   Viewing marriage as a sacred institution
    c.   Viewing mate as a best friend
    d.   Expressing affection in similar ways

6.   Which of the following statements is true?
    a.   Divorce is most disruptive to father-child relationships when it occurs early in the child's life.
    b.   Divorce is most disruptive to father-child relationships when it occurs late in the child's life.
    c.   Approximately 75 percent of children of divorce have infrequent contact with the noncustodial parent.
    d.   Approximately 80 percent of young adult children of divorced parents have weekly contacts with absent fathers.

7. Who benefits the most from the empty nest?
   a. Fathers
   b. Mothers
   c. Both parents benefit equally
   d. Neither parent benefits

8. Which of the following statements is true?
   a. Grandmothers but not grandfathers place value on sharing wisdom with grandchildren.
   b. Grandfathers but not grandmothers view the relationship with a grandchild as central.
   c. Grandfathers but not grandmothers are concerned with the continuity of the family line.
   d. Grandfathers but not grandmothers are concerned with the continuity of family experiences.

9. If a person is unable to make his or her own medical decisions, a legal document can specify this information. This document is called a(n)
   a. living will.
   b. durable power of attorney for health care.
   c. affidavit.
   d. advance directive.

10. A legal document that allows one person to make medical decisions on another person's behalf is called a(n)
    a. living will.
    b. durable power of attorney for health care.
    c. affidavit.
    d. advance directive.

Conceptual Questions

1. Forty-seven-year-old Gary has recently decided that he and his wife should have a child even though they had agreed to remain child-free when they first married fourteen years ago. He's also considering the possibility of starting his own accounting business and quitting his job at the large firm where he has worked for eighteen years. Vaillant would claim that Gary is experiencing
   a. generativity.
   b. neuroticism.
   c. extroversion.
   d. mid-life crises.

2. Emily is a very organized person; she's also persistent and motivated to achieve. Costa and McCrea would describe Emily as displaying
   a. openness to experience.
   b. extroversion.
   c. Conscientiousness.
   d. agreeableness.

3. According to the findings of the Mills Longitudinal Study, which statement is correct?
    a. Identity status is more important than roles in predicting a woman's ability to change successfully.
    b. Roles are more important than identity status in predicting a woman's ability to change successfully.
    c. By middle age, identity diffused women had married.
    d. By middle age, foreclosed women had ended their traditional marriages.

4. Adam and Maryann have been married for seventeen years. Their twin daughters are fifteen years old. What is their level of marital satisfaction?
    a. It is high but not as high as when they first married.
    b. It is at its highest.
    c. It is at its lowest.
    d. It is low but not as low as when the children were preschoolers.

5. Valerie and Kevin are both in their forties, and they will soon become first-time parents. How will they adjust to parenthood?
    a. In comparison to "on-time" parents, they will experience more stress.
    b. In comparison to "on-time" parents, their level of marital satisfaction will decline dramatically.
    c. They will be better prepared than "on-time" parents and adapt more easily.
    d. Their ability to adapt will be similar to that of "on-time" parents.

6. In comparison to white adolescents, African American adolescents
    a. report significantly higher levels of family control.
    b. report significantly less family intimacy.
    c. experience higher parent-adolescent conflict.
    d. disengage from their parents much earlier.

7. Which of the following scenarios is most likely?
    a. Irene is a white grandmother and is the primary caregiver of her six-year-old grandson.
    b. Irene is an African American grandmother and is the primary caregiver of her six-year-old grandson.
    c. Irene is a Hispanic grandmother and is the primary caregiver of her six-year-old grandson.
    d. Irene is an Asian grandmother and is the primary caregiver of her six-year-old grandson.

8. Beverly and Gina recently lost their seventy-two-year-old mother. They are now concerned about caring for their father and wondering about what to do with the house they inherited from their mother. Dane would describe Beverly and Gina's experience as
    a. stocktaking.
    b. reminiscence of memories.
    c. internalization and passage.
    d. despair.

9. Beverly and Gina recently lost their seventy-two-year-old mother. What are they likely to feel is the best resource in helping them cope with their loss?
    a. Spouses
    b. Religion
    c. Friends
    d. Their work

10. Lila is spending a leisurely day. She is most likely to be
    a. playing tennis.
    b. attending an art exhibit.
    c. either a or b
    d. neither a nor b

Answer Key

Key Concepts

1.   social clock projects
2.   normative
3.   nonnormative life events
4.   generativity versus stagnation
5.   mid-life crisis
6.   normative crisis model
7.   trait
8.   family life cycle
9.   curvilinear; the birth of the first child; when the children leave home/couple retires; adolescents
10. younger; fewer
11. "sandwich generation"
12. semiautonomous households
13. off-time
14. beanpole
15. daughters; sons
16. dormant; crises
17. Bereavement
18. physical symptoms
19. leisure
20. advance directive
21. living will
22. durable power of attorney for health care

Multiple-Choice Self-Test / Factual Questions

1.   Choice (b) is correct; nonnormative life events are not associated with any particular age. Choice (a), normative life events, are age-related. Choices (c) and (d), generativity and stagnation, are the positive and negative outcomes, respectively, of Erikson's seventh psychosocial stage of development.

2.   Choice (d) is correct. Roger Gould conducted the UCLA study. The other choices are incorrect.

3.   Choice (b) is correct; longitudinal data indicates stability of traits after about age thirty. Choice (a), cross-sectional data, is inconsistent. Choices (c) and (d) are incorrect.

4.   Choice (d) is correct; the primary participants of the Mills Longitudinal Study were young females, about twenty-one years of age. The other choices are incorrect.

5. Choice (d) is correct; wives but not husbands report agreement on expression of affection as a reason for successful long-term marriages. Choices (a), (b), and (c) are reasons reported by both husbands and wives.

6. Choice (a) is correct; divorce disrupts the father-child relationship most if it occurs when the child is younger. Choice (b) is therefore incorrect. Choice (c) is incorrect in that about 13 to 51 percent of children have infrequent contact with the noncustodial parent. Choice (d) is incorrect in that about 60 percent of young adult children of divorced parents have weekly contacts with absent fathers.

7. Choice (b) is correct; mothers tend to benefit more from the empty nest, probably because they are now free of doing the second shift or because they have put off or limited their independent activities until now. The other choices are incorrect.

8. Choice (c) is correct; grandfathers are more concerned with the continuation of the family line. Choices (a) and (b) are incorrect because both grandparents emphasize sharing wisdom with grandchildren and view the relationship with the grandchild as central in their lives. Choice (d) is incorrect because grandmothers are concerned with the continuity of family experiences.

9. Choice (d) is correct; an advance directive is a document that specifies what medical care can be given to an individual if the person becomes unable to make his or her own decisions. Choice (a), a living will, informs doctors about the person's wishes regarding life support. Choice (b), a durable power of attorney for health care, is a document that designates someone to make medical decisions on behalf of another individual. Choice (c) is incorrect.

10. Choice (b) is correct; a durable power of attorney for health care allows a person to make medical decisions on someone else's behalf. Choice (a), a living will, informs doctors about the person's wishes regarding life support. Choice (d), an advance directive, specifies what medical care can be given to someone if he or she becomes unable to make decisions. Choice (c) is incorrect.

Multiple-Choice Self-Test / Conceptual Questions

1. Choice (d) is correct; it is common for people to reexamine their earlier choices and to make necessary changes at the midpoint of life. Choice (a), generativity, is the positive outcome of Erikson's seventh psychosocial stage. Choice (b), neuroticism, is the tendency to experience negative emotions, such as anger and fear. Choice (c), extroversion, is sociability and a general tendency to experience good spirits and joy.

2. Choice (c) is correct; conscientiousness is associated with organization, eagerness to achieve, and persistence. Choice (a), openness to experience, involves being imaginative and curious and welcoming new experiences. Choice (b), extroversion, is sociability and a tendency to experience good spirits and joy. Choice (d), agreeableness, is a tendency for sympathy, trust, altruism, and cooperativeness.

3. Choice (a) is correct and choice (b) is incorrect. Choice (c) is incorrect in that middle-aged identity diffused women tended to have remained single. Choice (d) is incorrect in that middle-aged foreclosed women continued their traditional marriages.

4.   Choice (c) is correct; marital satisfaction is at its lowest when the children are adolescents. Choice (b) is incorrect in that marital satisfaction is at its highest before the birth of the first child and after the children leave home and the couple retires. Therefore, choices (a) and (d) are incorrect.

5.   Choice (c) is correct; older parents adjust to parenthood more easily than younger/on-time parents. Choice (a) is incorrect because they experience less stress. Choices (b) and (d) are inaccurate.

6.   Choice (a) is correct; African American adolescents report more family control and more family intimacy - therefore, choice (b) is incorrect. Choice (c) is incorrect in that parent-adolescent conflict in African American families is reduced by the shared intimacy. Choice (d) is incorrect.

7.   Choice (b) is correct; in 13 percent of African American households children are raised by their grandparents without their parents being present. The other choices are incorrect.

8.   Choice (a) is correct; stocktaking involves exploration of changes caused by the parent's death. The second task of mourning, choice (b), is reminiscence of harsh and meaningful memories, and this involves reviewing memories that were negative as well as those that were positive. Choice (c), internalization and passage, the third and final task of mourning, involves discussion about the present without denying the past. Choice (d) is incorrect.

9.   Choice (c) is correct; research indicates that people report friends as the most important resource in helping them cope with a parent's death. Choice (a), spouses, are reported as the fourth most important choice. Choice (b), religion, is reported as the sixth most important choice. Choice (d), work, is reported as the fifth most important choice.

10.   Choice (b) is correct; women are more likely to spend their leisure time engaged in social, home-based, and cultural activities. Choice (a) is incorrect in that men are more likely to engage in physical activity as part of their leisure. Choices (c) and (d) are incorrect.

CHAPTER 16

Physical and Cognitive Development in Late Adulthood

Learning Objectives

1. Define ageism and discuss the use of stereotypes of aging..
2. Discuss the changes that have occurred in life expectancy and resulting effects on population growth and distribution.
3. Identify the leading causes of death in the elderly and discuss gender and race differences in mortality.
4. Differentiate between cellular and programming theories of aging.
5. Define the Hayflick limit and the Telomere hypothesis and explain what these concepts suggest bout aging.
6. Distinguish between primary aging and secondary aging.
7. Discuss the aging changes in skin, nervous system, bone, and muscle, as well as the changes in the cardiovascular and respiratory systems.
8. List the risk factors of osteoporosis.
9. Describe the changes that occur in the various sensory systems especially visual and auditory changes.
10. Identify behaviors that promote or detract from health and fitness during the later years.
11. Discuss sexual function in late adulthood.
12. Discuss concerns about alcohol consumption and prescription drug use among the elderly.
13. Describe cardiovascular disease, cancer, and arthritis, emphasizing risk factors and means of reducing risk.
14. Define wisdom and differentiate between cognitive mechanisms and cognitive pragmatics.
15. Define plasticity and discuss the roles of environmental conditions and training in brain functioning.
16. Describe the changes in the brain associated with aging and distinguish between acute and chronic brain syndromes.
17. Compare and contrast multi-infarct dementia, Alzheimer's disease, and senile dementia.
18. Discuss depression and the risk of suicide in late adulthood.
19. Distinguish between continuous work and discontinuous work patterns.
20. List and explain Atchley's phases of retirement.

Chapter Outline

I. Aging and ageism

   A. Societies differ in their treatment of the elderly. In some societies, old age is revered.

B. In the United States, elderly people are viewed negatively, although this was not always the case. Age bias has changed dramatically in the United States over the past three centuries.

C. **Ageism** is the systematic stereotyping of and discrimination against people because they are old.

   1. Stereotypes can be positive or negative.

   2. Because stereotypes are based on generalizations of old people rather than on actual appraisals of individuals, they reflect preconceived notions or prejudices.

       a. Stereotypes include physical traits such as slow, feeble, and gray-haired.

       b. Stereotypes include personality traits such as cranky, repetitive, sweet, caring, pleasant, and storytellers.

D. Elderly individuals who defy the stereotypes are perceived as exceptions.

E. Ageism is common among professionals in medicine, psychotherapy, and research.

II. Physical development

Most elderly individuals continue to be productive contributors to their families and their communities.

III. Longevity

The average life expectancy in the United States has gone from forty-seven years in 1900 to seventy-five years today. Eradication of disease and improvements in diet and sanitation increase life expectancy. The population of the United States has been getting more diverse during this century with regard to ethnicity, social class, and income. Poverty levels have declined, and median income for people sixty-five and over has increased, although subgroups of the elderly population live in poverty or near-poverty.

A. Mortality

   1. Mortality rates began to fall in the late 1960s because of improvements in medical care and drugs and improved health behaviors.

       a. Men have made larger gains in life expectancy than women except at advanced ages of seventy-five and above.

       b. SES affects mortality and morbidity among the elderly.

   2. Women and men die from the same causes, although men have higher mortality from all the leading causes of death except diabetes mellitus.

       a. In late adulthood, the gap between men's and women's mortality rates narrows.

       b. The gender gap continues to widen with age for cancer, heart disease, kidney disease, and suicide.

       c.   There are racial and ethnic differences in mortality rates and mortality crossover.

- A Multicultural View: The mortality crossover

  B. Life expectancy

      1.   Although life expectancy has increased, lifespan has not changed because it refers to the maximum possible period of time a species could be expected to live if environmental hazards were eliminated.

      2.   For humans, the lifespan is one hundred and fifteen years.

      3.   The oldest verified age to which an individual has lived is just over one hundred and twenty-two years.

      4.   People 100 years old or older is a fast growing segment of U.S. population.

IV. Theories of aging

  A. The breakdown of the surveillance, repair, and replacement process of the body is known as **senescence**. This causes an individual to become more vulnerable to disease and mortality. Theories of aging attempt to explain senescence.

  B. **Cellular theories**, also known as wear and tear theories, focus on the processes that take place within and between the cells and lead to the breakdown of cells, tissue, and organs.

      1.   These theories explain the loss of function by repeated errors of transmission of genetic material resulting from toxins, pollutants, free radicals, and other factors that affect cell reproduction.

      2.   The older the individual, the greater the number of cells that will have errors and the greater the number of cells that will have multiple errors.

  C. **Programming theories** consider the maximum lifespan to be predetermined by the genes in each species through the number of possible cell replications. At birth, our eventual death is already built in; anything less than ideal environmental conditions may shorten our life, but nothing can lengthen it.

      1.   The Hayflick limit predicts that cells will replicate only fifty times.

      2.   The Telomere hypothesis explains how cells can continue to replicate beyond the Hayflick limit.

V. Physical functioning in late adulthood

Late adulthood is a time of loss in efficiency of body systems, but it is also a time of compensation. Primary aging is normal age-related changes that everyone experiences; secondary aging refers to the effects of illness or disease on the body. Often it is difficult to differentiate between the results of the two.

A. Slowing with age

   1. Motor responses, sensory processes, and intellectual functioning slow with age.

   2. The slowing down may be due to aging in the peripheral nervous system, the sensory receptors, and the nerves that transmit sensations.

   3. Health and physical fitness are more closely related to performance than is age.

B. Skin, bone, and muscle changes

   1. The most noticeable changes of late adulthood occur to the skin.

      a. The skin becomes more wrinkled, dry, sagging, and less regular in pigmentation.

      b. The skin is easily bruised, heals more slowly, and grows lesions.

      c. Irregularly distributed melanocytes cause "age spots."

   2. Demineralization causes bone degeneration, which is called osteoporosis. Osteoporosis takes place in a two-phase pattern.

      a. Women experience far greater bone loss than men do.

      b. Regular weight-bearing exercise, estrogen replacement therapy, and calcium supplements have been effective at slowing and even reversing osteoporosis in postmenopausal women.

   3. A progressive loss of muscle strength and speed occurs.

      a. Loss of muscle fibers results from atrophy due to disuse or to damage and atrophy of the nerve fibers that carry impulses to the muscles.

      b. Strength is maintained through physical exercise.

C. Cardiovascular system changes

   1. The changes in the cardiovascular system that began in early adulthood continue through middle and later adulthood.

   2. The heart has reduced maximum cardiac output and aerobic power.

   3. These changes are kept to a minimum by regular aerobic exercise and good nutrition.

D. Respiratory system changes

   1. The respiratory system becomes less efficient as we age but it is not clear whether these changes are due to primary or secondary aging.

   2. The decrease in function is gradual, but by late adulthood the loss is considerable.

3. The decreased efficiency of the lungs increases the risk of stroke or loss of brain functions.

4. Older adults compensate by using accessory muscles to facilitate respiration. Under conditions of stress, an older adult may have difficulty breathing or become fatigued.

5. These changes make older people more susceptible to chronic bronchitis, emphysema, and pneumonia.

E. Sensory system changes

1. Visual loss is part of the primary aging process.

   a. Loss of accommodation occurs in senescence, leading to the need for reading glasses.

   b. A cataract is a clouding of the lens and is the most common correctable cause of blindness.

   c. Glaucoma is increased pressure in the eyeball and can cause blindness.

2. Hearing loss is also a part of the primary aging process.

   a. Presbycusis is age-related hearing loss caused by changes in the conductive systems in the outer and middle ear and loss of hair cells and nerves in the inner ear, leading to problems with high-pitched sounds and consonants in normal speech.

   b. The percentage of elderly Americans with significant hearing loss increases with age.

   c. Noise is the largest contributor to hearing loss.

   d. Hearing aids can compensate for hearing loss to some extent, but are not helpful in all settings.

3. Primary aging affects both taste and smell, with age-related declines in smell being greater than those in taste.

   a. Taste buds do show reduction in numbers with age.

   b. The ability to recognize a large number of foods declines with age.

   c. The number of smell receptors begins to decrease at about thirty years of age with the peak age to detect odors between twenty and fifty.

•   Focusing On: Older adults have healthier lifestyles than young and middle-aged adults

F. Changes in sexual functioning. Few changes in sexual functioning occur in late adulthood.

1. The best predictor or sexual activity is having a partner.

2. Among older men and women, sexual activity has been shown to predict health, happiness, and longevity.

VI. Health behaviors in late adulthood

Increased physical vulnerability may make health and fitness in the later years more important than in early or middle adulthood. Beginning healthy habits in early adulthood can have cumulative benefits in later adult years.

A. Diet

   1. Nutritional concerns increase during late adulthood because at the same time caloric needs decline, the need for many nutrients rises.

   2. Not getting enough vitamins and minerals can increase risk for a variety of health problems.

   3. Activity level, gender, weight, height, genetic make-up, social environment, and socioeconomic status all affect dietary needs and nutritional deficits.

B. Exercise

   1. As people get older, routine physical activity decreases.

   2. **Hypokinesia** is a disease of disuse that causes degeneration and functional loss of muscle and bone tissue.

   3. Regular exercise prevents hypokinesia and has a number of other positive benefits.

   4. During the past two decades, adults have been exercising more frequently, particularly older adults.

      a. In some cases people in their sixties have higher exercise rates than those in their forties and fifties.

      b. Among older adults, more men exercise than women.

      c. Health professionals are often overcautious in prescribing exercises for the elderly.

C. Alcohol consumption. Although some alcohol consumption may add to a long life, heavy drinking poses serious problems for older people.

   1. During late adulthood, sensitivity to alcohol increases.

   2. Alcohol can reduce reaction time, impair coordination, and cloud mental abilities.

   3. Levels of alcohol consumption and the number of problem drinkers are lower in older age groups.

4. For some groups of the elderly population, alcohol consumption remains a problem.

    a. Elderly males are at greater risk for alcoholism than females.

    b. Research shows that health problems are associated with a greater probability of elderly individuals abstaining from alcohol, while financial difficulties are associated with a lower probability of abstaining.

D. Prescription drugs

    1. Elderly individuals are at high risk for adverse drug effects.

    2. Improper medications may cause physical, cognitive, and social dysfunction.

VII. Chronic illnesses

A chronic illness is one that cannot be cured but only managed and is a common feature of late adulthood. Chronic diseases are incremental, universal, and characterized by progressive loss of organ reserve. The key to preventing chronic illness is to delay reaching the clinical threshold. Chronic illnesses tend to affect all aspects of a person's life.

A. Cardiovascular disease

    1. Cardiovascular disease is the major chronic illness in the United States. Atherosclerosis is the most common heart disorder in the United States and may progress evenly or may result in a sudden catastrophic event.

        a. Narrowed or closed arteries wholly or partially block the flow of oxygen and nutrients to the heart.

        b. Temporary blockage may cause angina pectoris, and severe blockage may result in myocardial infarction.

    2. Coronary heart disease is common among males and elderly people in general. Other risk factors include family history, health-compromising behavior, personality type, and stress.

    3. Hypertension, or high blood pressure, can cause deterioration of the arterial walls and of the cell tissue, putting the person at risk for heart attack, kidney damage, and stroke. Risk factors for hypertension include genetic predisposition, obesity, poor diet, and, perhaps, personality characteristics.

B. Cancer

    1. Cancer is characterized by uncontrolled cellular growth and reproduction due to a dysfunction of the DNA. Cancerous growths can spread by invading other tissues and organs.

    2. Cancer is the second most frequent cause of death in the United States.

        a. Regular breast examination and mammograms are recommended for women forty and older.

b.   Professional digital rectal examination of the prostate is recommended for men starting at age fifty.

c.   A new blood test can also be used to detect cancer cells in the blood.

3.   Some risk factors for cancer include genetic predisposition, gender, socioeconomic status, ethnicity, lifestyle, diet, and marital status.

4.   The onset of cancer is related to uncontrollable stress caused by some life event. Stress may suppress the immune system and interfere with DNA repair. Personality also has an influence on the likelihood of developing cancer.

C.   Arthritis

1.   Arthritis causes the body to incorrectly identify its own tissue as foreign matter and attack it. It is the second leading chronic disease in the United States.

2.   Arthritis attacks the joints and connective tissue and causes inflammation, pain, stiffness, and sometimes swelling of the joints.

3.   Arthritis can be crippling.

a.   Osteoarthritis is the most common type of arthritis and affects weight-bearing joints.

b.   Rheumatoid arthritis affects the whole body rather than specific, localized joints. It is the most crippling and is most prevalent among people ages forty to sixty.

4.   Early diagnosis and treatment can prevent the disabling aspects of rheumatoid arthritis.

D.   Common symptoms in later years

1.   The kinds of symptoms that bother women and men are very similar, but are more frequent in women.

a.   Women's chronic conditions tend to be nonfatal and therefore have received less medical attention.

b.   Men's tend to be fatal or precursors to fatal conditions.

2.   Incidence of chronic diseases varies among racial/ethnic groups.

3.   Chronic diseases generally have their beginning in earlier life stages and often have their onset earlier as well.

a.   The great frequency of chronic illness is a result of people living longer.

b.   Some people adapt and compensate for losses despite suffering from chronic illnesses.

      c.   Physical fitness helps to maintain most body systems at high levels of functioning, although the levels are not as high as they were before because primary aging cannot be stopped.

VIII. Cognitive development

Some individuals show significant changes in intellectual performance in midlife, while a few show little decline even into their eighties. Several factors reduce the risk of cognitive loss.

  IX. Wisdom and cognitive abilities

Wisdom, expert knowledge and good judgment about important but uncertain matters of life, is a positive change associated with late life.

    A. Cognitive mechanics

       1. Cognitive mechanics refers to basic memory processes, which are likely to decline in late adulthood.

       2. Using techniques to improve memory can help, but the performance of elderly persons is still poor compared to young adults.

    B. Cognitive pragmatics

       1. **Cognitive pragmatics** refers to intellectual problems in which culture-based knowledge and skills are key in managing the peaks and valleys of life.

       2. Older adults can show higher levels of wisdom-related knowledge on tasks specific to their own age group than young adults.

   X. Cognitive plasticity and training

Plasticity refers to the ability of other neurons to take over the functions of neurons that have been damaged or lost.

    A. Animal research

       1. Research shows that environmental living conditions have an impact on the state of the cerebral cortex.

       2. Young, middle-aged, and old rats raised in an enriched environment show an increase in the growth of dendrites and a thickening of the cerebral cortex.

       3. Young, middle-aged, and old rats raised in impoverished environments have diminished cortices.

    B. Human research

       1. Individual differences exist in age-related changes in cognitive functioning and may be related to environmental factors.

2.   Research has focused on retraining abilities and processes that longitudinal studies have shown to exhibit earlier patterns of decline.

3.   Intellectual decline is not necessarily irreversible, and intervention strategies may allow for longer maintenance of high levels of intellectual functioning.

XI.   The aging brain

Age-related changes occur in the central nervous system. Brain weight and mass start to decrease gradually at age twenty; these changes are very small by age fifty and accelerate after age sixty.

A.   Brain changes

1.   Most brain changes are not apparent until age sixty, with the greatest loss in the sensory and motor areas and the smallest in the association areas.

2.   New evidence suggests that loss of neurons in the brain is not as significant as previously thought, and in fact regeneration of neurons is likely.

   a.   Plasticity enables other neurons to take over the functions of neurons that have been lost.

   b.   Some research suggests that the density of synapses increases with age.

3.   As the cardiovascular system changes, the blood flow to the brain is reduced.

   a.   Some neurons die, and others develop neurofibrillary tangles; the brain develops granulovascular degeneration.

   b.   The brains of elderly individuals with senile dementia show these structural changes.

4.   Most declines in mental functioning are related to changes in health and are not a function of age.

5.   Physical damage to the brain can cause organic brain syndromes.

   a.   **Acute brain syndromes** are caused by metabolic malfunctions and medication effects.

   b.   **Chronic brain syndromes** are characterized by irreversible changes in the brain and include Alzheimer's disease.

B.   Multiinfarct dementia

1.   **Multiinfarct dementia** is caused by vascular diseases and is characterized by a series of tiny strokes.

2.   The tiny strokes may go unnoticed at the time or may be accompanied by headaches or dizziness.

3. Diagnosing multiinfarct dementia is important because treating the hypertension and underlying vascular disease can slow the progress of the brain disease.

C. Alzheimer's disease

1. Senile dementia of the Alzheimer's type, or **Alzheimer's disease**, affects more than 11 percent of individuals over sixty-five years of age.

2. Alzheimer's disease is caused by degeneration of the brain areas in those portions of the cerebral cortex associated with memory, learning, and judgment.

3. The presence of senile plaques and neurofibrillary tangles in the brain is the basis for the microscopic diagnosis of Alzheimer's disease.

4. Forgetfulness and confusion are typically the first symptoms of Alzheimer's.

   a. As the disease progresses, the confusion becomes more intense and often includes belligerence.

   b. Later symptoms include greater confusion and hyperactivity.

   c. In the final stages sleep increases, then come coma and death.

   d. The course of the disease is usually seven to ten years.

5. Some evidence suggests that genetic defects are involved in causing Alzheimer's disease.

   a. Variations in APOE, a gene on chromosome 19, are associated with Alzheimer's disease.

   b. APOE can be used to identify those who are at greater biological risk for the disease.

6. Older adults may experience anticipatory dementia, which is the concern that normal age-associated memory changes are signs of the onset of Alzheimer's disease. This may discourage people with remediable memory complaints from seeking help.

7. Drugs are sometimes given to lessen the Alzheimer's patient's agitation. Memory aids can help patients in the early stages to maintain their functioning.

• Working with Mark John Isola, therapeutic recreation director: Helping Alzheimer's patients and their families

D. Senile dementia

1. The loss of brain cells causes **senile dementia**.

2. Senile dementia impairs orientation, intellect, judgment, and memory.

3. Slightly fewer than 5 percent of all persons over sixty-five suffer so severely from dementia that they require institutional care or a full-time custodian.

      a.   Mild to moderate dementia requires special attention to care and safety on the part of the family or caregivers.

      b.   It causes much personal anguish to see a family member unable to recognize loved ones.

    4.   Most older adults are in good cognitive health. Changes in functioning should not simply be accepted as the inescapable effects of age.

XII.   Mental health and aging

    A.   Depression is the most common psychiatric complaint of elderly adults.

    B.   Since symptoms associated with depression may be thought to be normal changes associated with aging or illness, they may go undiagnosed.

      1.   Elderly patients report physical but not affective symptoms.

      2.   Symptoms of depression may mimic dementia, leading to misdiagnosis.

    C.   Between 4 and 7 percent of older adults experience depression severe enough to require intervention.

      1.   Depression is more common in very old adults.

      2.   Chronic health problems, functional impairment, and reactions to medications are factors leading to depression during late adulthood.

    D.   Gender, race/ethnicity, and socioeconomic status are associated with depression among the elderly.

    E.   Untreated depression increases the incidence of suicide, especially among elderly, White males.

    F.   Effective treatments for elderly depression include pharmacotherapy and psychotherapy.

    G.   Men and women who report low physical activity may be at a higher risk for developing depression ten or twenty years later.

XIII. Work and retirement

Most Americans look forward to retirement in their later years. People who can control whether and when they retire can plan for and anticipate the change. The statistics on when people retire are contradictory.

    A.   What is retirement?

      1.   Leaving a career job is a significant life event but does not necessarily mean leaving the labor force.

        a.   Many employees do not stop working when they leave their full-time career jobs.

    b.   Research shows that those who leave between fifty-eight and sixty-one are the most likely to hold another full-time job.

    c.   Retirement may mean changed or reduced employment, not simply stopping work.

  2. Many adults, especially racial/ethnic minorities, have never held career jobs and thus never consider themselves to be retired.

    a.   Perceptions of a discontinuous work life make the line between work and nonwork indistinct and create ambiguity of retirement status.

    b.   In terms of retirement, women face problems similar to those of racial/ethnic minorities.

  3. Nontraditional retirement patterns are common among older Americans.

  4. Those who retire experience a series of phases as they adjust to their new status.

  5. Race/ethnicity, gender, health, pension status, and occupational level all affect retirement possibilities and choices.

    a.   People with poor health or who perform physically demanding work are more likely to leave the labor force, as are those with pension benefits.

    b.   Those who are healthy and those without benefits are more likely to continue working.

  6. How much individuals enjoy their work also influences retirement decisions.

    a.   Workers with boring, repetitive jobs are likely to choose retirement as early as they can afford it.

    b.   Workers forced into early retirement due to downsizing adjust the most poorly.

    c.   Workers with interesting jobs that give them high satisfaction are less likely to retire early and more likely to continue to work.

B. Well-being in retirement

  1. Sixty percent of retirees are relatively satisfied and adjust well to their new life circumstances.

  2. Health and financial security are the major determinants of life satisfaction after retirement.

  3. Occupational status also predicts retirement satisfaction.

Key Concepts

Directions: Identify each of the key concepts discussed in this chapter.

1. Stereotyping of and discrimination against people because they are old is called _____.

2. The maximum possible period of time a species could be expected to live if environmental hazards were eliminated is called _____.

3. _____ is the degenerative phase of the aging process that causes vulnerability to disease and mortality as the years go by.

4. _____ of aging focus on processes within and between cells that lead to breakdown. These are also known as _____.

5. _____ of aging focus on the maximum lifespan to be predetermined by the genes in each species.

6. The _____ states that sufficient telomere loss on one or more chromosomes in normal somatic cells triggers cell senescence.

7. Age-related hearing loss caused by changes in the conductive system in the outer and middle ear and loss of hair cells in the inner ear is known as _____.

8. _____ is increased pressure in the eyeball and can cause _____.

9. A clouding of the lens of the eye is called a _____, and it is the most common correctable cause of _____.

10. The best predictor of sexual interest in middle and late adulthood is _____ and _____ of sex in younger years.

11. The degeneration and loss of function of muscle and bone tissue as a result of disuse is known as _____.

12. Levels of alcohol consumption and numbers of problem drinkers _____ with age.

13. The leading cause of death in the United States is _____; it is caused by _____, the narrowing of the arteries that supply the heart.

14. A heart attack is also known as a _____.

15. Cancerous growths are called _____, and they occur due to dysfunction of the _____. The spreading of cancer to other tissues and organs is called _____.

16. Risk for stroke is greater among _____ women then _____ women, and this risk _____ with age.

17. The most common type of arthritis is called _____.

18. _____ affects the whole body rather than specific joints.

19. Expert knowledge and good judgment about important but uncertain matters of life is called

_____.

20. _____ refers to basic memory processes, such as visual and motor memory. These are likely to _____ in late adulthood.

21. _____ refers to intellectual problems in which culture-based knowledge and skills are primary, such as reading and writing skills. These may in late adulthood.

22. The ability of functioning neurons in the cerebral cortex to take over the jobs of neurons that are damaged or lost is known as _____.

23. _____ is a negative term referring to mental and physical infirmity of old age.

24. Pathological states of the brain caused by metabolic malfunctions, such as liver failure, are called _____. Such damage is _____ and _____.

25. Chronic brain syndromes include _____, _____, and _____. These conditions are _____.

26. When blood flow to the brain is reduced or blocked, depriving the cells of oxygen and nutrients, _____ is the result.

27. _____ is caused by degeneration of brain cells in portions of the cerebral cortex that are associated with memory, learning, and judgment.

28. Senile dementia is more frequent among _____ than among _____.

29. _____ is the most common psychiatric complaint of the elderly.

30. People who have _____ work patterns are less likely to consider themselves as retired than those with _____ work patterns.

Multiple-Choice Self-Test

Factual Questions

1. Which of the following is *not* a stereotyped image of the elderly?
   a. Greedy
   b. Idle freeloader
   c. Sweet
   d. All are stereotyped images of the elderly

2. The degenerative phase of the aging process that causes people to become vulnerable to disease is called
   a. senescence.
   b. septicemia.
   c. senility.
   d. telomerase.

3. Which statement is correct?
   a. Ability to smell odors declines by age sixty.
   b. Ability to identify an odor declines earlier than ability to detect smell.
   c. Ability to perceive the intensity of an odor begins to declines at about age seventy.
   d. Ability to identify an odor is more advanced in males than in females.

4. Regular exercise can prevent
   a. septicemia.
   b. senility.
   c. telomerase.
   d. hypokinesia.

5. Pain or tightness in the chest caused by temporary blockage of arteries supplying the heart is known as a(n)
   a. a myocardial infarction.
   b. a metastasis.
   c. angina pectoris.
   d. atherosclerosis.

6. Without using a memory technique, most people can remember how many words from a list?
   a. Six to eight
   b. Five to eight
   c. Five to seven
   d. Six to seven

7. Willis and Schaie's longitudinal training research indicates that older adults' cognitive performance
   a. shows considerable plasticity.
   b. shows minimal plasticity.
   c. shows no plasticity.
   d. shows plasticity in males but not in females.

8. Senile plaques are
   a. loss of input to neurons.
   b. new synapses that are created to replace old ones that have been lost.
   c. clusters of degenerating neurons.
   d. empty spaces within the brain.

9. A degenerative brain syndrome caused by loss of brain cells that impairs orientation, intellect, memory, and judgment is called
   a. Alzheimer's disease.
   b. acute brain syndrome.
   c. multiinfarct dementia.
   d. senile dementia.

10. Older persons commit what percent of all suicides?
   a. 25
   b. 42
   c. 17
   d. 5

Conceptual Questions

1. Dora is sixty-four years old and diagnosed with depression. Her doctor prescribes antidepressant medication for her but does not refer her to a clinician because he does not believe that she can function in the therapeutic environment. The doctor's behavior is most specifically an example of
   a. stereotyping.
   b. ageism.
   c. the influence of industrialization and urbanization.
   d. age segregation.

2. Paul and Belinda are both sixty-nine-year-old retired individuals. Paul lives with his sixty-six-year-old wife. Belinda is widowed and lives alone in a rural town. Who is more likely to be financially disadvantaged?
   a. Paul
   b. Belinda
   c. Paul and Belinda will have equivalent financial resources
   d. Answer cannot be determined from the given information

3. Dr. Crain believes that people age because they are biologically predetermined to do so. His view is most closely associated with
   a. cellular theories of aging.
   b. wear and tear theories of aging.
   c. programming theories of aging.
   d. the telomere hypothesis of aging.

4. On the basis of the discussion in the text, we can conclude that osteoporosis is
   a. a form of primary aging.
   b. a form of secondary (pathological) aging.
   c. an irreversible condition.
   d. more common in men than in women.

5. Janice is sixty-three years old. Which statement most accurately describes her sexual functioning?
   a. Her ability to enjoy sex has diminished in comparison to younger years.
   b. Her interest in sex has increased in comparison to younger years.
   c. Her interest in and ability to enjoy sex has remained stable over the years.
   d. She and her husband now have sexual intercourse more frequently than in younger years.

6. Who is *least* likely to experience hypokinesia during old age?
   a. David, who has never smoked cigarettes
   b. Sam, who has always made time for breakfast in the morning
   c. Rick, who has always been a light social drinker
   d. Wayne, who has always exercised regularly

7. Which types of skills are most required for people who work as museum tour guides?
   a. Cognitive mechanics
   b. Cognitive Pragmatics
   c. Procedural knowledge
   d. Fluid intelligence

8. Barney has been a life-long alcoholic. Which condition is he most likely to have in old age?
   a. Multiinfarct dementia
   b. chronic brain syndrome
   c. Alzheimer's disease
   d. acute brain syndrome

9. Who is *most* likely to be afraid of developing Alzheimer's in the future?
   a. Men
   b. Depressed people
   c. Unmarried people
   d. Married people

10. Who is most likely to retire early?
    a.   John, who is a chemical engineer
    b.   Archie, who is a taxi driver
    c.   Donald, who owns a neighborhood grocery store
    d.   Jim, who is a high-school basketball coach

Answer Key

Key Concepts

1.   ageism
2.   lifespan
3.   Senescence
4.   Cellular theories; wear and tear theories
5.   Programming theories
6.   telomere hypothesis of aging
7.   presbycusis
8.   Glaucoma; blindness
9.   cataract; blindness
10. frequency; enjoyment
11. hypokinesia
12. decrease
13. coronary heart disease (CHD); atherosclerosis
14. myocardial infarction
15. malignant tumors; DNA; metastasis
16. African American; white; increases
17. osteoarthritis
18. Rheumatoid arthritis
19. wisdom
20. Cognitive mechanics; decline
21. Cognitive pragmatics; grow or improve
22. plasticity
23. Senility
24. acute brain syndromes; treatable; reversible
25. multiinfarct dementia; senile dementia; Alzheimer's disease; irreversible
26. multiinfarct dementia
27. Alzheimer's disease
28. women; men
29. Depression
30. discontinuous; continuous

Multiple-Choice Self-Test / Factual Questions

1.   Choice (d) is correct. Choices (a) and (b) are negative stereotypes and choice (c) is a positive stereotype of the elderly.

2.   Choice (a) is correct. Choice (b), septicemia, is infection that has entered the bloodstream. Choice (c), senility, is a negative term referring to mental and physical infirmity of old age. Choice (d), telomerase, is an enzyme required for cell division produced by the telomere gene.

3.   Choice (b) is correct. Choice (a), ability to smell odors, begins to decline with age at about seventy years. Choice (c), ability to perceive the intensity of a smell begins to decline much earlier. Choice (d), ability to identify an odor, is better in females than in males at all ages.

4.   Choice (d) is correct; hypokinesia is muscle and bone degeneration due to disuse, and regular exercise can prevent it. Choice (a), septicemia, is infection that has entered the blood-stream. Choice (b), senility, is a negative term referring to mental and physical infirmity of old age. Choice (c), telomerase, is an enzyme required for cell division produced by the telomere gene.

5.   Choice (c) is correct. Choice (a), myocardial infarction, is another term for a heart attack. Choice (b), metastasis, is the spreading of cancer cells from their origin to other tissues and organs of the body. Choice (d), atherosclerosis, is the narrowing of arteries that supply the heart.

6.   Choice (c) is correct. The other choices are incorrect.

7.   Choice (a) is correct; studies indicate that intellectual decline and cognitive decrements from which some elderly people suffer are not irreversible. The other choices are incorrect.

8.   Choice (c) is correct. Choice (a) is incorrect in that axon sprouting and dendrite branching mean loss of input to neurons. Choice (b), Synaptogenesis is the creation of new synapses to replace old ones that have been lost. Choice (d), empty spaces within the brain, are called vacuoles.

9.   Choice (d) is correct. Choice (a), Alzheimer's disease, is a chronic brain syndrome caused by degeneration of neurons that are associated with memory, learning, and judgment in the cerebral cortex. Choice (b), acute brain syndromes, are caused by metabolic malfunctions, such as diabetes, and effects of medication, such as vitamin deficiencies. Choice (c), multiinfarct dementia, is caused by blockage of blood vessels that reduces or prevents blood flow to the brain.

10.   Choice (c) is correct. Choices (a), (b), and (d) are incorrect.

Multiple-Choice Self-Test / Conceptual Questions

1.   Choice (b) is correct; ageism is discrimination against people because they are old. Choice (a), stereotyping, is discrimination on the basis of a particular group membership. Choice (c), industrialization and urbanization, is commonly assumed to have distanced the elderly and their children from each other. Choice (d), age segregation, is separation on the basis of age.

2.   Choice (b) is correct; research indicates that among the elderly the most financially disadvantaged are women, people who live alone, and people who live in rural areas. Choices (a), (c), and (d) are incorrect.

3.   Choice (c) is correct. Choice (a), cellular theories of aging focus on cellular processes and breakdown of cells and organs. Cellular theories are also known as wear and tear theories,

choice (b). Choice (d), the telomere hypothesis, predicts that sufficient telomere loss on chromosomes in cells triggers cellular dysfunction and loss.

4.   Choice (a) is correct; osteoporosis is an extreme form of primary aging. Choice (b) is incorrect in that osteoporosis is not a pathological form of aging. Choice (c) is incorrect in that osteoporosis is reversible through medication and exercise. Choice (d) is incorrect in that osteoporosis is more common in women than in men.

5.   Choice (c) is correct; research indicates that sexual interest and ability remain relatively stable as people age; however, frequency of sexual intercourse decreases. Choices (a), (b), and (d) are incorrect.

6.   Choice (d) is correct; hypokinesia is bone and muscle degeneration due to disuse. This condition is preventable by regular exercise. Choices (a), (b), and (c) represent behaviors that generally improve adult health and longevity.

7.   Choice (b) is correct; the tasks of a tour guide call on people to use their existing knowledge and interpersonal skills, and these are components of cognitive pragmatics. Choice (a), cognitive mechanics, refers to basic memory processes such as visual and motor memory. Choice (c), procedural knowledge or "knowing how", refers to knowledge of procedures; for example, knowing how to bake bread or how to ride a bike. Choice (d), fluid intelligence, is ability at dealing with new, never-before-encountered situations.

8.   Choice (d) is correct; alcoholism, as well as metabolic malfunctions and medication effects, can lead to acute brain syndromes. Choices (a), (b), and (c) are incorrect.

9.   Choice (c) is correct; unmarried people, women, and people who believe Alzheimer's is inheritable are more concerned about developing the disease in later life. The other choices are incorrect.

10.   Choice (b) is correct; people who have physically straining and routine jobs tend to retire earlier. The job of driving a taxi fits this description. People with challenging white-collar jobs, choices (a) and (d), and those who are self-employed, choice (c), often choose to retire later.

CHAPTER 17

Psychosocial Development in Late Adulthood

Learning Objectives

1. Identify the factors that contribute to successful physical and mental health in the later years.
2. Compare and contrast the Harvard Grant Study and the Berkeley Older Generation Study.
3. Discuss the stability of personality in later life.
4. Describe Erikson's eighth stage of development and discuss indications of a successful resolution.
5. Compare and contrast the activity and disengagement theories of successful aging.
6. Describe the role of marriage in late adulthood and discuss how husbands and wives view each other.
7. Discuss the effects of having to deal with chronic illness.
8. Compare elderly husbands and wives as caregivers and discuss common coping difficulties of long-term caregivers
9. Discuss the effects of spousal death on surviving spouses.
10. Define the double standard of aging and evaluate how it affects sexuality in late adulthood.
11. Discuss dating and remarriage in the elderly and identify the qualities that elderly persons look for in a mate.
12. Discuss how older lesbians and gay men deal with relationships in the later years.
13. Describe the late adulthood years of individuals who never married.
14. Define social convoys and use this concept to evaluate older adults' relationships with family and friends.
15. Describe and evaluate the importance of grandparent-grandchild relationships.
16. Discuss the housing options of the elderly in terms of degree of independence.
17. Differentiate between assisted living and long-term-care facilities for the elderly and discuss the role of control in living conditions.
18. Describe the elderly's community involvement in volunteerism and continuing education.
19. Discuss the roles of religious involvement and spiritual integration in late adulthood.
20. Discuss the role of reminiscence and life review in the adjustment process of older adults.

Chapter Outline

I. Personality development in late adulthood

The vast majority of older men and women who are not cognitively impaired show considerable psychological resilience in the face of stress. They are more satisfied than younger adults with their lives, except with regard to their health. Old age brings many adaptational challenges.

A. Continuity and change in late life

1. Vaillant and Vaillant, using the Harvard Grant study, found five variables that contribute to late-life adjustment.

a. Long-lived ancestors predict physical health only.

b. Sustained family relationships predict physical and mental health.

c. Maturity of ego defenses assessed before age fifty contributes to psychosocial adjustment at age sixty-five.

d. Absence of alcoholism promotes health.

e. Absence of depression disorders promotes health.

2. There are several important limitations of the Harvard Grant study that prevent conclusions about women, less privileged men, or people in old-old and very-old late adulthood.

3. The Berkeley Older Generation study reveals five personality components that appear to be stationary across two time periods: intellect, agreeableness, satisfaction, energy, and extraversion.

a. The most stable trait was satisfaction.

b. The data show stability in satisfaction and intellect well into very old age, an increase in agreeableness, and a decline in extraversion.

B. Integrity versus despair

1. **Integrity versus despair** is the developmental task of late adulthood according to Erikson.

2. Wisdom comes from the conflict between integrity and despair.

C. Theories of successful aging

1. **Activity theory** argues that the maintenance of social, physical, and intellectual activity contributes to successful aging.

a. Older people who are aging optimally stay active and maintain activities or find substitutes for the ones they must give up.

b. One can be active without maintaining levels of activity typical of middle age.

c. Research found that activity level did not predict mortality or life satisfaction.

2. **Disengagement theory** views the reduction in the social involvement of the elderly to be the consequence of a mutual process between the elderly and society.

    a.   It assumes that aging individuals experience inevitable decline in abilities and want to be released from societal expectations.

    b.   There is little evidence that disengagement is normative.

3. Both theories place the burden of adjustment on aging individuals, independently of the circumstances in the world around them. Neither theory can account for the range of activity and life of successfully aging individuals; people have different levels of activity and satisfaction based on their personalities and life experiences.

II. Marriage and singlehood

Older married people appear to be happier, be healthier, and live longer than widowed and divorced people of the same age. As couples face retirement, relocation, and declining health, the marital relationship plays important support functions, especially for men.

A. Spouses as caregivers

1. Spouses serve as the first line of defense in coping with disease and disability.

2. Caregiving by spouses is unlikely to stop until deterioration of health of the caregiving spouse prevents it.

3. Chronic illness affects plans for daily living and requires that individuals integrate their illness into their lives.

4. Chronic illnesses can lead to interpersonal strains for patients and their families.

5. Chronic illnesses can also lead to positive outcomes.

6. Spousal caregivers are subject to emotional, social, economic, and physical strain.

    a.   The illness of the spouse removes emotional and social support and limits the personal freedom of the caregiver.

    b.   Stresses may be greater on recently married older couples who do not have a lifetime of shared experiences to draw on.

7. More women than men provide spousal care.

    a.   Research has found differences in husbands' and wives' responses to their spouse's need for help among the frail elderly.

    b.   Men and women experience spousal caregiving differently.

    c.   The relationship before the disease or disability influences how couples cope with the situation.

       d.   Since wives already do most of the household tasks, the change is greater for caregiving husbands than for caregiving wives.

  B. Widowhood

      1.   The death of a spouse causes disruption to self-identity and relationships with others.

      2.   The impact of widowhood depends on the age and social class of the widow.

      3.   Family relationships are affected by widowhood.

      4.   Men typically have other roles besides husband that are important to them, which may make widowerhood a less severe identity crisis for them. However, men rely more exclusively on wives as confidants.

      5.   Being widowed does not increase the risk of earlier mortality, but does have a significant impact on lifestyle. It also reduces family income for both genders.

      6.   Strong signs of psychological resilience from bereavement and the burdens of widowhood have been found.

•   Focusing On: The double standard of sexuality in late adulthood

  C. Dating and remarriage

      1.   Socially active older adults are more likely to meet people who are potential dating partners.

      2.   Health, driving ability, organizational memberships, and contact with siblings are all positively associated with dating.

      3.   Older adults tend to place more emphasis on companionship and are not experimenting with marital roles.

      4.   Dating has positive effects on feeling desirable and finding an avenue for self-disclosure.

      5.   Marriage in later life is not uncommon, but it is likely to be remarriage, with the major reasons being companionship and economic resources.

      6.   Older adults choose mates who have similar backgrounds and interests.

      7.   Successful late-life remarriage is more likely when there has been a long prior friendship.

  D. Older lesbians and gay men

      1.   An estimated 10 percent of older adults are lesbian women and gay men.

      2.   Long-term relationships are much more frequent among gay men and lesbians than is commonly assumed.

3. Lesbian, gay, and heterosexual couples do not differ on standard measures of relationship quality or satisfaction.

4. In a study, areas of concern for gay and lesbian correspondents were primarily the same as those for most aging adults: loneliness, health, and income.

5. Older gays and lesbians are a diverse population with special needs because their partners are not recognized by law.

E. Ever-single older adults

1. Only about 5 percent of older adults in the United States have never been married.

2. Ever-single adults have learned to cope with aloneness and to be autonomous and self-reliant.

3. Married and ever-single people report less loneliness than those formerly married.

III. Relationships with family and friends

Social convoy is used to describe the dynamic concept of lifelong social networks. Attachment and social support are important throughout the life course. Older adults tend to provide support for fewer network members than younger adults. The most important relationships are with spouses, parents, and children.

A. Siblings

1. Older adult siblings often form one of the strongest social support systems for the older adult, during good times and bad.

2. Siblings can act as confidants, caregivers, and cherished friends.

3. The death of a sibling changes the family constellation, and those who remain feel less buffered from their own mortality.

4. Research shows that African Americans tend to report more positive attitudes toward their siblings and to show greater interest in providing support for them than do Whites.

5. Gender is important to sibling relationships.

    a. Having a living sister is associated with large increases in sibling contact.

    b. Sister-sister ties are the strongest, and brother-brother ties are the weakest.

6. Siblings can be a source of social support.

B. Adult grandchildren

1. There is a continuation of the bond between grandparents and grandchildren that begins early in the grandchildren's lives.

2. On average, adult grandchildren do more activities with their grandmothers than with their grandfathers.

3. Grandchildren report being more influenced by their grandmothers than by their grandfathers in religious beliefs, sexual beliefs, family ideals, educational beliefs, moral beliefs, and personal identity issues.

4. Grandchildren rate their relationships with their grandmothers to be stronger than their relationships with their grandfathers.

5. Age, location, level of relationship, and contact level with parents influenced the contact between grandchildren and grandparents.

6. Cultural attitudes of different ethnic groups affect how grandchildren assist their grandparents.   Having many grandchildren may have an effect on grandchildren-grandparent relations.

C. Friends

1. Interaction with friends is more important to everyday well-being in later life.

2. Of all types of support, friends most often provide emotional intimacy and companionship.

3. Contact with friends is less consistent than with family. Health, economic problems, distance, retirement, or neighborhood changes may make interaction difficult.

4. The research on the effects of gender on relationships in later life is inconclusive.

   a. Some research shows that older women have more gender-homogeneous friendship networks than older men and are more likely to be involved in supportive relationships.

   b. Older men and women tend to have equally age-homogeneous friendship networks.

D. Fictive kin

1. Sometimes, the relationships between kin and friends become blurred.

2. The merging of voluntary and obligatory relations sometimes produces **fictive kin,** or constructed relationships.

3. Fictive kin provide flexibility in family caregiving for elderly adults but are not expected to fulfill the responsibilities of kin.

E. Childlessness

1. Studies indicate that being without children does not have a negative impact on well-being in later life.

2. Childless women tend to develop ties with friends as both companions and confidants to a greater extent than older adults who are parents.

3. Childless men place greater emphasis on friends as companions as well, but turn to relatives for confidants.

4. Siblings become a more important part of adults' social support networks in the absence of living parents or children.

IV. Problems of living: The housing continuum

Aging in place is the ideal for both gerontologists and elderly people. Elderly people prefer to grow older where they have been younger. They are likely to relinquish their own households only when they have limited economic resources and become frail or widowed. Frailty brings the need for housing modifications and special services.

A. Independent living

1. Home ownership is common among the elderly.

2. Taxes and home maintenance costs can be a financial burden for older adults, especially when health problems and functional impairments accumulate.

3. Elderly homeowners are more likely to become isolated or to receive less adequate care than apartment dwellers.

4. Elderly renters tend to be older than elderly homeowners and are more likely to be women and disproportionately African Americans.

5. Renting provides close-by neighbors, some security, and some social support, and renters are not responsible for yard and building maintenance. On the other hand, renters may not be allowed to modify their homes to help their functioning.

6. **Naturally occurring retirement communities (NORCs)** are housing developments that are not planned or designed for older people but attract a majority of residents age sixty or more.

   a. NORCs provide supportive social environments and access to services and facilities that can prolong independent living.

   b. Safety of the neighborhood is of primary importance to both young and old.

   c. Some NORCs located in the inner city lack necessary services and security.

B. Assisted living

1. **Assisted living** refers to some degree of help with daily living that enables older adults to age in place.

2. Assisted living provides formal and informal support.

3. Retirement communities provide a range of options from independent living to twenty-four-hour skilled nursing.

4. An elderly person needs assistance when unable to perform at least one daily activity.

   a. The largest source of help is relatives.

   b. With advancing age, more people rely on formal support.

5. Elderly or senior housing is federally subsidized and specially designed to meet the needs of old and disabled adults who are poor and have few other options.

6. Retirement communities are private, age-specific housing alternatives.

7. **Congregate housing** provides some communal services, such as a central kitchen and dining room.

• Working with Louise Staley, community worker: Helping holocaust survivors in late adulthood

C. Long-term care

1. Long-term care is a broad concept that refers to ongoing assistance to people with chronic illnesses and disabilities in a wide variety of settings.

2. Most long-term care is personal care and consists of help with everyday activities.

3. Between 30 and 50 percent of older people will spend a short time in a nursing home after an early discharge from the hospital.

4. Paid help is important and often combines informal caregiving with some formal services.

5. Adult day care can supplement family caregiving.

   a. It is a community-based group program designed to meet the needs of adults with functional impairments.

   b. A comprehensive program of social, physical, cognitive, and functional activities is offered to maximize remaining strengths and minimize deficits.

D. Control over living conditions

1. If the elderly person has to move for whatever reason, it is preferable to move to some space that he or she personally controls.

2. Satisfaction is related to degree of personal control over living conditions.

3. Negative effects on the health of older people have been found when their personal control is restricted.

4. A number of variables are improved when elderly are given responsibility.

5. Choice becomes one of the most important aspects of the housing continuum.

V. Interests and activities

The socioeconomic standing of the individual to a large extent influences how he or she spends his or her time. Health acts as a threshold for leisure, and financial security plays a critical role in supporting various activities. Education and occupation influence preference for activities. Developing **activity competence** is generally established in earlier adult years. Leisure pursuits of older people vary greatly. Past patterns of activity shape the way older adults use their time.

A. Community involvement

1. Community organizations include many different types of organizations designed to achieve a purpose or pursue some shared interest.

2. There is much stability in the people's general levels of participation in community organizations from middle age until their sixties, when involvement gradually decreases.

3. Volunteerism provides a link with the community.

a. Numbers of older volunteers are relatively low although many who do not volunteer would be willing to do so.

b. If the definition of volunteerism is broadened to include informal services, almost all retired adults do volunteer work.

4. Older volunteers face some problems.

a. They may be assigned tasks that are beneath their knowledge, experience, and dignity.

b. Sometimes volunteers are placed in positions without sufficient training.

c. Some volunteers prefer paid part-time work.

d. People who are retired may be unwilling to commit to a rigid volunteer schedule that might limit their freedom to travel.

e. Transportation is often a problem for older volunteers.

5. Elderhostel programs are another kind of community involvement.

a. These programs offer continuing higher education which includes service programs, performance programs, and intergenerational programs.

b. Research shows that these programs have many desirable personal and social outcomes for participants.

B. Religion and spirituality

1. Churches or synagogues are the organizations to which older people most frequently belong.

2. There is greater involvement of people over age sixty-five.

• A Multicultural View: Men and grief

3. Lack of church or synagogue attendance does not necessarily mean lack of religious involvement.

4. Religious institutions form an important source of social support among racial/ethnic minorities.

5. The few longitudinal studies of religiosity show that cohort differences may be more important than age differences. Aging baby boomers represent a movement religiosity to spirituality.

a. Religion generally refers to organized religion.

b. **Spirituality** refers to the human need to construct a sense of meaning in life and can occur within or outside of a specifically religious context.

6. Spiritual development appears to be age related but not age determined.

7. Spirituality has been found to influence one's perception of quality of life and will to live, even in the face of loss and infirmity.

8. Solitary activities can promote spiritual integration.

a. **Reminiscence** is the recall of past experiences and events and occurs among people of all ages.

b. **Life review** is an evaluative universal inner experience of older people that enables them to take stock of their lives as well as to prepare for death.

VI.   Looking back/looking forward

A.   Continuity within change

B.   Lifelong growth

C.   Changing meaning and vantage points

D.   Developmental diversity

Key Concepts

Directions: Identify each of the key concepts discussed in this chapter.

1. The concept of _____ refers to the maintenance of psychological adjustment and well-being across the lifespan.

2. Erikson's eighth psychosocial stage of development, _____, describes the tasks of late adulthood.

3. The _____ predicts that levels of activity in late adulthood that are similar to levels of activity in younger years will lead to successful aging.

4. The _____ predicts that successful aging will be experienced by those who reduce their social involvement and gradually withdraw from society.

5. _____ provide more hours of care and tolerate greater disability than other caregivers.

6. Death of a spouse generally causes disruption to _____ and _____.

7. The ability to form new intimate relationships in later life is a form of _____.

8. In later years, the major reasons for remarriage are _____ and _____.

9. The relationship quality of _____ and _____ is similar to the relationship quality of heterosexuals.

10. The key interpersonal relationships of ever-single women are _____, _____, and _____.

11. The term _____ describes lifelong social networks of family and friend relationships.

12. The relationship between adult grandchildren and their _____ tends to be stronger than those with their _____.

13. Interactions with _____ are more important than interactions with _____ to everyday well-being in later life.

14. Constructed relationships, such as godchild and foster parent, are known as _____.

15. Older adults are often _____-rich but _____-poor.

16. Housing that is not planned for the elderly but that attracts a majority of elderly residents due to its supportive social environment is called a _____.

17. Semi-independent living with some provisions for help is called _____.

18. _____ provides elderly residents with some communal services, such as a central kitchen.

19. Health and personal care offered to people with chronic illnesses and disabilities is called _____.

20. The skills and knowledge necessary to take advantage of opportunities for leisure activities are called _____.

21. _____ is a nationwide program of continuing higher education that offers one-week summer programs.

22. Research indicates that the _____ is the most important social institution for Hispanic elderly.

23. _____ is the human need to construct a sense of meaning in life that may or may not occur in a religious context.

24.   Recall of past experiences and events that promotes spiritual integration in late adulthood is called _____.

25.   A _____ helps older people evaluate their lives, resolve remaining conflicts, and make decisions.

Multiple-Choice Self-Test

Factual Questions

1. According to the Harvard Grant Study, which of the following does *not* contribute to late-life adjustment?
    a. Having long-lived ancestors
    b. Having sustained family relationships
    c. Having and using mature ego defenses
    d. Having financial stability

2. According to Erikson, what is the positive outcome for the conflict between integrity and despair?
    a. Wisdom
    b. Hope
    c. Love
    d. Care

3. Which of the following statements about institutionalization is true?
    a. A higher percentage of married women than men are institutionalized.
    b. A Higher percentage of married men than women are institutionalized.
    c. Married men spend more days in nursing homes than married women.
    d. The percentage of institutionalized married men and women is not significantly different.

4. For the elderly, widowhood has a significant, negative, and long-term impact on
    a. depressive symptoms.
    b. mortality.
    c. economic and social well-being.
    d. relationships with adult children.

5. Who is likely to report feeling most lonely?
    a. Ever-single people
    b. Formerly married people
    c. Married people
    d. Homosexual people

6. In comparison with African Americans, whites are more likely to describe their sibling relationships as
    a. intimate.
    b. loyal.
    c. hostile.
    d. congenial.

7. Grandchildren typically rate their relationships with grandmothers to be_____ their relationship with grandfathers.
   a. stronger than
   b. weaker than
   c. similar to
   d. less emotional than

8. A facility that offers semi-independent living and allows older adults continued living in the community is called
   a. a naturally occurring retirement community.
   b. assisted living.
   c. a congregate housing.
   d. long-term-care facility.

9. Activity competence refers to
   a. continued involvement in the community.
   b. the level of physical activity that a person's health status allows.
   c. the skills and knowledge necessary for taking advantage of available leisure activities.
   d. the extent to which a person chooses physical activity over more sedentary pursuits.

10. People who are judged to have mature faith tend to be
    a. men.
    b. women.
    c. very religious.
    d. over seventy years of age.

Conceptual Questions

1. Seventy-three-year-old Jacob has been retired for six years. He is not suffering from any major health problems and feels strong and energetic. For the past five years he has been volunteering at the local hospital, and he continues to play golf and tennis. Jacob's behavior and attitude is most closely related to the tenets of the
   a. integrity component of Erikson's eighth psychosocial stage.
   b. activity theory of aging.
   c. disengagement theory of aging.
   d. the concept of successful aging.

2. Six months ago Steve's wife was diagnosed with cancer and she has been receiving radiation therapy and chemotherapy. Which of the following is most likely to be Steve's reaction to his wife's condition?
   a. He wants to and willingly provides her with social support.
   b. Her illness makes him afraid and causes him to withdraw from her.
   c. He provides her with ineffective social support.
   d. He is unable to care for her and asks their children to take on the responsibility.

3. Sixty-four-year-old Betty recently remarried. One of her major reasons for the remarriage is likely to have been
   a. a need for a caregiver when illness strikes.
   b. a desire to improve her financial status.
   c. a need to have a lover.
   d. a desire not to be a burden to her adult children.

4. Penny is a retired teacher. She lost her husband two years ago. Which of the following relationships is most important for her?
   a. Her sister
   b. Her past teaching colleagues
   c. Her friends at her church
   d. Her children

5. Stephanie is very close to her godson, who has become "like a real son" to her. Most likely, Stephanie is
   a. a lesbian.
   b. ever-single.
   c. divorced.
   d. widowed.

6. Seventy-year-old Dick is a retired widower. He would probably prefer to live
   a. with his daughter and her family.
   b. with his son and his family.
   c. on his own.
   d. in an assisted living facility.

7. Christina lives in a facility in which she has her own private bedroom, bathroom, and living room. However, she shares the kitchen, the dining room, and the recreation room with other residents in the facility. Christina most likely lives in
   a. a personal care home.
   b. an assisted living facility.
   c. a naturally occurring retirement community.
   d. congregate housing.

8. Marie lives in a "high-self-determination" nursing home. Her satisfaction level is likely to be
   a. comparable to that of community-dwelling elderly.
   b. significantly higher than that of community-dwelling elderly.
   c. significantly lower than that of community-dwelling elderly.
   d. comparable to that of elderly living in "low-self-determination" nursing homes.

9. Larry and Lois are a married elderly couple. After retirement they moved into a retirement community. How is the move likely to influence their leisure activity level?
   a. Their activity level will remain the same.
   b. Their activity level will decrease.
   c. Their activity level will increase.
   d. Their activity level will increase temporarily and then change back to its pre-move level.

10. Patricia is attending an Elderhostel program. She most likely
    a. is a high-school graduate.
    b. holds a professional degree.
    c. is currently employed.
    d. is financially strained.

Answer Key

Key Concepts

1. successful aging
2. integrity versus despair
3. activity theory of aging
4. disengagement theory of aging
5. Spouses
6. self-identity; relationships with others
7. resiliency
8. companionship; economic resources
9. lesbians; gay men
10. blood relationships; constructed relationships; friendships
11. social convoy
12. grandmothers; grandfathers
13. friends; extended family
14. fictive kin
15. property; income
16. naturally occurring retirement community (NORC)
17. assisted living
18. Congregate housing
19. long-term care
20. activity competence
21. Elderhostel
22. church
23. Spirituality
24. reminiscence
25. life-review

Multiple-Choice Self-Test / Factual Questions

1.   Choice (d) is correct; financial stability is not related to adjustment during old age. Choices (a), (b), and (c) all contribute to late-life adjustment.

2.   Choice (a) is correct; the virtue of Erikson's eighth psychosocial stage, integrity versus despair, is wisdom. Hope, choice (b), is the virtue of the first stage - basic trust versus mistrust. Love, choice (c), is the virtue of the sixth stage - intimacy versus isolation. Care, choice (d), is the virtue of the seventh stage - generativity versus stagnation.

3. Choice (a) is correct; more married women than men are in institutions, possibly because men appear to be less tolerant of caregiving burdens. Therefore, choices (b) and (d) are incorrect. Choice (c) is incorrect in that women, not men, spend more days in nursing homes.

4. Choice (c) is correct; widowhood is related to reduction in family income for both genders but the financial strain is greater for women. Choice (a) is incorrect in that depressive symptoms associated with grief and loneliness are high during the first year following the death of a spouse but return to normal levels thereafter. Choices (b) and (d) are incorrect in that mortality and relationships with children are not affected by widowhood.

5. Choice (b) is correct; research indicates that people who are married or ever-single, choices (c) and (a), report feeling less lonely in comparison with those who were formerly married (i.e., divorced and widowed people). Choice (d) is incorrect because the level of loneliness of homosexual people is not significantly different from that of heterosexual people.

6. Choice (c) is correct; a substantially greater percentage of sibling relationships of whites are described as hostile in comparison with sibling relationships of African Americans. Choices (a), (b), and (d) are incorrect in that an overwhelming majority of sibling relationships of both whites and African Americans are described as intimate, loyal, and congenial.

7. Choice (a) is correct; relationships with grandmothers appear to be stronger than relationships with grandfathers, Therefore, choices (b) and (c) are incorrect. Choice (d) is incorrect in that relationships with grandmothers appear to be more emotional than relationships with grandfathers.

8. Choice (b) is correct; assisted living facilities provide some help to residents while they continue to live in the community. Choice (a), a naturally occurring retirement community, is housing that is not designed for elderly but that attracts elderly residents because of the supportive environment it provides. Choice (c), congregate housing provide elderly residents with communal services. Choice (d) is incorrect in that a long-term care facility provides health care and personal care and may be a nursing home or a boarding home.

9. Choice (c) is correct. Skill and knowledge about leisure activity opportunities is referred to as activity competence. The other choices are incorrect; they are not descriptions of specific concepts.

10. Choice (d) is correct; maturity of faith is strongly linked to age and increases with each successive decade. Maturity of faith is not related to gender, choices (a) and (b), or degree of religiosity, choice (c).

Multiple-Choice Self-Test / Conceptual Questions

1. Choice (b) is correct; according to the activity theory of aging, life satisfaction in old age is related to remaining involved in society. Choices (a) and (d), the Eriksonian concept of integrity and the concept of successful aging, are not theories of life satisfaction. Choice (c), the disengagement theory of old age, posits that in order to be satisfied the elderly should withdraw from society as it withdraws from them.

2. Choice (c) is correct; chronic conditions, such as cancer and AIDS, often cause fear and aversion in family and friends, who are torn between a desire to help the ill person and a desire

to escape a situation that their efforts often cannot reverse. Therefore, spouses are likely to provide social support that is not quite satisfactory. The other choices are not supported by data.

3. Choice (b) is correct; a desire to complement economic resources is one of the main reasons for remarriage in old age. Choices (a) and (c), a need for a caregiver in time of illness and a need for a lover, are reported as lesser reasons for remarriage. Choice (d) is not supported by data.

4. Choice (d) is correct; research indicates that relationships with spouses, parents, and children are more important than relationships with other relatives, choice (a); friends, choice (c); and coworkers, choice (b).

5. Choice (b) is correct; constructed relationships are very important for ever-single people. Divorced people, choice (c), widowed people, choice (d), and homosexual people choice (a), are less likely to rely on such relationships.

6. Choice (c) is correct; most elderly adults prefer to live on their own. The other choices are not supported by data.

7. Choice (d) is correct; congregate housing is primarily self-contained, with some communal services, such as meals. Choice (a), personal care homes,,, are neither self-contained nor self-sufficient. Choice (b), assisted living facilities, provide self-contained semi-independent living arrangements. Choice (c), naturally occurring retirement communities, attract elderly residents even though they are not designed specifically for the elderly.

8. Choice (a) is correct; high-self-determination nursing homes are client-centered - residents are not treated like children, and behaviors that promote the use of cognitive skills are encouraged. Consequently, the satisfaction level of residents in such facilities remains relatively high. Therefore, choices (b) and (c) are inaccurate. Choice (d) is incorrect because the satisfaction level of "low-self-determination" nursing home residents who have very limited independence is quite low.

9. Choice (c) is correct; people who move into retirement communities and other congregate housing increase their activity levels. Those who remain in their original communities decrease their activity levels, choice (b). The other choices are inaccurate and are not supported by data.

10. Choice (b) is correct; research indicates that Elderhostel participants tend to be well educated. Therefore, choice (a) is incorrect. Choices (c) and (d) are incorrect in that participants tend to be retired and financially stable.

Chapter 18

Dying, Death, and Bereavement

Learning Objectives

1. Distinguish between degenerative diseases and communicable diseases and explain how recent changes in the causes of death have influenced an attitude of death denial.
2. Discuss how attitudes about death have changed and identify the factors that have contributed to those changes.
3. Describe the development of children's understanding of death.
4. Describe how people of different ages think about their own death.
5. Summarize current attitudes toward end-of-life decisions, including advance directives and euthanasia.
6. Explain why death anxiety typically declines with age and increases with having unfinished business.
7. Discuss the impact of how a culture defines death on the culture's acceptance of and use of organ transplants.
8. Discuss the factors that contribute to suicide in the elderly.
9. Identify and describe Kubler-Ross's stages of dying and critique her model.
10. Define the concept of a "good death" and discuss cultural diversity in dying preferences.
11. Compare and contrast alternative settings for providing terminal care.
12. Differentiate between passive euthanasia and active euthanasia and discuss the concepts of right to die and physician-assisted voluntary euthanasia.
13. Distinguish among the terms bereavement, anticipatory grief, grief, and mourning.
14. Describe how a parent experiences the death of a child at different life stages.
15. Discuss the functions of funerals and other ritual practices that deal with death.
16. Discuss the developmental diversity in how people bury and mourn the dead.
17. Discuss the recovery process and the role of support groups in the adjustment to the death of a loved one.

Chapter Outline

- Focusing On: How children understand death

I. Attitudes toward death

Most Americans will live past age sixty-five and die from **degenerative diseases**, compared to in the past when most deaths, young and old, were from **communicable diseases**.

  A. Death has become less familiar in the twentieth century than ever before because of social and technological changes.

  B. The attitude toward death has been described as death denied.

1. Death has become private.

2. Mourning is denied.

3. Funerary rites are included that erase signs of death.

C. The result of the "death denied" attitude is that people feel uncomfortable about death, and adults send confusing messages about death to children.

D. Because of contemporary attitudes toward death, the dying often experience a social death before their biological death.

E. The **death awareness movement** has attempted to give people the opportunities to learn about death and dying.

II. Facing one's own death

In 1990, 72 percent of deaths in the United States were among people age sixty-five and older. As people age, recognition of their mortality increases. In middle adulthood, people start to estimate the amount of time they have left before they are likely to die.

A. Death acceptance

1. People both accept and deny the reality of their dying.

2. Late adulthood is associated with an increasing acceptance of death and increasing concern about the process of dying.

3. Fewer than one in five American adults have actually prepared any written advance directive. Although euthanasia and assisted suicide are actively discussed, few people seem ready to choose these options.

4. Older people talk about death more than younger people do and seem to be less fearful of it, but there are differences among male and female perceptions of death; fear of death is also related to religiosity.

5. There are a number of explanations of why older people are less fearful of death.

6. Unfinished business can interfere with the normative process of accepting death as one gets old.

• A Multicultural View: Definitions of death in Japan and North America

B. Elder suicide

1. It is important not to confuse age-related death acceptance with desire for death.

2. Leave-taking can help individuals control anxiety and reduce impulses to end their life through suicide, assisted suicide, or euthanasia.

3. Suicide rates are higher in later life, but cross-sectional and longitudinal data present different pictures.

4. Not all elderly are equally likely to attempt or commit suicide. There are several factors that put an individual at high risk for suicide, such as living alone, poor health, and being a white male.

5. Older suicides may be harder to predict and prevent compared to younger suicides, and older adults seem to communicate warnings of suicide less frequently.

6. Suicide at any age appears sudden and unexpected to the people left behind.

C. The dying process

1. Kubler-Ross interviewed more than two hundred dying patients and proposed five distinct stages through which individuals pass.

    a. Denial is the initial response; it is the refusal to believe the terminal diagnosis.

    b. Anger then may be displaced onto the family or medical staff.

    c. Bargaining with a higher being, asking for more time to do something good, may occur next.

    d. Depression is the stage in which the individual begins to acknowledge and mourn the impending loss.

    e. The final stage, acceptance, is reached only if the person is allowed to express and work out earlier feelings.

2. Research has challenged Kubler-Ross's stage formulation.

D. The good death

1. The **good death** is one that is appropriate to the person who is dying.

2. Improving the quality of end-of-life care in hospitals will require changes in the organization and culture of the hospital and active support from hospital leaders.

3. The death awareness movement has promoted conditions that can make the good death possible. Open awareness, as opposed to closed awareness, gives the dying and their loved ones more choice.

III. Caring for the dying

The way the dying are cared for influences the quality of their deaths.

A. Terminal care alternatives

1. Grief work is an initial phase of the bereavement process that entails anger, self-recrimination, depression, and taking care of unfinished business.

2. Home used to be where most elderly people died in the United States. Most deaths now occur outside of the home.

3. **Hospice** takes a holistic approach to death by attending to the physical, emotional, spiritual, and aesthetic needs of patients and their families, predominantly in their own homes. It is formally recognized by Medicare and private insurance companies.

4. The decision to die at home brings with it several difficult aspects for which many families are unprepared.

    a. Today's dying typically are much sicker and more fragile than they used to be.

    b. The most likely caregiver is a woman, and today a higher portion of women are employed outside the home. This situation increases the risk for potential emotional, physical, and financial stress.

    c. Home care is most appropriate when the patient is alert enough to relate to the caregiver and benefit from the familiar surroundings.

5. Nursing homes are the institutions other than hospitals in which Americans most frequently die.

6. **Palliative care** is designed to manage the pain and other symptoms so that the dying person can enjoy what remains of life; it is a part of hospice care.

    a. Hospice includes trained medical staff and trained volunteers; family members serve as caregivers.

    b. Hospice facilities are designed more like homes than hospitals.

    c. Most hospice care is provided at home.

B. Assisted suicide

1. Some terminally ill people choose to end their lives while they are still rational rather than suffer and be a burden to their loved ones.

2. Euthanasia is the voluntary ending of life when illness makes it intolerable.

    a. **Passive euthanasia** refers to not doing something to prolong life.

    b. **Active euthanasia** refers to taking steps to end life.

3. There is much debate over euthanasia and especially assisted suicide. Some believe that patients should have self-determination regarding the termination of their lives. Others argue that loosening the restraints on active euthanasia could lead to abuses by unethical and incompetent doctors.

- Working with Susan Gardner, social worker: Helping the dying and bereaved

IV. Bereavement

Bereavement is the experience of loss of a loved one through death. During late adulthood, deaths of loved ones become more frequent. Bereavement is made up of **grief**, which is the emotional response to one's loss, and **mourning**, the actions and manner of expressing grief.

A. Grief

   1. Grief occurs when we lose certain primary relationships.

      a. Relationships of attachment include spouses or partners, parents, and children. We count on these relationships for security. Grief follows the death of any single relationship of attachment.

      b. Relationships of community include friends, work colleagues, and other family relationships. Death is followed by distress and sadness, but not persisting grief.

   2. Grief is a natural process that occurs after the loss of a loved one, although it is very personalized and is influenced by the age of the deceased person and the relationship.

   3. The grief process has three overlapping phases.

   4. The grief one feels before the death of a loved one occurs is called **anticipatory grief**.

      a. A study showed that anticipatory grief is more likely if the elderly parent is ill for a long time and is not cognitively intact.

      b. Providing care during a prolonged illness can result in grief before the death and relief after the death.

   5. Grief is a powerful emotion that is stimulated by the actual death of a loved one.

B. Funeral and ritual practices

   1. Funerals are ritual practices associated with death; modern rituals focus on the expression of both grief and hope.

   2. Funeral rituals have three functions.

      a. They organize the appropriate disposal of the body.

      b. They contribute to the realization of the implications of the death.

      c. They assist in social reintegration and meaningful ongoing life.

   3. The functions of funerals take different forms in different cultures.

   4. Funeral rituals take different forms in different circumstances in the same culture.

   5. Funerals in America have been criticized for being too elaborate because of commercial pressure.

   6. There has been a countermovement toward simpler funerals and cremation rather than burial.

C. Mourning

    1. Mourning is the social experience of grief.

    2. In all cultures, there are some restrictions and some obligations for mourning.

        a. American society does not approve of mourning except within the rigid confines of the funeral.

        b. Jewish law and custom give mourners a structure that encourages feeling their loss and thus healing.

        c. Hispanic Americans also believe it is important to take time to express one's feelings of grief.

        d. Many Asian Americans believe death allows for a continued relationship between the deceased and the survivors.

D. Support groups

    1. Bereavement programs have been developed to encourage survivors to feel normal about their grief reactions and to offer empathy.

    2. Bereavement groups take several forms such as self-help groups, groups organized by hospices, and groups led by trained professionals.

E. Recovery

    1. Grief involves a process of transition. Survivors take on new roles and see themselves from a new perspective.

    2. Grief leads not simply to recovery but to change and transformation.

    3. Recovery is a return to previous levels of functioning, and there are several indicators of this return.

    4. Not everyone goes through the same grieving process to reach recovery.

V. Looking Back

    A. Continuity within change

    B. Lifelong growth

    C. Changing meaning and vantage points

    D. Developmental diversity

Key Concepts

Directions: Identify each of the key concepts discussed in this chapter.

1. Diseases that spread from person to person, such as smallpox and influenza, are called _____ diseases.

2. Diseases that typically lead to slow, prolonged, and painful deaths that are more common in late adulthood are known as _____ diseases.

3. The _____ has led to the analysis of cultural messages about death, increased sensitivity to the dying, and increased education about death.

4. _____ refers to dying with minimal technological interference and surrounded by family and friends.

5. Research indicates that approximately one-half of American adults approve of _____ and _____ becoming legal options.

6. Children begin to understand that death is irreversible at about age _____.

7. People who favor maintaining life regardless of the circumstances tend to be _____, to have _____ and to be more _____.

8. _____ people have the lowest risk of suicide, and _____ and _____ people have the highest risk.

9. Elisabeth Kubler-Ross's stages of coping with death are: _____, _____, _____, _____, and _____.

10. An initial phase of the bereavement process that involves anger, depression, self-recrimination, and taking care of unfinished business is known as _____.

11. _____ takes a holistic approach to death and attends to the physical, emotional, spiritual, and aesthetic needs of patients and their families.

12. Americans most frequently die in _____ and in _____.

13. _____ refers to managing the pain and other symptoms of terminally ill patients.

14. _____ involves not taking life-prolonging actions, whereas ----- involves taking steps to end life.

15. The process of getting over the loss of a loved one is called _____.

16. _____ is the emotional response to a loss; _____ refers to actions and manner of expressing grief.

17. Feelings of grief before the death of a loved one occurs is known as _____.

18. _____ are ritual practices, and they aid in _____ with the death of a loved one.

19. Jewish law and custom give mourners a structure called _____ for mourning and expressing their grief.

20. _____ is best defined as a return to previous levels of functioning.

Multiple-Choice Self-Test

Factual Questions

1. Death anxiety is higher among
    a. men.
    b. women.
    c. older people.
    d. religious people.

2. Which of the following does *not* increase the risk of suicide during late adulthood?
    a. Living alone
    b. Being alcohol dependent
    c. Having a mental illness that limits communication with others
    d. Being African American

3. When both the dying person and the loved ones know that the person is dying, this is referred to as
    a. good death.
    b. open awareness.
    c. closed awareness.
    d. period effects.

4. In most nonindustrialized nations, most people die
    a. in hospitals.
    b. in nursing homes.
    c. at home.
    d. in hospices.

5. Care intended to manage pain and other symptoms is known as
    a. hospice care.
    b. long-term care.
    c. ordinary care.
    d. palliative care.

6. Assisted suicide is
    a. not engaging in behaviors that will prolong life.
    b. taking steps to end life.
    c. helping with active euthanasia.
    d. helping with passive euthanasia.

7. Relationships with one's children are examples of
    a. relationships of attachment.
    b. relationships of community.
    c. secondary relationships.
    d. horizontal relationships.

8. Which one of the following is *not* a current purpose of funerals?
   a. They provide a structure for the appropriate disposal of the body.
   b. They assist in allowing mourners to share each other's grief and to recognize that life must go on.
   c. They help mourners recognize and acknowledge the irreversible nature of death.
   d. They are designed to appease the dead person.

9. White Anglo-Saxon Protestant American society
   a. has elaborate rituals designed to help mourners cope with the death of loved ones.
   b. does not approve of mourning except within the context of a funeral.
   c. believes that communication between the dead and survivors continues.
   d. displays significantly greater grief intensity in comparison with Latino society.

10. When a terminally ill person begins to mourn his or her own impending death, which of Kubler-Ross's stages is he or she in?
    a. Anger
    b. Bargaining
    c. Depression
    d. Acceptance

Multiple-Choice Self-Test

Conceptual Questions

1. Sixty-nine-year-old Janice has been in a nursing home for the past year since being diagnosed with stomach cancer. She has been isolated from most of her family and friends, who don't have much opportunity to visit her. Her most constant companions have been the nurse's aides at the home. We can say that Janice is experiencing
   a. death awareness.
   b. good death.
   c. social death.
   d. death anxiety.

2. Fifteen-year-old Tina was recently killed in a car accident. Her school friends will have the most difficult time adjusting to her death if
   a. school officials respond by continuing life as usual, without acknowledging the loss.
   b. school officials allow the student body to express their grief and provide them with time for bereavement.
   c. they attend their friend's funeral services.
   d. they are allowed to take a course on death and dying.

3. Assume that you have a health condition that significantly reduces your quality of life. If your opinion is consistent with research in this area, which of the following will you do?
   a. Ask for assistance in committing suicide
   b. Ask the doctor to end your life
   c. Refuse medical treatment
   d. Strive to continue living

4. Who is *least* likely to be accepting of death?
   a. Seventy-year-old Jim, whose wife died three years ago
   b. Carlos, who is Hispanic
   c. Murry, who is the primary caregiver to his mentally retarded daughter
   d. Craig, who is white

5. Katherine is refusing to accept that she has bone cancer. Although her recent suffering is consistent with the diagnosis, she believes the doctor has made an error and claims she probably has nothing more than arthritis. Which of Kubler-Ross's stages is she in?
   a. Denial
   b. Anger
   c. Bargaining
   d. Depression

6. Judd is dying at home. Which of the following is most likely to be true?
   a. He is dying from a secondary infection, such as pneumonia.
   b. He is fragile, confused, and dependent on caregivers even for basic needs, such as feeding.
   c. He is continuing to receive treatment for his illness.
   d. He is unaware of his terminal diagnosis.

7. Ellen has been in a coma for two years, and there is no hope of her recovery. Her family and doctors have decided to withhold medications, such as antibiotics, from her when she develops an infection so that she may die. This is an example of
   a. active euthanasia.
   b. passive euthanasia.
   c. assisted suicide.
   d. palliative care.

8. Millie recently learned that her father has been diagnosed with cancer and has six to eight months of life left. Millie is sad and depressed and grieving the loss of her father, even though he is still alive. Millie is experiencing
   a. mourning.
   b. bereavement.
   c. anticipatory grief.
   d. grief.

9. Julie remarries six months after her husband's premature death. Julie is most likely to be
   a. African American.
   b. White.
   c. Japanese American.
   d. Mexican American.

10. Which question is a bereavement counselor *least likely* to ask in order to determine the vulnerability of the bereaved?
    a. "Tell me about the loved one you lost."
    b. "Tell me how she died."
    c. "How did this death affect your family?"
    d. "Is anyone blaming you for her death?"

Answer Key

Key Concepts

1. communicable diseases
2. degenerative diseases
3. death awareness movement
4. Good death
5. euthanasia; assisted suicide
6. ten
7. African American; lower SES; religious
8. Married; widowed; divorced
9. denial; anger; bargaining; depression; acceptance
10. grief work
11. Hospice
12. nursing homes; hospitals
13. Palliative care
14. Passive euthanasia; active euthanasia
15. bereavement
16. Grief; mourning
17. anticipatory grief
18. Funerals; coping
19. shiva
20. Recovery

Multiple-Choice Self-Test / Factual Questions

1. Choice (b) is correct; women express more anxiety than men, choice (a). Also, death anxiety is lower in people who are older, choice (c), and more religious, choice (d).

2. Choice (d) is correct; suicide is extremely rare in the African American culture at all ages. The other choices all contribute to the incidence of suicide during old age.

3. Choice (b) is correct; open awareness, when both the dying person and his or her loved ones are aware of the impending death, has been more common since 1969. Prior to this, closed awareness, choice (c), when the loved ones know but the dying person does not know, was more prevalent. Choice (a), good death, refers to dying without much technological interference and surrounded by loved ones. Choice (d), period effects, refers to the impact of a unique stressor on the suicide rates for a particular age group.

4. Choice (c) is correct; in nonindustrialized countries, most deaths occur in the person's home. Institutionalized death, choices (a), (b), and (d), has become the norm in industrialized nations, such as the United States.

5. Choice (d) is correct; palliative care refers to pain management, and it is not intended for treatment. Choice (a), hospice care, represents a holistic approach to death and may be given in a person's home or at various acute-care facilities. Choice (b), long-term care, refers to medical care provided for chronic or otherwise debilitating conditions. Choice (c), ordinary care, refers to basic care, such as feeding and cleaning, without taking extraordinary measures to prolong life.

6.   Choice (c) is correct; assisted suicide was illegal in all states but Oregon in 1998. Choice (a) is
      passive euthanasia. Choice (b) is active euthanasia. Choice (d) is incorrect.

7.   Choice (a) is correct. Choice (b), relationships of community, include friends, colleagues, and
      extended family. Choice (c), secondary relationships, are equivalent to relationships of
      community. Choice (d), horizontal relationships, occur between those who occupy similar
      statuses and roles, for example, husband and wife.

8.   Choice (d) is correct; according to anthropological research, funerals originated out of fear and
      a desire to appease the dead. Choices (a), (b), and (c) represent contemporary purposes of
      funerals.

9.   Choice (b) is correct; white Anglo-Saxon Protestant society views grief as something to be
      mastered, and mourners are expected to return to normal functioning following the funeral.
      Therefore, choice (a) is incorrect. Asian/Asian American and Mexican cultures believe that
      communication between the deceased and the survivors continues, choice (c). Choice (d) is
      incorrect in that Latinos display significantly greater grief intensity in comparison with whites.

10.   Choice (c) is correct. Choice (a), anger, is the second stage, in which the person displaces his or
      her anger on to medical staff and family/friends. Choice (b), bargaining, is the third stage, in
      which the person asks from some higher being for more time to engage in good behavior.
      Choice (d), acceptance, is the last stage, in which the person acknowledges and accepts his
      impending death.

Multiple-Choice Self-Test / Conceptual Questions

1.   Choice (c) is correct; social death is the result of the isolation that many institutionalized
      patients suffer as a consequence of being apart from their families and friends. Choice (a),
      death awareness, refers to increased sensitivity to the process of dying, as well as to the dying
      individual. Choice (b), good death, refers to dying in the company of one's friends and family
      and with minimal technological invasion. Choice (d), death anxiety, refers to fear and concern
      about one's own dying.

2.   Choice (a) is correct; adolescents respond with grief to the deaths of people for whom they care.
      The best psychological adjustment occurs if the death is acknowledged and a time for mourning
      the loss is experienced. Consequently, choices (b), (c), and (d) all represent helpful strategies
      for adjustment.

3.   Choice (d) is correct; research indicates that more than half the respondents favor a decision to
      continue living even if they were to have a terminal illness and lacked quality of life.
      Respondents selected choices (a), (b), and (c) less frequently.

4.   Choice (c) is correct; parents who have dependent children are less accepting of death and are
      afraid of what will happen to the child when they are no longer alive to care for her or him.
      Choice (a) is incorrect in that older people who do not have "unfinished business" or
      responsibilities often are more accepting of death. Choices (b) and (d) are incorrect in that
      research that explores racial/ethnic differences in acceptance of death is very limited and results
      are not clear.

5.   Choice (a) is correct; denial involves a refusal to believe a terminal diagnosis. Choice (b), anger
      over impending death, is usually displaced toward medical staff and loved ones. Choice (c),

bargaining with a higher power, usually involves asking for extra time to do good things. Choice (d), depression, involves mourning one's impending death.

6. Choice (b) is correct. Choice (a) is incorrect in that people are more likely to die from primary diseases, such as cancer, which cause severe debilitation. Choice (c) is incorrect in that people who die at home are more likely to be receiving palliative care rather than treatment. Choice (d) is incorrect in that most people who die at home are aware that they are dying.

7. Choice (b) is correct. Choice (a), active euthanasia, involves taking steps to end life. Choice (c), assisted suicide, refers to helping with active euthanasia. Choice (d), palliative care, refers to pain and other symptom management.

8. Choice (c) is correct. Anticipatory grief is experienced while a loved one is in the process of dying. Choice (a), mourning, refers to a culturally accepted manner of expressing grief. Choice (b), bereavement, refers to the process of recovering from a significant loss. Choice (d), grief, refers to the emotional response to a significant loss.

9. Choice (a) is correct; African Americans are more tolerant of quicker remarriage following the death of a spouse than whites, choice (b), Japanese Americans, choice (c), and Mexican Americans, choice (d).

10. Choice (d) is correct; counselors are less likely to ask specific questions and more likely to ask general and broad questions, choices (a), (b), and (c).